AF531428

EDUCATIONAL ADMINISTRATION

EDUCATIONAL ADMINISTRATION

Dr. Digumarti Bhaskara Rao
M.Sc., M.A., M.A., M.Ed., Ph.D.
Reader
R.V.R. College of Education
Srinivasa Nagar Colony
Guntur–522 006
Andhra Pradesh
India

DISCOVERY PUBLISHING HOUSE
NEW DELHI-110002

Reprinted – 2025

ISBN: 978-81-7141-842-8

Educational Administration

Published by:

DISCOVERY PUBLISHING HOUSE PVT. LTD.
4383/4B, Ansari Road, Darya Ganj
New Delhi-110 002 (India)
Phone: +91-11-23279245; 23253475; 43596065
Mobile: +91 9811179893 / +91 9871656464
E-mail: discoverybooksindia@gmail.com
orderdphbooks@gmail.com
namitwasan9@gmail.com
web: www.discoverypublishinggroup.com

Printed at:
Infinity Imaging Systems
Delhi (INDIA)

Preface

At a glance, education and administration appear to be two different disciplines. But, education requires perfect administration, while administration needs administrators, who should necessarily be highly educated. Thus, both are inter-related.

Administration in the area of education is a difficult job. Normally, administration is based on the plank of tough handling and strict discipline, often imposed by force. It is here, where ordinary administration differs from educational administration. Educational administration can not work successfully with a harsh attitude and a heavy hand. Educational institutions are run in a democratic and empirical manner. That's why, educational administrators should first of all be educationists and then administrators.

The abovesaid distinction makes Educational Administration, a different discipline. Today, all good teachers are required to be able administrators, so that they can hold positions of authority, where they have to take important decisions and execute them successfully.

There is a dearth of good books on Educational Administration, as a seperate discipline. Hence, this comprehensive book, which covers all the aspects and dimensions of this relatively new but vast subject.

Hopefully, this book would serve as a textbook and as well as a good reference for teachers, teacher-students and students in general.

Editor

Contents

1
Introduction

The need for a general theoretical perspective on school administration has long been recognized. As early as 1916, Mort lamented the lack of comprehensive theory in the field, charging that it is largely made up of rules of thumb. His own principles, however, seemed to have been more humanitarian than theoretical. He stressed the importance of the individual, local participation in the school system, and called for administrative simplicity. A book of essays edited by Halpin constitutes one of the important statements of the need for systematic theory in administration. In that volume Thompson describes the core of administration as a complex of "simultaneously variable factors" rather than a set of specific techniques, and he calls for a theoretical approach which stresses processes and relationships rather than techniques.

Basic Theory

One reason that theorization has not nourished among educational administrators in the past must be related to the fact that many of them have had to be involved in the mundane, technical aspects of organization, which perhaps has smothered some of their natural theoretical curiosity. One writer observes that most literature on school administration over the past twenty-five years deals with the technical aspects of organization, the legal and physical matters of organization which include details from purchasing and maintenance to performance ratings of teachers, and this writer attributes the basis of this former era to the "efficiency cult." Charging that the so-called "principles of administrative theory" are little more than sheer doctrine, Cornell calls for an analysis of educational administration from the standpoint of social structure — that is, such features as operations, coordination, interaction, customs and informal organization, he believes that these, not the more technical elements, are the essential processes of administration.

Currently, there has been a more widespread awareness that the administrator is not the "manager" who is aloof from his organization, but that he is rather a worker who is a part of it. This awareness alone forced widespread acceptance of the view of administration as human interaction, which in turn has increased the relevance of social science and interdisciplinary research for administrative skills. This renewed enthusiasm for a social science of administration, however, has created still other problems, as Halpin notes. Science is a "sacred cow" in our culture and, as Halpin cautions, it tends to be sanctified by scientists and administrators alike who take themselves too seriously and tend to accept speculation of truth regardless of the validity of the speculative statement. This faith in science can be especially embarrassing to the social scientist whose wildest speculations may be regarded as confirmed knowledge. Yet, if theorization is wanted, someone must be willing to take a chance occasionally; however, such speculation must not be confused with scientific generalization.

From the social scientist's point of view the faith in science may be equally disappointing when it evident that what he wants is not confirmed knowledge information useful in solving the practical everyday problems that administrators face. Since much social science theory does not have this objective, administrators are sometimes disillusioned with theoretical analyses. Thus, the social scientist is disappointed to learn that even those administrators who verbalize about the potential utility of sociological theory sometimes are not willing to support it in terms of necessary research, nor to accept some of its discomfiting and disconcerting conclusions.

These precautionary statements suggest that it is necessary for the social scientist, the educational theorist and the practitioner alike to formulate some common understanding about both the nature of scientific theory and the direction in which the field is expected to evolve if a full-fledged theory of scientific administration is to materialize.

There is much common sense at the basis of all theory. One of the fundamental reasons for theory development was provided more than six centuries ago by William of Ockham. Sometimes known as the "principle of parsimony" Ockham's dictum is perhaps best known as "Ockham's razor." The dictum maintains, in effect, that understanding becomes clearer as we are able to explain a variety of effects with very few principles. Or, put another way, understanding of phenomena is least complete when a different principle is required to explain every observation.

One particularly coherent statement about the general function of theory is the following by Bernard Bass:

> In any science, our aim is to understand the phenomena we study. We understand a phenomenon when we are able to account for it by means of a sat of principles, principles which are sufficiently general to apply in various combinations to other phenomena. We check our principles through testing the accuracy of our predictions, using the principles. Finally we may achieve control over the phenomena by appropriately using the principles.

Basic Features

As an extension of common sense, theory consists of some of the same essential elements. The difference is in the degree of self-conscious precision with which each element is used. What are the essential elements of theory? Merton suggests six types of activities that are often considered to comprise social theory: methodology, general orientation, analysis of concepts, post-factum interpretations, empirical generalizations, and quantified knowledge.

Methodology: Precision of generalization usually increases with refinements of measurement. Measurement enables typologies to be transformed into variables; for example, when temperature became measurable, the single concept "heat" replaced the common sense hot-cold typology. Indeed, the primary utility of gross classifications generally resides in their promise of eventual transformation into such variables. Authoritarian and representative bureaucratic types of bureaucracy, is an example of a gross dichotomy which will eventually be refined into not one, but a set of variables, including the degree of centralization and standardization, the degree of specialization, the amount of personality, and a relative stress on rules and record keeping. It should not, however, be assumed that dichotomies always represent opposite ends of the same continuum, for they often turn out to represent different classes of events: for example, bureaucratic and professional characteristics of organization, discussed later, are probably two different kinds of continua rather than polar opposites of the same continuum.

The advantages of methodology which make it most useful can also be its shortcomings. Merton charges that there is often more attention paid to the methods of hypothesis testing than to knowledge of the theory from which the hypotheses are derived. It is to expected that in a technique-oriented, practical culture, "how-to-do-it" disciplines and "methodologies" will have a special place, but it may obscure the more basic aim of science, the discovery of knowledge. Correctly understood, method is not separate from theory; method is part of theory. The methods used to arrive at a conclusion influence that conclusion; this implies that the theory being tested should determine the methods used. To assess personal attitudes toward power, for example, questionnaire methods are often adequate; but to understand the actual operation of power, risking individuals about their beliefs may produce conclusions with gross inaccuracies, particularly because, laymen have usually not been trained to observe power systematically and also because power is often self-incriminating.

The demand for precision is often motivated by a desire to copy the physical sciences. It is part of a general glorification of "the scientific method." That "method" seems to amount to a ready-made "prescription" revealing the way knowledge is discovered, the scientific method seems to promise the investigator that if certain rules are followed "an act of science" is being done.' The most popular of these rules states that hypotheses must be proposed before investigation begins. The rule implies that the connection between knowledge and the process of knowing has already been determined. It is significant that important hypotheses often emerge in the process of investigation, initiated without preconceived hypothesis. Insistence by educators and fund granting agencies on prior statements of hypotheses or similar rules represents a confusion between the process of theory construction and retesting of established theory. It often leads to sterile, unthoughtful research because attention is directed away from significant events which may have the misfortune to be unrelated to the initial hypothesis. More refined methods become necessary at advanced stages of hypothesis testing, but at the elementary stages of theory development the more creative rather than the more exacting skills of the scientist are required.

Despite the prestige and ultimate utility of the mythological "rigor," validated and reliable instruments, and well-formulated hypotheses that are preferred by the private and government foundations sponsoring research on such problems, a premature attempt to imitate the more advanced sciences at this point would be not only pretentious but misleading. "Let's not," says Hall, "make the mistake of rushing toward a unified theory! There can be no theory of school administration as an operating field of endeavour until there are well-tested theories explaining all the relevant operations in all the situations which make up the administrative field."

Because the orientation sets the context for inquiry, it is extremely crucial (Administrative theorists are still debating their orientation)—whether social relationships are the core of discipline in the organization, and whether value prescriptions, lists of functions and tasks, and endless lists of other concepts are essential subjects of investigation. Social Scientists are also still arguing over a general orientation and are not even agreed on types of variables that ought to be accounted for. Some are still debating whether a social science is possible. One theorist, for example, proposes that a theory of administration must include such variables as value patterns, situational patterns, aptitudes, skill and knowledge, personality, physical energy and capacity of the administrator in addition to individual and organizational performance. This is indeed a comprehensive list, but admittedly too abstract to be meaningful until these types of variables are refined under more specific situations. The crucial question is which variables are important. One primary move in this direction is being made by Haas and others who are studying the possibility of an empirically derived typology of organization using ninety-nine variables. No one project could possibly consider all relevant variables and their specific applications, there must, therefore, be a conscientious selectivity at this stage of the theory construction. Because of the elementary level of theory construction in the field, this book will have achieved its purpose if it does little more than suggest guidelines for an orientation to administrative theory by illustrating the types of variables that promise to be important.

The Concepts

Language provides a perspective. Concepts sensitize the observer. Concepts point to important aspects of the situation to observe and implicitly determine what is not to be observed. Therefore, conceptual development is a crucial phase of theory construction.

It is difficult to define a concept because it is normally used to stand for the very words one must rely on to describe it. A concept is a kind of "bucket term" – and it is useful because, analogously, it is easier to carry the bucket than what is in it. Theory is, of course, a particularistic form of conceptualization; the theorist must deal first of all, therefore, with concept construction and must exercise both care and precision in their construction. It is to this task that the theorist applies operational definition. Such definitions not only provide a measure of logical precision to the particular theorist's constracts, but they also protect him from others' meanings (which might be quite different) for the concepts he is using. Bass has characterized this quality of operational definitions as follows:

The operational definitions and their meanings are critical for empirical verification of the adequacy of the theoretical model developed to account for the phenomena under study. But their meaningfulness to the public has nothing to do with the validity of the deductive proofs of the relations between the constructs defined by the operations.

Thus, if a reader understands that morale in an organization means *esprit de corps*, then whatever principles or theorems relating to morale that a particular theory produces will be applied in that reader's case, to *esprit de crops*.

The terms post factum refers to interpretations of observations after they haye been made, as opposed to empirical testing of predesigned hypotheses. Explanations construed in this way after the facts can be extremely consistent, and hence convincing, but precisely because they are convincing, they may obscure alternative explanation. Moreover, since new explanations can always be constructed to account for the exceptions, this type of explanation is not subject to disconfirmation. Yet, despite these inadequacies post-factum interpretations are extremely useful as plausible starting points during the creative stages of theory construction. There is no mistaking that school administration had been at the creative stage at least until about 1961, post-factum explanations are as vital to the following chapters as reviews of more rigorous studies.

Objective Study

Establishing empirical generalizations constitutes of the main theoretical tasks. These generalizations are sometimes mistaken for theory. For instance, the discovery of a correlation between the level of administrative success and amount of scientific training might be construed as a "theory." This is not precisely theory, although it is true that empirical generalizations are important elements of theory.

Before a generalization may be considered appropriate, several conditions must be fulfilled. First, there must be more evidence that confirms the statement than disconfirms it. This seems obvious enough, but untested hypotheses are easily mistaken for generalizations. Complete confirmation would require a systematic search for evidence to modify or refute the hypothesis, but sometimes all that one investigator is able to do is provide example that support the hypothesis. In this sense, initial investigations take the form of a "grand jury investigation" to determine whether there is a "case" or in other words, whether there is reason to explore the hypothesis further.

Second, the conditions under which the generalization is valid must be specified. So long as the prediction occurs under the stated conditions, the statement is true regardless of the infrequency with which these conditions might occur. For instance, it may be found that Catholic school administrators are less geographically mobile than Protestant administrators, but the generalization is limited to the South and not in the North. Any such limitation does not destroy the statement's validity and theoretical utility. The point is that generalizations need not be "universal" – that is, applicable to all situations (even the law of gravity is limited by vacuums). At the early stages of theory formulation, exact limits often remain unknown, and the theorist must content himself with establishing whether or not certain relationships occur at all and must postpone more refined analyses of the limiting conditions for further research.

Finally, precision of generalization, is increased as the exact form of the relationship is discovered. Crude hypotheses are usually only first approximations which assume a simple linear relationship. For example, it may be hypothesized that the level of ambition progressively declines with age; it could be true up to a point, but a more refined analyse might reveal that near the age of retirement it rises again. Increased precision in stating the nature of the relationship is essential at the later stages of theory construction, but cannot be demanded during the initial stages.

Knowledge in Nutshell

Although theory consists of generalizations, one generalization does not equal theory, nor does a body of generalizations in themselves constitute a theory. For theory to exist, the empirical generalizations must be related logically. This logical component is an essential feature of full-blown theory. The test of theory, in turn, is whether other generalizations can be derived from it.

To be tenable such a postulate rests partially on the confirmation of the derived statements. If true it would apply to other minority groups as well. If it does not apply to Negroes, Italians, and Puerto Ricans, the initial premise must be modified. This is, of course, a simplified illustration.

There are two common misunderstandings about theory: (1) that it is speculation, and (2) that its goal only to predict. The tendency to distinguish between "theory" and empirical fact is a false understanding of the term. Correctly understood, an empirical theory is fact—that is an organized body of empirical generalizations (and the assumptions on which they are based). The other misunderstanding is that the goal of theory is only to predict. If theory is a logical set of laws, then the goal is not to predict, but to derive other laws. Once such a logical relationship is established, prediction more easily follows. While prediction is, of course, extremely important, its importance to theory construction rests merely on its utility as a tool of science; it is employed to test the validity of theory. That is, if a derivation does not accurately predict, of course, the theory is inadequate. But the ability to predict in itself is not the distinguishing feature of theory. A set of random -predictive statements does not constitute theory, no matter how practical they may be.

This point is not purely academic, because a search for predictive statements often proceeds differently from a search for theory. For example, if it were learned that body build is related to administrative success, the person who visualizes prediction as his goal would be satisfied, but the theorist would be puzzled. While prediction may have great utility and while it may be a point of merging interest between practitioner and theorist, it is not a substitute for the scientific goal of theoretical explanation. So long as school administrators demand of social science only that it solve their practical problems of management, they are not, no matter how great their faith in social science, directly contributing to the development of explanatory theory. Of course, practical research may bear some theoretical implications, by accident if not by design, but zeal for practical solutions may actually divert investigations which otherwise would have been more directly focused on explanatory work.

The whole question of the relevance of theory to daily problems partially involves the question of what is practical. It is not entirely clear that solving the daily problems is more practical than developing more fundamental understandings about them. It is not by accident that the most advanced of the applied sciences – notably medicine and engineering are grounded in such theoretical disciplines as physiology and physics. In the words of Walton, "It is perhaps because of impatience with theorizing and because of eagerness to get at practical applications of our knowledge that we overlook the essential practicality of sound theory, out of which sound practice can be developed." Yet, at this point even many of the sympathetic administrators who otherwise express a fondness for "theory" tend to retreat under the daily pressures of work to what seems for the moment the more practical affairs of administration.

Implications: Empirical theory, then, may be deemed as a logically coherent body of confirmed generalizations that have in common certain assumptions and concepts that can be specified with a degree of precision. Theory develops, when it does, as a result of a series of modest attempts to imaginatively think through problems in conjunction with rather close and systematic observations. Despite some claims, there is no formula for achieving this success. In order to evaluate the current state of progress intelligently, it is imperative to first identify the particular stage of theory construction that the field has achieved. A realistic appraisal of the current state of administrative theory reveals that social science is still wrestling with problems of the elementary stages of orientation and conceptualization. Criticism must fall within the range of reason set by this current level of theory. The contemporary theorist cannot properly be criticized for failing to provide a full-blown theory before its basis has been established. Such criticism often reflects the disappointment of persons who are zealously interested in achieving the more advanced stages of theory without bothering about the preliminary turmoil. This book is hardly dedicated to the promulgation of that turmoil but the authors are resigned to live with some of it for a while longer. We are aware, however – and comforted by that awareness – that theory is, above all else, heuristic – that is, theory begets theory. And perhaps at this point, we are back to common sense. There is startling scientific clarity in the adage that one must crawl before he walks.

Perhaps it is also well to remind ourselves that in the field of administration rigorous and systematic study of organizational process must candidly recognize the difficulties imposed by the bifurcation of practice and science.

Theory construction probably best begins with an exposure of the critical underlying assumptions. The assumptions of the theoretical or entation to be developed in subsequent chapters are outlined below.

1. There are certain administrative problems which are shared by all types of organizations. Educational administration does have much in common with other administrative fields from which insights can be drawn.

2. The nature of administrative problems and effective principles are more a function of the organizational structure in which the administrator works than of his line of work. That is the nature of administration is as much determined by such conditions as the size of the organization, and whether it is privately or publicly controlled and whether it is complex or simple, than whether it is educational, business, or political. (This does not mean that the administrator can function in ignorance of his particular institution; on the contrary, in order to exert leadership in any area he must appreciate its basic values and goals. However, given a school administrator and businessman each of whom understands his respective field, the similarities and differences in the problems they face will be greatly influenced by whether or not they work in the same size of organization and so on).

3. The administrator works with organized groups rather than directly with individuals themselves. The problems of administrators are better understood from the perspective of social organization rather than from the psychology of individual.

4. The educational leader is not a "manager" aloof from the organization, but an art of it. Therefore, administration is best understood as a relationship between persons and

groups rather than techniques and rules of administration. Accordingly the factors of subordination, co-operation, conflict, and principles of leadership, co-ordination and organization are the primary tools that administrators must understand. With regard to relationships, administration must be understood from the standpoint of the subordinates – that is, the teachers as well as the superior's stand point. This will mean that "school administration" is not an exclusively executive function, but that it is distributed throughout the organization in terms of these interrelationships between teachers and supervisors.

5. Modern organization is characterized by internal contradictions among the various principles on which they are organized. These contradictions, often produced by environmental pressure, are a source of internal conflicts "built" into the organization itself. The administrator and his employees "inherit" problems from the situation.

6. The important supervisory and leadership decisions concern the regulation of these internal contradictions and environmental pressures. The operating decisions often inadvertently lead to organizational "drifts" between social policy and practice.

7. The significance of these contradictions within organizations has been insufficiently stressed in the past, and much of normal theory, consequently, amounts to little more than assertions of myths about organization. A theory of organizational process as well as structure is needed.

8. Validated knowledge ought not be confused with the process of theory development; codified theory can not be achieved without beginning systematic analysis at less ambitious levels. Synthesis of abstract hypotheses with illustrative material and concrete examples is a convenient point of departure.

Sometimes assumptions are most clearly exposed by the model of society which the investigator imagines.

2

Fundamentals of Education

Education is never ending. It starts with the birth of an individual and then it goes on till the last day of the individual. Education makes an individual a real human being. It is an essential human virtue. Man becomes man through education. He learns something at every moment and on every day. Education equips the individual with social, moral, cultural and spiritual aspects and thus makes life progressive, cultured and civilized. About education, P.O. Bannerji said, "It is the development of the power of adaptation to an ever changing social environment."

Gone are the days when education was the right of a privileged few. Now all have the equal right to be educated as education has become *sine quo non* of civilisation.

What is Education ?

Let us understand the word 'Education' etymologically :

First view is that the word 'education' is derived from the latin word 'Educatum' which means 'to bring up' or 'to nourish'.

Second view is that the word 'education' is derived from the latin word 'education' which means 'to find out', or 'to draw out'. Naturally here in the process of education, 'effort is to draw out' rather than 'to put in'.

Third view is that the word education comes from the Latin word 'Education' which means the 'act of teaching or training'.

Initial Views

1. According to Rig Veda, "Education is something which makes a man self-reliant and selfless.
2. According to Upanishads, "Education is that whose end product is salvation"
3. The well known Indian Economist Kautilya says, "Education means training for the country and for the nation.
4. The Indian Philosopher Shankaracharya considers education as "the realisation of the self."
5. Swami Vivekanand considered education as "the manifestation of divine perfection of existing in man."
6. According to Vedantic view point. The essence of man is spirituality. We need an education that quickens, that kindles the urge of spirituality inherent in every mind."
7. According to Mahatma Gandhi, "By education I mean an all round drawing out of the best in child and man-body, mind and spirit."
8. Guru Nanak said, "Education is self-realization and service of the people."
9. Aurobindo Ghosh puts forth his view on education as. "Helping the growing soul to draw out that is in itself".
10. Rabindra Nath Tagore says, "Education means enabling the mind to find out that ultimate truth which emancipates us from the bondage of the dust and gives us the wealth, not of things but of inner light, not of power but of love, making this truth its own and gives expression to ."
11. In the words of Zakir Hussain, "Education is the process of the individual mind" getting to its full possible development. It is a long school which lasts a life-time."
12. According to Swami Dayanand, "Education is a means for character formation and righteous living."

13. In the words of University Education Commission Report (1948-49): "Education to the Indian traditions, is not merely a means of earning a living; nor it is only a nursery of thought or a school for citizenship. It is initiation into the life of spirit, a training of human soul in the pursuit of truth and the practice of virtue. It is a second birth, divitiyam janma."

14. According to the Report of Indian Education Commission (1964-66), "Education ought to be related to the life, needs and aspirations of the people and thereby made powerful instrument of social, economic and cultural transformation."

The Other View

Concept of education as given by a few popular Western thinkers is as given below:-

1. Plato's view: "Education is the capacity to feel pleasure and pain at the right moment. It develops in the body and in the soul of the pupil all the beauty and all the perfection of which he is capable of."

2. According to Aristotle, "Education is the creation of a sound mind in a sound body....It develops man's faculty, especially his mind, so that he may be able tb enjoy the contemplation of supreme truth, goodness and beauty in which perfect happiness essentially consists."

3. Socrates said, "Education means the bringing out of the ideas of universal validity which are latent in the mind of every man."

4. In the words of Comenfus, "All who are born as human beings, need education because they are destined to be real men, not wild beasts, dull animals and clumps of wood."

5. Thompson said, "Education is the influence of environment on the individual with the view to producing a permanent change in his habits of behaviour, of thought and of attitude."

6. Pestalozzi remarked, "Education is natural, harmonious and progressive development of man's innate powers."

7. Adams said, "Education is a conscious and deliberate process by which one personality acts upon another in order to modify the development of the other by the communication and manipulation of knowledge."

8. Froebel's view, "Education is the unfoldment of what is already enfolded in the germ. It is the process through which the child makes internal external."

9. In the words of Milton, "I call, therefore a complete and generous education that which fits a man to perform justly, skillfully and maghanimously all the offices, both private and public, of peace and war."

10. According to T.P. Nunn, "Education is the complete development of individuality so-that he makes an original contribution to human life according to the best of his capacity."

11. John Dewey says, "Education is the process of living through a continuous reconstruction of experiences. It is the development of those capacities in the individual which will enable him to control his environment and fulfil his possibilities."

12. Herbert's view, "Education is the development of good character."

13. In the words of Redden, "Education is the deliberate and systematic influence, exerted by the mature person upon the immature, through instruction, discipline and harmonious development of physical, inteliectual, aesthetic, social and spiritual powers of the human being, according to individual and social needs and directed 'towards the union of the educated with his creators as the final end."

14. Draver says, "Education is a process in which and by which knowledge, character and behaviour of the young are shaped and moulded."

15. According to Kant, "Education is the development in the individual of all the perfection of which he is capable."

16. According to Ross, " The aim of education is the development of valuable personality and spiritual individuality."

In a limited sense, education is confined to the school and the University instruction. Education starts from the day a child is admitted in a school and it ends when the child completes studies and leaves at the college or University stage. Here education is limited to class room teaching. It is formal in nature. The different examinations passed indicate his success of education. This type of education is intentional and not incidental. It is consciously received education and it is imparted by the institution through an organised way. The curriculum of studies is also of definite type. Here everything is pre-planned and education is given by the teachers in the class room controlled situations. Here education is synonymous with instruction.

in the broader sense, education means the totality of experience gained by an individual from birth to death. It is not the communication of information by the teacher. It is also not just the acquisition of knowlege by the student. The fact is that it is the total development of the personality. Here learning is through any agency such as home, street, school, society, temple, play-ground, cinema etc. In this regard William H. Kilpatnck said, "From the broad point of view, all life heartfully lived is education." Here the curriculum 'for studies is unlimited and also indefinite. Mark Hopkins says, "Education in its widest sense includes everything that exerts a formative influence."

Edward Thring said, "Education is the transmission of life, by the living to the living." in short we can say that education is life and life is education.

T. Raymont remarked: One is educated by one's vocation, by home life, by friendship, by marriage, by parenthood, by reaction, by travel, and so forth."

According to the Report of international Commission on the development of education - "Learning to be' ......human beings keep on learning and training themselves throughout lives, above and through the influence of the surrounding environment and through the experiences which mould their behaviour, their conceptions of life and the content of their knowledge."

Narrow and broad meanings of education have to be reconciled. Surely they are complementary to each other. The following lines by the well known educationaists satisfy the whole thing:

According to Gibbons : "Every person has two educations : one which he receives from others and one more important, which he gives to himself."

Wbitehead said: "There is only one subject matter of education and that is life in all its manifestations."

1. Education is a tri-polar process where teacher taught and social environment act and react with one antoher.
2. Education is a never ending venture.
3. It is a process where some purpose/purposes are aimed at and efforts accordingly are made to attain them.
4. It is a life-long process.
5. Education is preparation for We through Me experience.
6. It is a process of individual development.
7. It is dynamic.
8. It is rotated to time, place and social set up life.
9. It is both theoretical and practical.
10. It is science as well as art.
11. It is an instrument which is used to attain better life.
12. It is an essential human virtue because man becomes man through it.
13. Education is essentially a process of growth and development which goes on throughout life.
14. Education is the modification of behaviour.

15. Education is getting new knowledge and a new reactions.
16. Education is adjustment with the environment.

Instruction is an integral part of education. The process of instruction generally goes on in the class room situations. Some knowledge is put into the mind of the child and he is expected to memorise it.

According to international Dictionary of Education: "instruction is often used synonymously with teaching but often specific teaching is akin to the skill of training rather than to education in a broader sense. It may be audio-visual, correspondence or individual.".

It includes the activities dealing directly with the teaching of students. It is given for improving the quality of teaching.

The following are the characteristics of instruction:

1. Instruction is an integral part of education. It often goes on when a group of learners are there. It is not possible in the vacuum.
2. Instruction is not spontaneous. Rather it is pre-planned activity.
3. It helps in giving knowledge systematically.
4. Instructions are instructor oriented. The teacher is the giver and the child receives instruction passively.
5. The process of instruction goes on in a limited context only.
6. It is mostly examination oriented. The purpose of giving instruction is enabling the student to pass the examination.
7. The person who gives instruction does need language, proficiency.
8. Its main limitation is that it does not develop interest in the students. It also does not imbibe any values in the learners.

Training is an integral part of education, we compare education with, a circle training is then a segment of circle, in training, practical activity is involved) Training helps an individual reach a set standard of behaviour. There is always a set programme to be followed. Thus in the air force, training is given to make the individual an expert pilot. Training is given for car driving, scooter driving etc. In all these cases, some instructor is always there to give training.

Thus training is a specific programme of vocational preparation. It is a planned and systematic sequence of instruction under competent supervisor. It may include refresher and reorientation training for professionals.

Training is a time bound process. After the expiry of certain period, we say that training is over. Then the person becomes a fit person in that field.

The following are the characteristics of training:

1. Training is given in a formal way. Some agency is always working behind it.
2. In training, there are rigid rules and regulations and those have to be observed carefully.
3. Training is given by expert person of the field.
4. It is a practical activity.
5. Framing may or may not make an individual socially efficient.
6. Through training, the expert tries to formulate a set type of behaviour of the individual. Arguments or reasoning of any type are not welcome here.
7. Training is a part of education. Education aims at all round development of an individual whereas training imparts some practical skill or skills.
8. It is a time bound process.

Indoctrination is an activity which helps in forming beliefs. Some ideas are infused in the minds of the learners from the beginning. Those ideas are continuously put in the mind and thus ideas become their firm beliefs. Once the ideas or beliefs are fixed in the mind then time can't easily shake off those deep rooted ideas or beliefs from them.

Broadly, indoctrination is the attempt to inculcate or fix in the individual a certain pattern of beliefs or habits. It may occur in any teaching learning situation. More strictly, it is an attempt to insinuate into the experience of the individual any doctrine whether social, political, economic or religious.

People are indoctrinated to believe certain things. In the process of indoctrination, there is almost negligible scope for reasoning.

Education brings desirable changes in beliefs, attitudes, values etc. Naturally education is something bigger and indoctrination is a part of it.

The following characteristics of indoctrination show its nature:

1. Indoctrination shapes the beliefs and transmits knowledge.
2. There is no scope for reasoning.
3. It makes the individuals believe certain things. There may or may not be any rational thinking behind.
4. Indoctrination is a sort of strategy which may be used as per the desire of the doer or as per requirement of the situation.
5. It is a part of education.

In this fast changing arena of life, indoctrination can be used as a strategy and the results can be wonderful. To bring about desirable social change, indoctrination may be used to make the people believe certain things.

Various Levels

Education is an organised and imparted can be classified as under:

1. Formal Education 2. Informal Education 3. Non-formal Education.

Formal education is that which is provided in a formal way by observing all types of formalities. It is a pre-planned type of education, where specific alms are well fixed in advance, methods of teaching are decided and knowledge is given to the selected pupils by the selected teachers. This type of education ts imparted in the schools, colleges and universities where the learners abide toy the rules and regulations of the agency of formal education. Formal type of education is also provided in the library. It is limited to a specified period.

It is a consciously received education for which deliberate efforts are made both by the teacher and the learner. This type of education is well-organised and so it may anywhere in the school or outside the school. There, is a well-defined and clear cut curriculum. It is not confined to the schools only. In short, we can say that any teaching where there is instruction, supervision, definite aims etc., is called formal education. No matter whether it is given in the school or at home.

1. It is a well-known type of education well-cared for, well-aspired for and well-advocated.
2. Many tyes of formalities are observed here.
3. There is set of curriculum. Effort is there to modernise it as far as possible.
4. There are fixed goals and conscious efforts are always on to achieve the goals.
5. It is an organised type of education. Its show off is made as good as possible. It is made public to attract more and more learners.
6. It is a well-planned activity with fixed time table specially prepared for It.
7. Both the teacher and the taught make conscious efforts in the process of teaching learning.
8. The place of education and the timings are fixed here.
9. This type of education has a beginning and also the close.
10. Surely the syllabi are completed

11. Examinations are held in a formal way and results announced keeping in view the goals fixed up.

Advantages

1. A student is able to sit in the company of other students of the same age group. That increases peer relationships, fellow feelings for one another.
2. In the formal system, many students get the opportunity of being together in different classes for a good deal of time. They have better understanding with each other.
3. It makes the students learn things in a disciplined way. That gradually imbibes the quality of self-discipline in the students.
4. Here education is a continuous process and naturally it develops in the learners the habit of reading continuously.
5. "Education is in accordance with the growth and development of the different faculties of the learners. Thus it helps in having well cared for growth and development of the learners.

Disadvantages

1. Good and bad students, gifted and backward are generally made to sit together in the same class and taught by the same teachers. This shows down the ongoing rapid progress of the gifted pupils.
2. Every student has to wait for the expiry of the academic session and then only he/she gets promotion of the next class.
3. A few students may be keen to cover up more syllabus in less time. That is obstructed here in Indian system of formal education.
4. There are strains on the minds of the learners.
5. It is more or less unnatural way of teaching learning. There is artificial situations created when teaching-learning is conducted.

6. There is need of motivating the students. Sometimes student may fail to learn anything inspite of motivation by the teachers.

Education for which no formalities are observed is known as informal type of education. In this type of education, there is modification of the behaviour of the learner but no conscious efforts are made for it. Whatever is learnt here is not preplanmed. It is rather incidental. Here neither the teacher nor the lean is conscious of the process of teaching learning. For example, a person goes to the playground for physical exercise and there comes across someone who tells him very good ways of utilizing leisure time. Surely in this situation one acted as a teacher and the listener was a student but none of them was conscious of the fact that the process of teaching learning occurred informally. In this way through our daily routine of life, teaching learning may take place and we are quite unaware of it. This type of education is known as informal education. It is a casual type of education which is received through daily experiences and activities.

In this type of education there are no pre-determined aims, no definite curriculum, no well thought methods of teaching, no qualified and trained teachers and no definite place of education. Here education is received by the company of friends, relatives, community etc. Whatever as education is received plays a very important and significant role in the life of the education. This type of education may result into learning something wrong or bad. That is negative education and that may create some problems.

1. This type of education is informal because no formalities are observed here.
2. No conscious efforts are made either by the teacher or the taught.
3. It is in no way pre-planned activity.
4. It is incidental.
5. No formal goals are fixed up.
6. No formal means are used to attain the goals.

7. There are no fixed/appointed teachers. Any and eveybody can be a teacher in an informal situation.
8. Here a situation might crop up where the student may teach a teacher something.
9. There is no prescribed curriculum and no time-table is observed.
10. There is none who organises this type of education. It is all a matter of chance that teaching in learning occurs.
11. There is no fixed place for it.
12. This type of education is never completed and there is no fixed syllabus.
13. There are no examinations of any type.
14. It is all a natural way of teaching-learning.

Advantages

1. There are no strains of any type on the mind of the learner.
2. It is a natural way of teaching learning.
3. The learner is self-motivated in the process of learning.
4. Most of the learnt things are situational as they are learnt in one situation or the other. So they are remembered for a long time.
5. In this type of education there is no dependence on rote learning.

Disadvantages

1. It does not give much confidence to tne learner. Inspite of good knowledge, the learner may feel inferiority complex in a group of highly educated persons.
2. Here education is received in the absence of a so called 'guru' the teacher. One may not learn the right things.
3. Whatever is expected to be learnt in the company of equal age group, that is missed here. Class fellow feelings,

discipline, good habits, attitude etc. may not be acquired properly and rightly.

A Comparison between Formal and Informal Types

The following points of comparison indicate clearly the difference between formal and informal types of educations:

1. Here all type of formalities are are observed.
2. Goals are fixed in a formal way.
3. Proper means are used to achieve the goals.
4. Conscious efforts are made both are by the teacher and the learner and in the process of teaching-learning.
5. Apparently it is an artificial way of teaching-learning.
6. Anybody may acters teacher in a situation. Even a student may, some times, play the role of a teacher in some situation.
7. There is prescribed syllabus here.
8. No time-table. Things happen out of chance or by mere coincidence as they say.
9. Efforts are there to teach in accordance with the prescribed syllabus.
10. Syllabus is completed through .the and formal type of education,
11. It is always organised type of education-Some organised body is no is behind the establishment of hind or the school.
12. The schools at a fixed place.
13. Work schedule is fixed.
14. Rules and regulations are there and obedience of those is mandatory, for all the learners of that school.
15. Restricted type of freedom is to be given to the learners and the teacher.

16. It is started at a particular age, for is continued and thus over the years it is completed. Start is not possible at all stages of age.

17. Its result is always good eehicatioft because every-thing is pre-planned and the process of education goes on under supervision.

Non-formal education has become popular during the recent past. Non-formal education is in between the formal and informal types of education, It is midway, because it is partly formal and partly informal. It is both intentional and incidental. This type of education is imparted outside the format school system.' For providing this type of education, there are no' restrictions of any type learners of any age group in service anywhere or unemployed can seek admission and receive education. A few examples of this system of education are open school, open university, correspondence course etc.

The system of non-formal education is parallel to formal education.

The only difference is that in this system there is flexibility almost at every step i.e. In admission, mode of instruction, curriculum etc. There are rules and regulations but there is no rigidity. Here different media are used for educating the people. Surely this approach is education to the doors of the learners who could not or are unable to receive formal education due to any reason.

Some experts put forth their views on non-formal education:

1. According to Coombs'. "Non-formal education is one which is imparted through organisation and institutions, outside the formal education institutions."

2. Handerson's view. "Non-formal education is far wider and more inclusive than schooling, which imparts wider experiences out of school."

3. In the words of McCall's : "Non-formal education is the entire range of learning experiences outside of the regular graded school system."

4. According to Bremworks: "Non-formal education differs from formal education from the promixity to immediate action, work and the opportunity to put learning to use."
5. In this regard, international Education Commission put forth the view: "Non-formal education is a life-long process and it emphasises the informal and non-formal education for those, who left education at certain stage of life and now they have felt the necessity."
6. Harbulsm's view: "Non-formal education is the only means of filling the gap between the 'schooled' and "unschooled' population."

A few Characteristics of Non-Formal Education are as:

1. It is fully learner-centred approach because its convenience, needs and requirements of its surroundings are fully recognised here.
2. It is life-oriented and enviornment based. It enriches life with new experiences.
3. It catters to the needs and requirements of one and all. Learners in all walks of life and of every age group are able to receive eduation.
4. There is a good deal of flexibility to help the learners.
5. It develops positive attitude in the learners and thus helps them to become self-reliant.
6. In curriculum and methodology, there is too much of flexibility so as to encourage all types of learners.
7. It is an open system of education without any rigid rules and regulations.
8. There is a good deal of diversification of courses so as to benefit all types of learners.
9. It is a voluntary type of education provided through non-formal means.
10. It is continuing education and for this purpose appropriate facilities are created.

Advantages

1. One can earn while learning. One becomes self-dependent and self-confident.
2. Habit of hard work is developed.
3. There is proper use of leisure time. Usually the student of non-formal edcuatlon wants to use the free time in studies.
4. It helps the learners to achieve their goals of life. Even the fast changing goals are possible to be achieved.
5. Through non-formal education, one can cover up one's deficiency in any aspect and thus is able to improve one's standard of living.

Disadvantages

1. A student may receive the desired type of degree/ certificate diploma but many a time he does not enjoy full confidence as the regularly studied learner enjoys.
2. A student is not able to study regularly. He/she studies day and night near the examination and thus chance factor and luck play a good deal of role in his career.

Out of the formal, informal and non-formal types of education which is of greater significance for us or for the society? We can't say that we need more the formal type or our greater need is the informal type of education. Also we can't decidedly say that non-formal education is more significant. No individual can have all education in formal ways only or through informal ways only or through non-formal process of education. Whatever may both individual and whatever may be his/her environment, there is need of formal, informal and non-formal type of education. All these three types put together are able to bring about proper growth and development of the individual. So there is need of the three-one or two out of these can't be equivalent to the unfunctioning of the three put together.

3

Educational Aims

In every walk of life, aims are of unique importance. Without fixing up aims, the work that we take up remains dull and cheerless aims. In fact it makes the process lively, and they also provide satisfaction at the end. In the field of education aims are very essential. Undoubtedly, education is a purposeful and planned activity. It makes a man quite fit for the society. Therefore, we should try to fix up aims in advance and then make efforts to achieve them.

Education without an aim is quite meaningless. In the words of John Oewey, "An aim is a foreseen end that gives direction to an activity or motivates behaviour." An aim to predetermined goal which inspires the welfare activities of an individual, after careful thinking and proper planning it is achieved. In fact, an aim is that predetermined goal which stimulates human activities to achieve it.

The Fundamentals

1. They emerge out of the existing conditions.
2. They are tentative. They can be revised as per need and requirement.
3. They are well-defined.
4. They are flexible.
5. They are related to the life and aspirations of the people.

John Dewey suggested the following criteria for aims of education:

1. Good aims are related to real situations of life. They grow out of these situations and they can be achieved only under these situations.
2. Good aims are flexible. These should be flexible enough to meet the demands of changing circumstances of life.
3. A good aim represents a span of diverse activity. The real objective in pursuing an end is not the end itself but the course of the activity itself which constitutes the core of education.

There is a great importance of aimes of education. All scholars philosophers and educationists have laid great stress on the importance of aims in education. Being a systematic and planned activity, education loses much of its significance without clear-cut aims. According to Encyclopaedia of Modern Education, "Education is purposeful and ethical activity. Hence it is unthinkable without aims." in fact, without aims neither an individual nor an institution is capable of realising its potentialities."

Educational aims are important due to the following reasons:

1. Aims are necessary as they give direction to an act. Education is a planned activity. It has certain aims in view. The aim as a foreseen end as it gives direction to the education process. Without aims, the educator is like a sailor who does not know his destination and the pupil is like a rudderless vessel which may be drifted along somewhere ashore.
2. Aims allow us to act intelligently. John Dewey has aptly remarked, "Acting with an aim is all one with acting intelligently." Thus by keeping the aim in view, one knows what one is doing and why one is doing it. It saves wastage of time and energy.
3. Aims help in assessing the outcomes of the education

process. They are necessary because they help in measuring the success and failure of work done in the school.

4. Aims are necessary for efficient school administration. They help the school authorities in organising, equipping and managing the school. This refers to the selection of teachers, curriculum, planning, proper library equipment, planning of various activities etc. Each activity is guided by educational aims.

5. Aims give direction to the work of the pupils. Once the pupils are clear about the aims, they are likely to co-operate and work with zeal for the achievement of these aims.

6. Aims are useful for parents and general public. Parents and general public can appreciate the work of the school in the light of aims. Aims put restraint on the undue criticism from the parents.

7. Aims give continuity and significance to education. Education is a continuous process. It has an intrinsic continuity. It is the aim that gives continuity and significance to the series of events and experiences that make up what we call education. So aims are potential seeds from which grows the plant of a well-defined educational policy. Aims help us in acting with meaning.

Aims are the core of a workable philosophy of education. Without philosophy, an educator could not have aims and without aims he could not have a practical philosophy.

Aims are an integral part of the fabric of the educative process. They enable an individual to continue his education. As such, an aim is not an end ; it is only a means to an end.

Aims are both within and without the educative process. Ward G. Reader rightly points out, "Education finds its aims both within and without the educative process. It must be kept in mind the interests and the abilities of the pupil and prepare him to share in democratic living both now and when he becomes an adult."

Affecting Factors

Many factors contribute to the determining of educational aims. These factors touch every phase of human life and also reflect socio-cultural trends. The following factors usually determine aims of education :

1. *Philosophy of Life.* Aims of education have direct relationship with the prevailing philosophy of life. Different thankers and philosophical thoughts influence the course of education and its aims. Idealism emphasises self-realisation and divine perfection as the aims of education. According to the natural-view point, self-expression or self-gratification should be the aim of education. The pragmatic school of thought views life as the process of socialization of an individual. Similarly, existentialism, realism and other philosophical view points recommended their own aims of education.

2. *Human Nature.* Educational aims have often been decided keeping in view the human nature. Idealists regard 'unfolding the divine man' as the aim of education. To naturalists, the aim of education is "self-expression."

3. *Religious Factors.* Though there is no state religion in India, yet different religious view points influence the aims of education. The denominational institutions run by different religious organisations have to work to realise the goals accordingly.

4. *Political Ideology.* No system of education can rise above the political ideologies of the country. In other words, political ideologies influence aims of education in a significant way. According to Brown, "Education in any country and at points reflects value of the ruling class." Under a totalitarian system, the aims of education are different from those under a democratic political system.

Under a democratic set-up, the-aims of education are flexible. The goal of education is the good man who is to be educated for life of freedom. Education aims at developing the full personality of each individual, irrespective of caste, creed, class or religion.

Under a totalitarian system, the aim of education is to propagate the state ideology. It is, in fact, indoctrination. The good of the individual lies in his working for the good of the state. Thus he dies for the state.

5. Socio-Economic Problems. Socio-economic problems of a country determine the aims of education. In India, we have a number of socio-economic problems. One of the objectives of education may be to establish a socialistic pattern of society which is in tune with the democratic set-up of the country. Similarly, the educational system of the country is expected to produce socially and economically independent citizens who can contribute to the betterment of the country. In the words of Secondary Education Commission Report (1952-53) : "As political, social and economic conditions change and new problems arise, it becomes necessary to re-examine and re-state clearly the objectives which education at each definite stage, should keep in view."

6. Cultural Factors. Socio-cultural heritage of a country largely determines the aims of education. Education has to preserve and develop the cultural heritage. The changing and developing pattern of culture directly influences the aims of education.

7. Exploration of Knowledge. Present age is the age of science and technology. There is almost an explosion of knowldege. Education today, has become cience-oriented and technology-based. It is thus evident that exploration of knowledge is an important factor in determining the aims of education.

Education must represent these factors and be related to the realities and problems of life.

The Background

Aims of Education as history reveals, differed from time to time. Here below are given the aims of education which were popularly advocated at different times:

Ancient India

1. To infuse in the learners piety and religiousness.
2. To form good character.

3. To develop the personality fully.
4. To inculcate civic and social duties.
5. To promote social efficiency and happiness.
6. To preserve and propagate culture.

In Medieval India

1. Propagation of islam.
2. Spread of education among Muslims.
3. Extension of islamic kingdom.
4. Development of morality.
5. Building of character.
6. Propagation of 'Shariyat'.
7. Achievement of material well being.

British Rule

1. Consolidation of British empire.
2. Recruitment of clerks.
3. Spreading English Literature.
4. Promoting craze for English articles and English textiles.
5. Preparing a class of interpreters of English laws.
6. Translating literary master pieces of Indian religious books into English.

Aims of Education are related to time and space. They are also changeable. The history of educational development in India stands evidence to this fact. There have been different aims of education in different periods. A brief account of aims of education in chronological sequence is given below :

Aims of Education in the Brahmanic Period. The aim of education during Brahmanic period was an all-sided development of man. Education was regarded as a means of salvation or emancipation. The chief aim of education was to unfold the spiritual and normal power of the individual. Education was thus determined by religious values.

The Aims of Buddhist Education. The aim of education during Buddhist period was to create a sense of equality among all, 'Satya' and 'Ahimsa' were the directive principles of this system of education. The child was taught to control and suppress his worldly desires in accordance with the eightfold code of conduct enunciated by Lord Buddha.

Aims of Education during Muslim Rule. The aim of education during the Muslim period was to prepare an individual for the wordly life as well as for the spiritual life. It was education of islamic culture and scriptures which regulated human behaviour accordingly.

Aims of Education during British Rule. The aims of education during British rule were different. The system of British education was implanted in this country with purely political motives. It aimed at dividing Indians spiritually and intellectually into the English-knowing class of men and non-English-knowing masses of people. It was in accordance with Macaulay's "Downward Filtration Theory."

Change in Society

Aims of Education need careful fixation. They have to be in accordance with the needs and requirements of the individuals, the society, the nation and the situations prevailing all around. Aims of education have been different at different times. After the independence of the country Pt. Jawahar Lal Nehru remarked, "Great changes have taken place in the country and the educational system must be keeping with them. The entire basis of education must be revolutionised." The society today is facing a number of problems. Social, political and economic conditions of the country are fast changing. It is, therefore, very important that we should assess everything carefully in the light of present situations and fix up aims of education which are suitable for the people of free India in every way. Suggested aims of education are :

1. Individual Aim of Education.

2. Social Aim of Education.
3. Vocational aim of Education.
4. Character Building Aim.
5. Spiritual Aim of Education.
6. Harmonious Development Aim.
7. Cultural Aim of Education.
8. Knowledge Aim of Education.

Various Factors

Individual aim of education means that education should develop the individuals according to their interests and capabilities. It meas free growth of individuality, helping every boy and girl to achieve the highest degree of individual development. Individuality is the ideal of life. An individual is the central figure in the social setup of life. All social institutions exist for the betterment and improvement of the individual. The individual is the end and these social institutions are the means. It is the fullest development of the individual. Education aims at training and development of the individual. It is only this type of individual who comes out as a good citizen.

The individual aims of education have been emphasised by various thinkers. Their view points are as under:

The Naturalists like Rousseau believe that "The central aim of education is the autonomous development of the individual." According to him, "Everything is good as it comes from the hands of Author of Nature, but everything degenerates at the hands of man. God makes all things good. Man meddles with them and they become evil." This group of thinkers believe that man and citizen cannot be trained simultaneously. In short, education must secure those conditions where every individual is allowed to have a free play of his personality. He is free to develop his inherent, powers the highest potentialities of self.

The biologists believe that every individual *is* unique in his own way. G. Thompson believes that "Education is for the individual. Its function being to enable the individual to survive and live out its complete life. Education is imparted to preserve the individual life. Education is given for the sake of the individual to save him from destruction. Community exists for the individual, not the individual for the community. Community being the means and individual being the end, education should not set the means over the end." Therefore, individual and not society should be the centre of all educational efforts and activities.

According to the psychologists, education is an individual process. No two children are identical in intellectual capacity. Education must be individualised. Then only they can be benefitted fully.

The modern progressive thinkers also hold the view that the ultimate good of society lies in discovering the hidden value of the individual. In the words of Sir Percy Nunn, enters the human world except in end through the free activities of the individual men and women and that educational practice must be shaped to accord with the truth."

Each individual child should hold the key positions in the educative process. There is much force in the individual aim of education. However, individual aim, in its extreme form, is not desirable. The social aim has its own values and justification. This extreme and one-sided view of individual aims has teen criticised.

The individual aim of education has been discussed on account of the following points:

Isolated Individual a figment of imagination. "An isolated individual" as, T. Rayment says, "is only a figment of imagination. We cannot conceive of an individual living and developing in isolation from society."

An Individual is a Social Being. In the words of John Dewey, "As a social being he is a citizen growing and thinking in a vast complex of interactions and relations." So an educational activity that does not swear by the social end, consequently fails even to serve the individual.

Inherently Defective. The idea of autonomous development may be misinterpreted as giving absolute freedom to the individual. It may take the form of unchecked self-expression' or 'self-assertion.' If we ridlcute all social conventions or moral laws which form the basis of society. *Sir-fierey* Atowrngntly *sects.* Individuality develops only in a social atmosphere.

The critics of individual aims believe that the individual left to himself, is an animal, selfish and undisciplined. Thus it is against the spiritual nature of man.

Individual must be Made Fit for the Society. Rusk says that the aim of education is not development of individuality but the enrichment of personality. Education must transform him from individual being to social being. He must be fit to live in the society.

The Basis of Individual's greaters is Social. The contribution of great men (individual being?) wen not isolated from the society. Their greatness was due to their assi xlation of the rich Heritage of the society. They worked against some social background. Hence the very basis of their great contributions was social.

In all, individual aim of education in its extra form is one sided. It is not in tune with the socio-political set-up of the country. It may adversely affect the economy of the country as well. Those who believe in it are self-centred and perhaps selfish. It is all right to a limited extent. Society or state aim also very important.

A man in isolation is not considered good. He is known by the company he keeps or the society he belongs to. Surely the society or state is superior to the individual. That is my view-point of supporters of social aim of education.

In its extreme form,.social aim regards individual only as a tool of society. He is subordinate to the society. Moreover, it cannot ive without society.

Below are given the arguments o: those who are in favour of social aim of education:

An Individual is an Integral Part of the Society. He is born in society and he grows and develops in society. Sodety should be given more importance as compared to the individual.

The Individual is Born with a Number of Raw Instincts. The society gives training to him. The good sodt environment makes him a man. Social environment need be cared for more as compared to the individual.

Education is Under the Control of the State. State or society is to determine 'what' and 'how' of education. What should be taught to the individual and how it should be taught are determined by the society. Therefore, social aim is more important.

Society Makes the Individual Civilized. It teaches him the lesson of citizenship. So the society or the social aims need be given more importance.

Security, Peace and Justice exist in Society. They are properly maintained in the society only. It is, therefore, urgently needed on the part of the individual that he should give importance to society.

Thus, we find that the social aim of education completely overpowers the individual.

Social aim of education in its extreme form has been criticised in many ways. It is certainly one-sided view. The following are the points of criticism:

1. It is unpsychological bcecause it does not take into account the capacities and interests of the individual. Man becomes a means to an end. He has to sacrifice his own interests.
2. It suppresses individual freedom, develops narrow nationalism and ignores the individual completely, it leaves no scope for the individual personality to flourish.
3. It ignores the needs, desires and interests of the individual and also suppresses his creative power.
4. It tries to make the individual just a tool of the state. He forgets his own individuality and becomes a blind servant of the society.

5. The desires and aspirations of the individual are ended and he has to work for the good of the society. Thus education makes an individual a tool of the society. It may make the individual narrow-minded and in them there may develop all hatred for the society.

Are individual aims of education sufficient in themselves? Can we go on fully with their support? No, it is not possible. An individual cannot be thought of in a vaccum. Support of the society is a must for him. He is an integral part of the society. We shall have to think of betterment of society through the increase of education. Education is a very good weapon to cut off the itching sharpness of individual and social aims of education. They have certain drawbacks and those must be ended. Then the two — individual and soda! aims of education be synthesised. Surety,they are contemporary nature. Each one wilt become a support for the other. That way then, they will serve the purpose in far better ways.

Synthesising the individual and social aims of education will create healthy and conducive environment which will ensure proper growth and development of the individual. There will be nothing bad for the individual no suppression of his creativeness. Better individual will give rise to a group of better individuals and that will naturally improve the society in every day.

Every individual has got the capacity to make the society grow and develop full. Everyone wants to see it prospering. For this achievement, the individual will have to be prepared for the self-sacrifice for the society. Education serves that purpose fruitfully. Education has two fold purpose : "The perfection of the individual and good of the community. Isolated individual is the figment of imagination.

An individual is like a plant and society is the soil or earth. No plant can grow in the absence of soil or earth. Social medium is needed for the proper growth of the individual. In the words of John Adam "individuality requires a social medium to grow, without social contacts we are not human." According to Ross, "individuality is of no value and personality is a meaningless term, apart from the social-environment in which they are developed and made manifest. Self-reallsation can be achieved onty through social services and the social-ideas of real value can come into being only through free individuals who have developed valuable individuality. The circle cannot be broken."

There is no conflict between self-realisation and social service as aim of life. It is, undoubtedly, right to say that the true aim of education is the highest development of the individual as a member of the society.

A few experts gave their views to favour it :

(i) Adams, "Self is realised in society through social interaction."

(ii) MacIver, "Socialization and individualisation are two sides of a single process."

(iii) Nunn says, "individuality develops only in a social atmosphere where it can feed on common interests and common activities."

(iv) in the words of Mahatma Gandhi, Gandhi sees no conflict between individual and society. He says, "I believe that if one man gains spiritually, the whole world gains with him."

(v) According to Humayun Kabir: "If one is to be creative member of society, one must not sustain one's own growth, but contributes something to the growth of society."

Thus we find that both the individual and the society are needed for making life full of fragrance and worthy of living. Initiative of the individual is important at its own place and social contact is needed to give the individual proper recognition and right-direction. Both supplement each other. So by synthesizing the two we shall be able to make the individual and the society grow and develop fully.

The Objectives

Livelihood is important because without bread and butter, living is not possible. Education, therefore, must enable an individual to stand on his own feet and he should be able to earn for his living. Only a living person has certain needs and requirements. A dead person has no desire, no aspiration and no requirements. When we talk of a living person, we surely see to it from his all around point of view. An individual needs education in order to live. He needs education in order to live well. He needs education to do various things of life in a better way. They are possible with the help of money only. According to Secondary Education Commission, knowledge gained is useless if an individual cannot make both ends meet. Without a vocation, the individual is a drag and parasite on others. A social parasite cannot be called a free man. He begins to feel free only when he is economically independent. Vocational education, thus, exercises a liberalising effect on man. There is no vocation without education. Every vocation has an educational value. Education with the vocational aim in the background will prepare each individual for an occupation. Vocational aim of education is also known as 'Bread and Butter aim', 'Blue Jacket Aim' and 'White Collar Aim.'

It has been rightly said that "Vocational Education is an education of most effective kind, for lack of which those who merely go to school, suffer all their lives." in the words of Gandhiji, "True education ought to be a kind of insurance against unemployment."

Solves Economic Problems. Vocational aims make a person fit for some vocation. He becomes sound economically. In this age of material crisis, the problem of unemployment and underemployment are causing many economic problems. When education is vocation centred, it will help a lot.

Gives Social Status. Vocational aims bring vocational efficiency. With more money, a person feels satisfied in the society. It gives him good social status.

Suits the Average Learners. In every classroom, there are different types of learners. The good and brilliant are able to do well in studies. But the average types of learners find studies a big problem. Vocational education helps them, because it is suitable for them.

Helps in Moral Development. In the absence of vocation centred education, many students would become misfit for society. They will do every type of bad deeds to earn money for their living. Vocational education thus makes them morally good.

Makes a Person Active. In vocational education, the learners are able to develop their interests in the vocation. Quite a number of them are able to excel.

Makes Learning Useful. Vocational education makes learning useful. Here some vocation is of primary importance. The study of so-called traditional subjects is secondary.

A few experts pirt-forth their views as under:

Spens Report, "Preparation for vocation is an important part of our education."

Hartshome's view, "Vocational education is an education of most effective kind, for lack of which those who merely go to school, suffer all their lives."

Demerits

1. Only vocational aim is not sufficient for an individual. Some studies are also needed. Social and cultural aims are in no way of lesser importance.
2. It is a narrow aim of education.
3. It is too much materialistic.

It we have a professionally good doctor or a professionally good engineer, it is not sufficient. There is need of a good man in each one of them. So just vocational aim is not sufficient. All other aims which make an individual a good person, are also fleeced.

Character is very important in the case of every learner, every teacher, every professional and above all, every person. In the absence of a good character, the whole personality stands zeroed. It is the soul of human body. Education for character is of top-most importance. It gives the man confidence and courage. A man of character is a man of word, is a true national, is a true citizen, and above all, a true human-being. India needs today men of character. In them lie the hope and future prosperity of the nation. Only persons of character make the nation great and strong.

In the present day life, when there are erosion of higher values, education for character is the only way to solve the problems. Definitely the society of today is badly in need of higher values of life—Truth, Beauty and Goodness.

The chief aim of education should be 'character building.' Herbart summed up the concept of education as 'Morality.'

Swami *Vivekanand* says, "We want that education by which character is formed, strength of mind, is increased, the intellect is expanded and by which one can stand on one's own feet."

John Dewey says, "The establishing of character is a comprehensive aim of school instruction and discipline."

Raymont says, "The teacher's ultimate concern is to cultivate, not wealth or muscle, nor fulness of knowledge, nor refinement of feeling, but strength and purity of character."

'Gandhiji very dearly said, "Character building is the aim of education. I would try to develop courage, strength, virtue the ability to forget onself in working towards great aims. I should feel that if we succeed in building the character of individual, society will take care of itself."

in the words Radhakrishannan, "The troubles of the whole world including India and the fact that education has become a mere intellectual exercise and not the acquisition of moral and spiritual values."

Personal Examples of Teachers and Administrators. The teachers and the Administrators working in the schools should be living good examples of character. The learners come in contact with them every now and then and they observe them and watch them carefully at every moment. Only good teaching personnels will be able to imbibe the qualities of good character in the learners.

Encourage the Students to Read' Good Books. The teachers should recommend the study of good books to the students. Biographies of great men were really great in the true sense of the word should be purchased for the library. Such books should be within easy access of the students. Then naturally the students will read those books and learn lesson for all times to comes.

Moral Education as a Subject. Moral education as a subject should be introduced in the school curriculum. The different textbooks of all subjects of among or more education as a subject among me youths will naturally improve upon their moral behaviour. The earlier we start with this, the better it would be for the future of society and the nation.

Celebration of Birth Days. The school should actually celebrate the birthdays of great religious leaders and saints. Instead of declaring a holiday on such days, celebration of the day highlighting the achievements and contributions of those great men will help the learners to learn many good things. Naturally it will improve upon their moral behaviour.

Projects for Honesty. A few projects for honesty may be started in the school. Students' Post Office, Students' Co-operative Store, Students' Canteen etc. may be started. The students should be given the charge of these activities under the guidance of some teacher and they should run it on 'No Profit, No Loss' basis. This will imbibe in the students qualities like sincerity, honesty and hardwork which will make them an asset for the society.

Lectures by Persons of High Moral Values. Some religious persons who are really saints of the society should be invited to the school for a lecture on moral education. Speech by them based on their studies and experiences of life will create interest in the students and also help them in becoming morally better students.

Merits

1. A person without character is like a man with body and without soul. So character building aim of education is really of primary importance.
2. Everybody needs be good human being. That is not possible without character. Therefore, character building as aim of education should be given top-most importance.

Demerits

1. Let there are not too much moral values. If we do so, other aspects of life stand neglected.
2. What is good and what is bad need to be known to everyone. Character aim is moral and that is for all. In its absence, it will be difficult to live well in a social group.

Education for culture is education to improve upon cultural aspect of the society. That improvement can be there only it we have the past and the present cultures available with us many good things we want to preserve, we want to refine and transmit in order to enrich our culture all the more. Cultural aspect of life is significant in its own way.

Cultural aim in narrow sense means dress, manners, way of life etc. In broader sense, it means good habits; good thoughts, etc. Surely cultural aim of education is grace to human life. Humanyun Kabir has rightly emphasised the importance of culture in the words : The continuity of culture and traditions is an essential condition for the survival of a nation" Culture is the foundation, the pifthary thing—it should snow itself in the smallest detail of your conduct and personal behaviour, how you sit, how you talk, how you dress, etc, inner culture must be reflected in your speech, the way in which you treat visitors and guests and behave towards one another and your teachers and elders.'

4

Salient Features

Continuing with the conceptual milieu of educational administration, we give attention in this chapter to the tasks of educational administration. These task areas constitute the major subject matter of educational administration. Scholars spend years developing theory and knowledge in each of these areas, and any well-developed school system must employ persons with expertise in these subject fields. The conceptual knowledge used in the performance of all jobs in just one of these task areas cannot be included in one volume. Consequently, the discussion here only presents the major task areas and offers illustrative concepts for each area to provide an overview.

A comprehensive study of the task areas of educational administration was done as a part of the W.K. Kellogg-sponsored Southern States Cooperative Program in Educational Administration. The critical task areas included in this taxonomy were as follows: (1) instruction and curriculum development, (2) pupil personnel, (3) community school leadership, (4) staff personnel, (5) school plant, (6) school transportation, (7) organization and structure, and (8) school finance and business management.

Also described were the specific jobs (and accompanying statements of theory and knowledge) that needed to be performed in each task area. In reviewing this 1955 study, it is interesting to see the changes that have occurred. For example, in 1955 the study group stated one job task as "Promoting the General Welfare of the Staff." If the school superintendents of districts having collective bargaining attempted to apply this to teachers, as was described in 1955, they would be accused of paternalism by leaders of teacher unions and of abdicating their managerial responsibilities by their boards of education.

On the other hand, many of the tasks stated in 1955 are still relevant. The conditions under which they must be performed and the performance techniques are different, yet these jobs must still be accomplished. Therefore, even though circumstances have changed during the last twenty-five years, there is considerable stability in the kinds of administrative tasks to be performed.

The areas presented here are arbitrary categories of a total administrative function. They are not separate entities, but interrelated parts.

Development of Organisation

The formal organizational arrangements of schools at the district, state, and national levels are presented in Part Two. In this section we discuss some of the tasks traditionally associated with administrative organization.

Basic Problems

The discussion of theories of organizational behaviour demonstrated the age-old problems of bringing people with individual needs and organizational demands into congruence. Theorists who plan rational organizational designs are confronted with the problem that humans frequently act irrationally. Waldo reminded us that both the internal and external environments of school systems are not totally rational. A rationally prescribed organization usually does not function as expected and frequently fails to accomplish goals, especially if those involved do not adjust to the unexpected.

One manifestation of this irrational behaviour is when power is sought or purposes of self-aggrandizement. Energy that could have been used to attain organizational goals is spent in empire building and conflict, and the potential of the organization is never realized. Therefore one of the conceptual problems of school administrators is how to maximize cooperation and minimize power conflicts.

Problems of rationality occur in both formal and informal organizations. Informal organizations both react to and influence formal organizations even controlling the formal organization of some schools. As Barnard suggested, informal organizations (e.g., office cliques, friendship groups, faculty Cliques) may help facilitate the tasks of formal organizations. Or, as Griffiths implied, they may positively affect the decisions of the formal organization.

Organizational Structure

One of the basic concepts for organizational development is that structure should be based on the purposes of the enterprise. No organization representing several conflicting purposes ever accomplished much.

When most of our educational organizations were initiated, those involved probably had a general idea of their goals. Persons were assigned various roles to perform in carrying out the mission. As the organization grew in complexity and changes in personnel occurred, the perceptions of organizational mission became blurred and numerous problems emerged (e.g., problems of communication, decision making, value conflicts).

Unless a means exists for organizational renewal, the members of an organization may in time lose sight of purpose. In this situation the organization may feed upon its own inadequacies rather than focus on goals. Parkinson presented a humorously critical analysis of how grotesquely ineffective a bureaucratic organization can become when people in it lose sight of purpose. Consequently, one of the main functions of those engaged in organizational development is to help the personnel achieve a sense of mission – to come to terms with their objectives. Once the organizational mission has been defined, leadership can focus energy on other needed improvements.

Aims and Objectives

The structuring of school organizations (work division, assigning responsibilities, and so on) has to be decided. The bureaucratic model is the most prevalent concept guiding the establishment of educational organizations. However, most people have a stereotyped idea of the nature of bureaucratic organization, which Woodring so well expressed as follows:

> Bureaucracy, though an accepted part of modern life, is rarely defended. Even the meaning of the word is unclear. It is generally assumed that it has something to do with red tape, petty rules, and massive confusion. In a bureaucracy there is a piling up of layer on layer of administrative authority, which makes it necessary to submit all reports with seven carbon copies in order that one may be filed at each of the various echelons. A typical bureaucrat is thought to be a stupidly determined little man who always gets to work on time and likes order. His purpose in life is to see that all rules are followed to the letter and that fresh ideas are frustrated. His ultimate horror is to find an IBM card that has been bent folded, spindled, or mutilated.

The real meaning of bureaucracy, as defined by Weber, is much different from this popular concept of the term. Nevertheless, when enough of the principles advanced by Weber become corrupted in practice, the worst consequences of bureaucratic organizations emerge to make Woodring's statement a regrettable reality.

Recognizing the tendency of the bureaucratic organization to expand upon autocratic features, many school administrators have made major alterations. Most of these are in the form of massive committee structures for participative planning and decision making and attempted decentralization of control in the interest of greater democracy. Thus the bureaucracy is used for the execution of policies, and not for policy decision making. Democratic processes for planning and policy development are substituted for top executive control.

Some believe that bureaucratic organization should be completely abandoned in favour of some form of pluralistic or collegial type of organization. Thompson, Argyris, and Bennis are among many who have directed strong criticism at the bureaucratic type. The term collegial organization is taken from the traditional illustration of the college, where there are provisions for academic freedom and faculty control of academic matters. Those, in the administrative hierarchy provide leadership and services to make the system function well, rather than functioning as all-directing industrial tycoons. In the collegial organization professors may have higher salaries than administrators, which is very different from the typical bureaucratic structure.

The differentiated-staff movement in the schools has some of the elements of the more democratic or collegial model. For instance, teachers are assigned professional functions and greater control over program development, not unlike those of professors in a college. Caldwell pointed to the increased decision making of teachers in differentiated staffing.

Because the collegial concept provides for the abandonment of monocratic control and provision is made for democratic processes of decision making on educational policies, communication in the organization is different. Communications flowing downward no longer are necessarily greater in number than those flowing upward. Those concerned with the development of programs are better charaterized as a community of equal scholars than as management over labour.

As stated previously, most educational organizations resemble bureaucratic-type organizations. This is especially true of the very large school systems. The growth of collective bargaining may enchance the bureaucratization of large educational organizations so that.they look like big industrial companies. If education does go the route of private industry, school administrators may have much control over the purposes of education, and teachers will bargain about wages and working conditions, thus giving up the collegial model and firmly establishing the bureaucratic model.

Regardless of the type of organizational model educators use, the structure must provide for (1) a way in which tasks can be divided among personnel; (2) a means through which decisions can be made; (3) the establishment of communication channels so that work can be coordinated; (4) the maintenance of organizational effectiveness to meet unforeseen problems; (5) an effective climate of flexibility cooperativeness, personal security, creativity, and organizational renewal; and (6) the establishment of appropriate operational (e.g., elementary, middle, junior high, senior high schools).

System at Work

The task of establishing effective relations with state and federal agencies has grown in importance as their funding of education has increased, and because this trend is likely to continue administration of this task will be of growing importance. Also involved is the establishment of cooperative relations with non-educational agencies on the local, state, and national levels.

Public school administrators must always remember that the schools are subject to public control. Therefore processes should be included for the appropriate participation of parents and other citizens in planning activities and establishing goals. This has usually been attempted through citizens committees, parent-teacher organizations, cooperative school studies, and so on.

This process must include the development of an effective relationship with the board of education. Great difficulty is encountered in school districts where the board and professional educators have not learned how to work together to establish and attain goals.

Development of Curriculum

The instructional program of an educational organization consists of the curricular opportunities offered pupils and the instructional methods through which these opportunities are delivered. Once the educational goals of the organization are known, leadership in the development of the instructional program becomes of primary importance.

Fundamental Programmes

Decision making about the school curriculum is frequently supercharged with conflicting philosophies of education. Some very troublesome questions must be answered, and each of these may have several answers, depending upon one's values. Finding answers to these questions is the greatest conceptual problem faced by school administrators. What is the function of the school in the society? What is the nature of the culture in which the school functions? What is the nature of the learning process? How do people grow and develop? What is the nature of knowledge? What is the nature of the physical environment for learning?

Although all these questions must be satisfactorily answered, in the school district the areas of knowledge to be taught, of experiences to be offered, and of methods to be used become the focus of conflicts. Persons with a traditional view emphasize the three R's and traditional college-preparatory subjects, whereas some "modernists" may not even indicate a specific body of knowledge to be taught. Agreeing on a theory of learning as the basis for the delivery system is again a value choice. Theories of learning must be examined in relation to goals.

As emphasized throughout this section, goals are the basis for all responsible administrative activity. Little can be accomplished in the classroom unless teachers focus upon tasks related to clearly understood and personally appreciated goals, and all administrative activity must be consistent with this goal—task focus. The goals of the schools should be attainable. They should be socially relevant, individually challenging, and speak to the compelling needs of the culture.

The educational goals must be meaningful to the educators directly concerned with program development. The test of meaningfulness is how useful the goals are in developing programs. Translating goals into specific programes is immensely important because this is where educators can determine whether they know what they want and need.

Numerous statements of the goals of education have been produced by various groups. In 1918 the Commission on the Reorganization of Secondary Education propounded the Seven Cardinal principles as follows: health, command of the fundamental processes, worthy home membership, vocation, citizenship, worthy use of leisure time, and ethical character. Some attempts to establish goals in recent decades were by the

Educational Policies Commission, National Committee for the Project on Instruction, and American Association of School Administrators.

There are untold lists of these goals, which have been prepared by national, state, and local groups. Some of these lists are so general as to be devoid of social direction. For example, the Seven Cardinal Principles could be as applicable in a Russian school as they would be in an American school. To be meaningful, the statement of organizational purposes must be thoroughly legitimized and internalized intellectually by school administrators, teachers, and a preponderance of the clients of the schools. Moreover, they must be spelled out in detailed objectives. This means that processes must be established to encourage as many persons as possible to participate in the development of the school mission.

The process of translating the goals of the school into a school curriculum is a difficult one. There is the problem of selecting from available knowledge and the problem of how to structure this knowledge to facilitate attainment of objectives. The presentation of what is to be taught involves a concept of how children grow and develop. There are conflicting views on the subject, all of which seem to have academic respectability.

As illustration of this point is the subject curriculum linked with the principles of behavioural psychology. In relation to the educational goals, one structures (or packages) what needs to be learned in various subject areas (or disciplines). The principles of behavioural psychology (e.g., operant conditioning) may be followed in structuring the instructional materials. Behavioural psychology may also undergird the delivery system (e.g., methods of teaching, media). Hansen's description of the curriculum in the Amidon Elementry School in Washington, D.C., is illustrative of the subject approach to curriculum design.

The subject curriculum, which was based on this conceptual design, is not acceptable to many parents and educators who hold different beliefs about the nature of learning. For example, those believing in experimentalist views of knowledge and accepting

Gestalt principles of psychology believe that pupils should be more active in what and when they learn. The experimentalists are concerned about persons learning how to think through real-life situations.

The point of this discussion is that numerous alternative choices of curriculum designs are available, and a value choice must be made. No amount of data will prove empirically what the design of curriculum should be. However, well-defined school goals should help administrators and teachers make this choice.

Recognizing the burden of school leaders in keeping up with the many curriculum alternatives, the American Association of School Administrators publishers material on curriculum trends. In a recently published curriculum handbook, specialists in various fields of study indicated emerging concepts in curriculum, emerging concepts in the organization of knowledge, and emerging concepts of instruction.

Teaching and Instruction

School administrators face difficult decisions concerning the organization of instructional services. For illustrative purposes, some problems in organizing instruction follow.

An obvious problem involves the organization of the school district into school centres.

Although most school districts use some aspects of the graded school as a means of organizing pupils for instruction, some have developed various form of non-graded organizations. How teachers should be organized for instructional services has also been a point of continuing concern. The self-contained classroom and departmentalized patterns have been used widely. However, other school districts have moved to other patterns, such as teaching teams. There have been recurrent waves of interim independent study organizations since Washburne initiated the Winnetka Plan in Winnetka, Illinois.

Another aspect of instructional organization is the so-called tracking procedure. Various approaches to ability grouping are used. The controversy over heterogeneous versus-homogeneous grouping has not been resolved. This involves how pupils should be assigned to designated grades, teams, or other groupings.

Decisions about an instructional procedures are followed by the need for decisions about support services. Of primary importance is the task of providing the necessary materials and facilities. Although instructional materials alone do not make an instructional system, appropriate materials are absolutely essential in any learning system designed. The same can be said for the physical facilities and equipment.

Modern instructional programs must be supported by appropriate supervisory services and by well-organized in-service programs. The ultimate aim of supervisory services is to provide better instructional programs congruent with program goals. Moreover, opportunities must be provided for administrators and teachers to evaluate cooperatively the effectiveness of the educational programs.

5
Important Issues

During their efforts to develop theory in educational administration, They are impeded by three substantive problems:

1. They are not clear about the meaning of theory,
2. They have tended to be pre-occupied with taxonomies and have confused these with theories,
3. They have not been sure of the precise domain of the theory we are seeking to devise. Let us examine each of these in turn.

The construction of a theory demands an act of creative imagination. This is a tough assignment that many of us are not equal to, nor can we get help from a how-to-do-it manual. Theories cannot be produced on demand; they evolve, and they evolve in many shapes and in many different degrees of precision. The building blocks of which they are composed — the constructs, the postulates, the assumptions — may be molar or molecular. Thus, Parsons' "input" and "output" of social organisation and Hemphill's leadership acts are concepts of different orders. A theory may be broad and eclectic in its range, or narrow and specific. Shartle, for example, in formulating his theoretical framework for the studies of behaviour in organisations, has deliberately sought constructs from a variety of disciplines and has sketched his ideas on a broad canvas. The components of theory may also differ in the ease with which testable hypotheses can be adduced from the postulated model. The Getzels and Guba have tested empirically several specific hypotheses about roleconflict derived from their model. On the other hand, the tri-dimensional concept of the jab, the man, and the social setting, to which Griffiths refers, is essentially a taxonomy rather than a theoretical model in the strict sense of the term. For this reason, it does not lend itself to the derivation of specific, testable hypotheses.

Consequently, it is not surprising that we may sometimes wonder about the meaning of theory. Theories do not come in a standard brand; we find them in packages of different size and shape, wrapped in different ways, and labelled differently. One must respect these differences and must recognize that theories, like the human beings, who create them, follow different courses of development and grow at different rates. We must avoid rejecting a theoretical proposal simply because it still has a few rough edges. But it is one thing to respect these differences; it is another to deny them. The crux of the problem is that the term "theory" carries the burden of too many different meanings. Fiegl has stated the problem well:

A set of propositions may be called a "theory" for various reasons. It may be because these propositions are highly inferential—either because of the sweep of their generalisations or because of the remoteness of the concepts from those of direct observation. That is, we tend to regard assumptions as theoretical if they are only very incomplete or very indirectly confirmed. This customary terminology does not altogether recommend itself for the simple reason that a well-confirmed set of propositions could then not be called a theory. Yet, such is the ambiguity of our terms, that by a "theory" in the empirical sciences we may mean anything from a style or jargon of mere descriptions, from a mere classification, inventory, or typology to a full-fledged hypothetico-deductive system; from a bold guess or a suggestive working hypothesis, a programme of research, to an elaborate model in either analogical or purely abstract mathematical terms.

In educational administration this issue in complicated even further by the fact that some writers have used this term in the sense of "value theory", to refer not to how administrators do behave but how the ought to behave. This confoundment between the "is's" and the "ought's" of behaviour is responsible for a greater failure in communication between educators and social scientists than any other issue. No one will deny that we need normative standards—in the ethical meaning of the term—for how administrators ought to behave, but these prescriptions do not constitute a theory. These standards cannot be secured through the methods that we must use for constructing a theoretical model in science. In this model we must confine our attention to how administrators do behave. In short, the description or events and their evaluation must be kept distinct. To state the issue in other terms: the immediate purpose of research is to enable us to make more accurate predictions of events, not to prescribe preferential courses of human action.

Miller has noted our problems of communication in educational administration and has urged us to use words with greater precision. One place at which we might start is with the concept of "theory". Specifically, we may want to examine the advantages and the disadvantages of restricting this term to the meaning assigned to it by Feigl:

In order to provide for a terminology which will not constantly involve us in a tangle of confusions; I propose to define a "theory" as a set of assumptions from which can be derived by purely logico-mathematical procedures, a larger set of empirical laws. The theory thereby furnishes an explanation of these empirical laws and unifies the originally relatively heterogeneous areas of subject matter characterized by those empirical laws. Even thought it must be admitted that there is no sharp line of demarcation (except a purely arbitrary one) between theoretical assumptions and empirical laws, the distinction at least in the sense of a gradation, is illuminating from a methodological point of view.

One more terminological suggestion may help. Let us speak of scientific explanation wherever more specific or more descriptive statements are derived from more general or more hypothetical assumptions.

Main Problems

The first major problem, then, in developing theory in

educational administration is that we do not share a common understanding of the meaning of theory.

Note that according to Feigl's definition, a taxonomy, or classificatory scheme, is not a theory. To say that a proposal is only a taxonomy is not to disparage it, for even in the physical and biological sciences we find taxonomies that have served as useful precursors to theory. The difficulty is that taxonomies can become alluring in their own right and that sometimes we are tempted into offering them as "genuine" theories.

There are three related snares that we must watch out for in establishing taxonomies. First, the number of classifications we establish is limited only by the size of our vocabulary. The cogent question is whether the verbal categories we posit correspond to events in the "real" world, whether the event assigned to these categories are in fact mutually exclusive. It requires no great imagination to produce new sets of verbal categories—lists of skills and competencies, and various tabulations to describe the components of the administrative process. But for research purposes we must still demonstrate that one set of categories permits us to make a better prediction of events than another. The merit of our rubrics must be determined not by their Trendex ratings but by the quality of hypotheses that can be generated from them, by the extent to which they improve the accuracy of our predictions.

The second snare in using taxonomies is that we run the risk, say, of mixing oranges and battleships. We seldom are sure that the rubrics we have established are at a similar level of ordinality. There is the further danger that we may mix phenotypic and genotypic categories quite indiscriminately. The essential snag, of course, is that the taxonomic method— as we have ordinarily used it in education—is based upon the Aristotelian as opposed to the Galilean mode of thought. The taxonomic approach therefore fails to take advantage of the very shift in emphasis which has brought about such great progress in the physical and biological sciences.

The third share in using taxonomies is the fallacy of assuming that, if we juxtapose two or more taxonomic schemata, we can somehow or other produce a theory. We discover, however, that even when we force two taxonomies into mating position, nothing happens; the conception of theory demands greater fertility than taxonomies possess. Why? Because the classification of similarities and differences does not in itself permit us to specify the order of the phenomena we study or to define the relationships that obtain among them. This must be accomplished by a creative act of a different kind. Taxonomies have their place, but they do not automatically grow into theories. Nor do all taxonomies have good potentials for being developed into theories. Much depends upon the type of events that are classified and the exclusiveness of the categories into which the events are sorted. But even the best of taxonomies, or the best two or more taxonomies taken in conjunction, will not yield a hypothetico-deductive theory.

Much research energy in educational administration has been dissipated through the failure to recognise the snares of the taxonomic method. One need only examine the bulk of the studies conducted through the CPEA. We can charge off our early mistakes as "good learning experience", but it is difficult to condone dogged persistence in repeating these same mistakes.

In sum, then, our second major problem in developing a theory of educational administration is that we have tended to be too pre-occupied with taxonomic methods.

Finally, we have not been sure of the precise domain of the theory we are seeking. Administration is a practical art, pursued by men in a world of action. Yet a theory of administration can be practical only in a limited sense: it can permit us to declare that if you do x, consequence a will result; if you do y, consequence b will result. However, the theory itself cannot give us information on whether consequence a or consequence b is more desirable for a given organisation at a given time. Accordingly, when we say that we want to develop theory in educational administration, it is important for us to find answers to certain questions. What is the domain of the theory that we are trying to forget? What kinds of predictions are we seeking to make? To make these predictions with sufficient accuracy to warrant our efforts, how molar can we afford to make the components of the theory? How molecular? It is not enough to say that we intend to make better predictions of behaviour and of other events; we must also specify the level of events and the kinds of behaviour with which we propose to deal.

This is the place, too, where we must be sure to keep our "is's" and "ought's" straight, where we must be prepared to take all our hidden value assumptions out into the open and make them explicit.

Hence, there are three major questions about theory that we must examine. The first is: What is the minimum number of value assumptions we must invoke in order to construct a satisfactory theory of educational administration? And the corollary: Can we agree on these assumptions? The second question concerns the molar-molecular issue. Should we seek to articulate molar theories, such as Parsons' and Shartle's with theories of a more molecular type, such as Hemphill's and Getzel's ? If we agree that this is desirable, then how do we achieve articulation? The third question relates to possible differences between administration and the special province of educational administration. Obviously, business administration, hospital administration, public administration, and educational administration have many characteristics in common. To the extent that we can, indeed, identify g (or general) factor, a theory of administration is meaningful. But there are s (or specific) factors, too, that distinguish educational administration from other forms of administration. These g and s factors require examination.

These, then, are the major substantive problems that impede the development of theory in educational administration. It will not be enough to "solve" these problems; they will have to be "resolved". And resolved means re-solved— solved again and again. Now, let us turn to the major communicative issues.

Even in this brief attempt to discuss the problem of developing theory in administration, questions about the use of language arise. Practitioners and theorists must work together in developing theory and must be able to communicate with each other. Unfortunately, because of differences in their training, background, and day-to-day sphere of operations, the members of these two groups tend to think about events in different ways—and with different time-perspectives. The way they think, the concepts and ideas they use, and the conceptual frameworks within which they organize their ideas are different. This does not mean that one way is right and the other wrong. Each can be right for its own purpose. Nor does it necessarily mean that the two approaches are irreconcilable.

We must guard against castigating the practitioner as being purely empirical. The general run of practitioner is no more purely empirical than many social scientists. There are scientists so utterly empirical that their research never gets off the ground. On the other hand, there are scientists and administrators, too, who consistently soar in the clouds. They forget that every theory must be rooted in the actual world of experience. In cloud soaring, the scientist has an advantage, he can get away with flights into space for a longer time than the administrator; he is not as promptly called to account. But he, too, must eventually relate his theory to the "real" world.

The scientist has no monopoly on theory: effective administrators have invariably based their decisions upon somekind of theory of administration. The administrator, however, does not usually state this theory explicitly: he may not even recognize it as such. The explicitness with which a theory is stated contributes to the ease with which we can examine it, subject it to criticism, and modify it. But let us not make the mistake of assuming that explicitness, in itself, guarantees a better theory. A good theory can suffer through lack of explicitness, but a poor theory, no matter how explicit, will remain sterile.

When the practicing administrator and the social scientist encounter each other, several intriguing reactions occur. The scientist is quick to see shortcomings in how administrators perceive their problems. He notes especially the lack of "operationally defined" terms and the intermingling of facts and value judgments. Consequently, the probing character of the scientist's questions can help the administrator better understand his own problems. The administrator, however, does not always detect shortcomings in how social scientists formulate problems. He often allows himself to be too impressed by the scientist's technical jargon: he is afraid that by asking questions he may expose his naivete. This is unfortunate, for hokum can suffuse the scientist's language just as easily as it can bog down the language of the practical man. Yet because science is a sacred cow in our culture, the pronouncements of scientists have been sanctified. Nor has this situation been relieved by scientists who trade upon the obscurity of their own jargon. What we forget is that no change in the wording can make a trivial idea profound: we sometimes mistake complexity for profundity.

The administrator's hesitance in questioning the scientist results in a loss for both groups. The social scientist loses the wealth of ideas that practical men can contribute; he loses an important feedback on his own theorizing. Similarly, the administrator losses either by contenting himself with a superficial acceptance of what the scientist has to say or by categorically rejecting as impractical all that the scientist has to offer. In either event, the schism between the two groups is made more pronounced. Despite pious protests on both sides that theory and practice are an integrity, these adjurations become an empty catechism, while each group, de facto, continues to play its own game by itself.

Each set of players has its own defense mechanism. The scientist becomes increasingly disdainful in casting his pearls of wisdom—and I have chosen this metaphor deliberately because of the attitudes of many social scientists. The scientist concludes that it is not his responsibility to communicate his ideas clearly to the ultimate consumer. On the other hand, the practitioner consoles himself with the knowledge that he is on the real firing line, that what he contributes to his school system is more important than any misty theory.

To circumvent these language difficulties, we must be sure that we understand the referents of the concepts we use. This understanding can be achieved only through patient and respectful questioning and cross-questioning. We shall have to learn to be tolerant with each other, and we must be willing to ask questions that appear naive. Naive questions are disarming; they puncture the balloon of hokum that gives our jargon a false impression of substance. In addition to patience and respect, it would be well for us to bring to our task a good sense of humor. In many ways administrators and scientists take themselves too seriously. What we need most, perhaps, is the freshness of approach that marked the little boy in *The Emperor's New Clothes.*

We already agree on the interdependence of practice and theory. Incantations on this score need not be repeated: we must, however, vivify this point through a rich supply of concrete examples, so that administrators will be better able to relate their day-to-day experiences to appropriate theoretical frameworks. We need to build bridges between our theories and live, concrete case material. Sargent and Belisle and Griffiths have made a start in this direction.

The third source of problems in developing a theory of educational administration is motivational: what are our personal motives in working on this problem? This is a delicate issue, but it demands examination.

Administrators and social scientists alike must guard against personal motives that are less than lofty. We are part of our culture, and there are values in our society that can lead us astray in our effort to develop a theory. The present comments will be confined to only three of these values. First, as we noted earlier, in the high value our society places on Science, with a capital S. The second and third values have been identified by Shartle in his list of value dimensions. The second is newness—that new ideas and things are better than older ones. The third is change—that frequent changes are better than infrequent ones.

People in the advertising business know how to capitalize upon all three of these values. By putting a TV pitchman into a white coat they give a greater credence to their claim for THE BIG CHANGE: Wheezies, with their NEW scientific filter, with 20,972.68 separate filter traps, will not produce lung cancer. Observe the shrewd touch of including the 68 filters: this "accuracy" makes the statement more scientific.

In the world of everyday affairs we are all barraged by appeals to change, to something new, appeals often bolstered by the argument that the new is more scientific. This applies to detergents, automobiles, and movements to education. For example, there is a tendency in education to join new movements not so much because of their intrinsic soundness, but simply because they are new, "Progressive" education, the look-and-say method of reading, and group dynamics have each, in turn, been embraced with greater enthusiasm than understanding. Fads and styles in education, like the length of women's skirts, have had their ups and downs and have been pursued and accordingly. We would like to hope that our pursuit of theory in educational administration is based upon appeals of less transitory revelation. Our task deserves a stronger commitment than this.

However, one must be wary of succumbing to such temptation. For example—and with no intention of presumption— John Dewey and Kurt Lewin were less dogmatic and less zealous about their own ideas than were disciples. Consequently, our progress in developing useful theory in administration may depend, at least in part, upon our ability to keep this endeavour from being viewed as a new movement. Progress will be steadier and more constructive if we can discourage as prospective co-workers those eager individuals who, in perceiving the effort as a new bandwagon, aspire to increased status by being among the first to jump on it.

To repeat, our purpose is to enrich our understanding of administration. The fact that our effort to devise theory is new, that it reflects change, and that it wears the white cloak of science guarantees the achievement nor the intrinsic merit of our objective. Although the values of science, newness, and change have a positive side, they can also become meretricious. Consequently, our effort should not be construed simply as a new gimmick for educational administration, nor should it be proffered as a panacea.

Likewise, we must not let our ideas degenerate into slogans. Expressions such as "research design," "action research," "group dynamics," and "the whole child" have been used so loosely and with such abandon that they have been debauched of meaning. "Administrative theory' will become another empty slogan if we use it as a rallying cry and proselytize in its name.

Some of us will need the examine our motives rather carefully. Are we seeking a better understanding of theory, or are we trying to promote the idea of theory? These motives are starkly different. In seeking a better understanding of theory, and through patient application to the development of better theory, we shall gain greater acceptance for this approach. But this acceptance will come about through the merit of what we actually accomplish, not through claims of what we intend to accomplish. Neither a particular theory nor the idea of theory are things to be sold, to be marketed as an advertiser might market a new breakfast cereal.

Teachniques in Vogue

Most administrators develop skilfull techniques to secure support for the programmes they initiate. This often is necessary in education, and for this reason some promotional ability on the part of the administrator is useful. But because these promotional skills have proven effective in other areas, a few of us may be tempted to apply them to the present endeavour. This would be a mistake, since it would reflect motives alien to our purpose. Our gains must be measured by the integrity of the ideas we generate, not by the number of supporters we enlist. In education we have paid so much obeisance to the dogmas of democratic method that we have failed to stipulate those areas where the method does not apply; we have failed to observe, for example, that the merit of a theory cannot be assayed by majority vote.

Social scientists, too, are not innocent of contaminated motives. Few are as crass as one former colleague who declared, "A theory is better than money in the bank. You can't get ahead in this field unless you publish a theory- any theory." The promotion system in American universities, with its premium upon the length of a professor's publication list, does little to discourage this attitude. Furthermore, Professor Zilch likes to be able to refer to Zilch's theory even if it consists of nothing more than two fugitive ideas held together with Scotch tape. As Zilch, or one of his brethren, once declaimed, "I don't care whether they understand me, damn me, or praise me, just as long as they quote me." These premises lead to a pre- occupation with theory for the sake of theory. The theorist becomes concerned chiefly about the elegance of his creation and is motivated by the admiration he expects from other theorists who are playing this same narcissistic game.

The theory, of course, is only a model, and it has no more reality than its creator endows upon it. Brass's observation on this point is pertinent:

> There is another very grave danger in the use of models. After a scientist plays for a long time with a given model he may become attached to it, just as a child may become, in the course of time, very attached to a doll (which is also a model). A child may become so devoted to the doll that she insists that her doll is a real baby, and some scientists become so devoted to their model (especially if it is a brain child) that they will insist that this model is the real world.

When social scientists and administrators come together there is a danger that the negative aspects of their motives will be accentuated. The scientists, not quite prepared to answer the questions of practical administrators, may tend to regress to the "theory for the sake of theory" position. The administrators, on the other hand, following the line of least action, may be inclined to support the idea of theory without fully comprehending its meaning. The interplay of these defence mechanisms can create for both groups an illusion of greater agreement than actually exists.

Further Scope

One purpose of administrators and scientists working together is to provide better reality-testing for their ideas; without this, the scientific method sacrifices its most important self-corrective feature. Thus continuing the quotation from Bross, we find:

> Now things are not that bad at the scientific level largely because of the self-corrective features of the sequential process of model-making which provide a periodic return to the real world after each excursion into the symbolic world. The test of the model acknowledges, as it were, the supremacy of the real world. If the model fails to predict what will happen in the real world, it is the model that must give way. This is the standard of scientific sanity:

This standard will guard us against a search for the theory of educuational administration and will help us recognize the possibility of alternative explanations. The scientist's predicament in this regard has been nicely stated by Einstein:

In an endeavour to understand reality we are somewhat like a man trying to understand the mechanism of a closed watch. He sees the face and the moving hands, even hears it ticking, but he has no way of opening the case. If he is ingenious he may form some picture of a mechanism which could be responsible for all the things he observes, but he may never be quite sure his picture is the only one which could explain his observations. He will never be able to compare his picture with the real mechanism and he cannot even imagine the possibility or the meaning of such a comparison. But he certainly believes that, as his knowledge increases, his picture of reality will become simpler and simpler and will explain a wider and wider range of his sensuous impressions.

Thus, as various theories of administration are presented to us, we need not ask, which is right? Each may help us make better predictions of events, and for this reason may appear "good" or "right". But note, as Einstein observes, that the scientist can never be quite sure his picture is the only one which could explain his observations. The fact is that we can never open the case to find out what really makes the watch tick.

This should teach all of us concerned with theory development some sense of humility, a sense less conspicuous among social scientists than among physicists and biologists. Specifically, we may do well to examine the principle of complementarity that Niels Bohr has enunciated in the field of atomic theory. This principle, in slightly paraphrased form, states: The use of certain concepts in the description of nature automatically excludes the use of other concepts, which, however, in another connection are equally necessary for a description of the phenomenon. From this perspective, the dilemma of free will versus causality is resolved; both "explanations" are needed, and in their own right both are tenable. The application of Bohr's principle to the social sciences has not been examined—let alone spelled out. But if we view various theories of administration in the spirit of Bohr's principle of complementarity rather than construe these theories as competing explanations of the truth, our progress will be healthier. This attitude may also alleviate some of the obnoxious symptoms of young investigators freshly pregnant with theory.

There is no intention to paint as a villain every scientist who devises a new theory, to imply that his motives are solely those of self-aggrandizement. Nor need we denounce categorically administrators who conscientiously seek to promote the idea of theory. Both scientists and administrators may operate with perfectly decent motives; the ends they avow may be perfectly laudable. But the means most readily available to them within their respective milieux may contaminate these ends and may in fact, subvert their personal motives. Consequently, we must all be alert to the devious ways in which our motives can be corrupted by the social pressures under which we operate. This awareness will not guarantee the elimination of such corruption but may reduce its likelihood.

To recapitulate, our problems in developing theory of educational administration may be classified under three general headings; substantive, communicative, and motivational. For purposes of presentation, these three sources of difficulty have been discussed in order, in the knowledge that the problems we encounter within a specific context can never be attributed to a single source of difficulty apart from the other two. Most of our difficulties stem from problems of communication, from the fact that we do not always make our concepts clear. Unfortunately, even when a writer defines his concepts with startling precision, there is no assurance that his readers will receive his concepts in this way. Their own predilections may prevent them from incorporating into their own thinking the writer's ideas. This is why repeated feed-back is needed between communicator and recipient.

What are the implications of these remarks? We must listen to each other with respect. We must feel to raise critical —even damning—questions, but without malice or antagonism, and stand ready to answer such searching question, but without defensiveness. We must all recognise that we are engaged in solving what Hemphill refers to as a "mutual problem". To accomplish this, each of our cooperating disciplines must forego any claim to a monopoly on wisdom.

If the lessons we have learned for NCPEA, CPEA and UCEA mean anything, then the success of the future will depend upon liberal portions of two ingredients. The first, of course, is complete respect for each other's intellectual integrity. The second is patience—the patience to listen and to explore each other's ideas through questioning and cross-questioning in an effort to comprehend what we are saying to each other. More than mere verbal acceptance is necessary; we must form a basic understanding as well. This kind of listening is tough work, but there is no alternative.

6

Structural Setup

The cultural context in which the organization operates determines its ends. The values of the broader society, and the fact that education is a culture-wide institution, have an undeniable influence on policy formulation. However, the institutional values which regulate and guide education are not always compatible with the goals of a particular organization or school. The administrator is sometimes forced to choose between the welfare of his school and the improvement of education. Such a choice constitutes a fundamental aspect of educational leadership. The interplay between organizational and social leadership deserves some brief comment.

Theory and Practice

Much modern administrative thought stubbornly encourages a mythical separation of value and fact of "policy formulation," and "administration." This analytical separation is difficult to maintain in practice. Which is a matter of policy and which is application of the policy: "learning social studies," "learning history," or a course in American history in the eleventh grade? Each of these statements has been treated by school boards as a policy function within their province. Moreover, the distinction conveniently justifies a passive administrative posture toward policy formulation, and produces in administrators a characteristic retreat from concern with long-range planning and purpose. It also encourages its counterpart, an excessively technical orientation. Accordingly, one writer states of educators: "....Those concerned with administration too seldom look beyond the machinery of administration to see what purpose it serves..." Newlon's study of eighteen textbooks of administration between 1882 and 1932 reported that fiscal administration, business administration, buildings and equipment were, at that time, the prominent emphasis in courses for preparation of administration. None of the texts were concerned with purposes or factors that influence policy.

Harlow has held that the most neglected and yet among most important aspects of administrative preparation is concerned with the processes of purpose definition. He states, "...public, wide-scale education is not a given in any social order; it is a creation. It comes into being as the servant of social purpose. Its content and processes are altered to accommodate changes in these purposes. And education itself bears most intimately upon the formation and revision of the purposes which it in turn is required to serve.

Later writings in educational administration have included statements of purpose, and objectives for education. Moehlman's book, School Administration, which was popular during the 1940's and early 1950's devoted a substantial amount of space to the background of educational science, and purposes of education. Yet, even then, and to some extent today, the statement that the purpose of administration is to "facilitate instruction" was accepted as a raison *de etre* for administration. This has become a well-worn cliche among school administrators. It really says nothing except that administration is dedicated to providing machinery, tools, and techniques to develop that which is already set up. The emphasis has been on means, techniques, and operational recipe for "banking a good cake." Ends and means have been considered inappropriate concerns for school administrators. Consequently, to this day the organizational objectives of school organization, as they apply to the internal organization, have not been clearly denned, and very little study or thought has been given to the extent of conflict between the internal organizational objectives of school and the broader societal objectives of education. Developing from this orientation is an ideal image of an administrator who is a skilled technician but essentially neutral, and therefore adaptable to any goal that is hired to serve.

This "cult of efficiency," the stress of technique-orientation, as it has been called, not only reverses the relative theoretical importance between ends and means, but it obscures the impact that purely technical decisions may have on organizational purposes. The seemingly technical decision to organize schools in terms of the so-called "comprehensive classroom," by including non-intellectual and intellectual students in the same classroom, has made it very difficult to emphasize scholarship in the contemporary classroom. It is misleading to visualize organizational purposes as given, in view of the fact that they are continually being modified by the "technical" decisions that are being made every day. Even so mundane a decision as the purchase of new desks, which on the surface appears to be a purely technical problem best determined by the logic of efficiency, places limits on policy formulation; the use of funds in this way commits the organization to use out-dated textbooks for another year, for example. Once a technical decision has been made, it may be simpler to change policy than reverse the initial decision. Because of the interdependence of means and ends, the administrator is forced into a position of institutional leadership, whether it is recognized as such or not.

Although they are created as a technical expedient to achieve certain institutional goals, organizations readily become embodied with value and transformed into temples of tradition. Thus, the five-or six-period day, the summer vacation, and educational television are defended, or resisted, because they disturb traditions and for sentimental reasons other than their demonstrated educational value. This fusion of organizational technique with institutional value is the process whereby means become transformed into ends.

Institutions in the Making

The institutionalizing process has a significant influence on both the nature of internal relationships and on the leadership role. Established ways of doing things provide a source of personal satisfaction, a sense of continuity, a fixed plan of action, and a fixed personal image, all of which commit personnel to a particular way of organizing, But all of this may be costly, for it binds the organization to specific aims and procedures, limits the freedom of leaders, and reduces the organization's ability to adapt to changing conditions.

While reducing the organization's adaptability, Structural institutionalization increases its autonomy, because institutionalization does fix the operation and the responsibilities for it more precisely, external social forces will have less effect upon the organization. One writer suggests that the opportunity and need for strong institutional leadership diminishes as institutionalization proceeds; the need to standardize declines as the homogeneity of personnel increases. Conversely, schools with numerous and ambiguous goals require strong internal leadership; leadership is dispensable only in fully institutionalized stable organizations, and then at the expense of their flexibility.

Vital Side

Institutionalization is a two-way process. Besides the fact that the internal operations become infused with value, the organization is forced to live up to the board institutional values that define the purpose of the school. That is, the institutional setting forces upon the administrator a responsibility for improving education which involves more than the concern with his own school. As Selznick points out, the leader is in a position, to act as an "agent of institutionalization" exerting influence over the haphazard direction of institutions. Because of his official position, and the implications that the decisions which pertain to his school may have throughout the institutional fabric, the executive of the local school does in fact help to shape and direct the development of education in this country.

A leader who is aware of his institutional leadership responsibility will probably proceed differently from one who is not. In fact, Selznick believes that the most serious default of leadership is failure to face up to the problems of institutional success while seeking organizational success. Of this Selznick says, "he [the leader] fails if he permits sheer organizational achievement, in resources, stability, or reputation to become the criterion of his success. A university led by administrators without a clear sense of values to be achieved may fail dismally while steadily growing larger and more secure." The administrator who resists consolidation, who ignores the problems of his colleagues in other school systems, who fails to support his colleagues before the state legislature or their own school boards, and who seeks to advance his school at the disadvantage of other schools, is failing as an institutional leader even while improving the welfare of his own school. His failure to recognize the implications of his actions for institutional development may permit the organization to drift along a course of short-run adaptations to unintended institutional changes which ultimately sacrifice student and social welfare. But for those leaders who recognize them, institutional considerations provide another aspect of the environment which must be taken into account The institutional leader will not sacrifice the welfare of education in the name of his school's success. It is this fundamentally moral character of the institutional leadership which makes the administrative task so difficult and challenging.

Internal decisions may be viewed either in terms of the environmental forces which shape them, or in terms of their potential effects on the environment. The decisions which most directly involve the broader society, such as personnel policies and proposed cooperation with other organizations, are usually more crucial ones. At such times, the organization must reappraise its general aims and adapt them without seriously corrupting the institutional values. It is precisely these decisions which have been ignored by the stress on routine problems of management.

Process of Governance

Because of the strategic limitations which the environment places on policy formulation, Selznick proposes that the leader's ability to maintain institutional values depends on his autonomy, that is, independence from outside pressures. As schools are exposed to the demands of outside groups, the special identity and the standards and ethics of professional educators are endangered by countless compromises with public pressure groups.

Selznick proposes that administrative decisions should take into account the different capacity of subordinate units to defend their values from outside pressures. One defense is to attach weaker divisions to stronger units which are capable of defending themselves. However, the risk remains that the stronger unit will encroach on the goals of the subordinate unit. For example, a school administrator may have to justify a large expenditure of funds for data-processing equipment for purpose of research and self-study in education. Because research divisions are not usually recognized as justifiable operations by the public, the data-processing equipment is often incorporated into a stronger, more acceptable department, such as business and finance. But as a result, the research and study tends to be dominated by the finance department, with an emphasis on finance and business rather than learning or instruction.

From this analysis, it is apparent that the decision capacity of administrators can be improved by more effective methods of analyzing power structures. This is not equivalent, Selznick points out, to more "human engineering," "Human engineering" stresses skill in getting others to accept decisions, but ignores the basic problems of decision-making itself. Nor will improved decision capacity be achieved by more concern with be "public relations," the role of the leader is not defined by his ability to create harmony, which can be achieved regardless of what the end may be. Analysis of decisions must focus on the forces that deter the organization and the pressures which bear on it to sacrifice its distinctive competence, its social purpose.

Such an intensive analysis requires, first of all, a "systematic" view of organizations that is, executives must be cognitively capable of conceiving the organization as a total entry. Such a cognitive view necessitates a rather abstract reconstruction of the organization's significant components; a model meets such requirements and one that is useful and appropriate is that of Talcott Parsons.

According to Parsons, there are four basic levels of organization in a social system which may be said to constitute a structural hierarchy. These levels extend from the most highly unified at the top to the most highly differentiated at the bottom. "At the Bottom of the structure, the social system is rooted in the concrete human individual as a physical organism acting in a physical environment." This individual participates in processes social interaction through various roles. At the top is the society as a total system such as a single political collectivity which institutionalizes an integrated system of values. Thus, at the bottom where there are many millions of individuals, the system is highly segmented and differentiated; while at the top of the system, unity is attained through the medium of a common culture and a generally homogeneous value system. The various levels may therefore be interpreted as constituting intermediate structures which are necessary to the functioning of the general system.

The lowest level Parsons designates as the technical of primary level of the system, and as such it produces outputs of significance to other levels and receives inputs from other primary sub-systems. The next level may be designated as the managerial. Two further levels as the institutional and the societal.

Parsons asserts that all social systems are organized about two major axes and when these axes "are dichotomized, they define four major 'functional problems,' with respect to which they differentiate." These four functional categories apply at any of the four fundamental levels of organization referred to above.

The first of the two major axes represents the relationships that exist between the organization itself and its external environment:

External
Internal

The second axis of differentiation is ".....central to what Durkheim called the 'division of labour' through which parts are differentiated and concomitantly integrated through 'organic solidarity.' It is analogous to the differentiation between means and ends in terms of action as such." When these two axes are dichotomized, they produce the following schema:

	Instrumental (Means)	Consummatory (Ends)
External	The problem of adaptation	
The problem of goal-attainment		
Internal	The problem of tension-management	The problem of integration

Practical Difficulties

In the above schema, the dichotomization of the two organizational axes generates what Parsons has termed variously as "imperatives," and "functional problems." He has used the latter term in his more recent writing.

Although the four functional-problem dimensions may shade into each other, they must be considered as qualitatively differentiated categories. The four categories that are derived are (1) adaptation—the external-instrumental reference; (2) goal attainment—the external-consummatory reference; (3) latency (or in some of Parsons' writings, pattern-maintenance and tension-management)—the internal-instrumental reference; and (4) integration—the internal-instrumental reference. The processes which involve these functional categories, or organizational problems, generate what is known as an "action cycle."

Chandler Morse provides a lucid interpretation of these categories. He points out that goal-attainment represents the termination of an action cycle. By the same token, an action cycle of a subsystem terminates when it has completed its contribution (at any given moment in time) to the functioning of the larger system. Thus, a school system completes an action cycle when it contributes high school graduates to society. This represents the ultimate goal of the school even though there may be a number of highly important intermediate goals—for example, changes in behaviour of pupils as they progress through school. More acceptable behaviour therefore acts as an output of the school and an input for the societal system because it is required by the societal system in its various functioning.

Adaptation, according to Morse, involves the process of mobilization of the means for goal-attainment and tension-management. The adaptive problem is that of properly perceiving and rationally manipulating the external world for the attainment of ends. The two best simple examples of the adaptive function as inter-related task-conditions are public relations on the one hand, and the securing of facilities, personnel, supplies, and so on, on the other hand, which allows the system to continue to operate as a system pursuing culturally prescribed goals.

Integration is the process of achieving and maintaining appropriate emotional and social relations (1) among those directly cooperating with the goal attainment process, and (2) in the system of action viewed as a continuing entity. The integrative problem generates those management tasks associated with holding cooperating units "in line" and of creating and maintaining "solidarity" despite emotional strains which normally accompany goal-attainment; important to this also is the development of whatever devices are necessary to the sharing of rewards in the cooperation process. In other words, integration concerns the mutual adjustment of units or subsystems from the point of view of their contributions to the effective functioning of the system as a whole.

Latency or tension-management, is an interlude between successive goal-attainment phases. It is not a period of inactivity, but rather the activities consist of restoring the energies, motives, and values of cooperating units and do not explicitly advance the larger system toward its goals. Generally, this function refers to the maintenance of the structural pattern of the system. Such functions in the public school system could be those of pupil accounting, building maintenance, preparation of lesson plans, in-service training, and general house-keeping responsibility.

The most important thing to remember about this theory of action is that for each level of the hierarchical structure of organization, the next operational level is the most significant. If it is remembered that Parsons specifies four levels in the hierarchy—the technical, or primary; the managerial; the 'institutional; and the social—then for a school system we have:

Political entity .... Societal level

Fiduciary boards	....	Institutional level
Administrators	....	Management levels
Teachers and pupils	....	Technical, or primary levels

Using the paradigm developed by Parsons, Curtis surveyed as many studies as he could find (going back to 1890) which dealt with the functions of the school superintendent in an attempt to determine which of the four functional problems were dominant. Among other things, he concluded that the superintendent "has primarily been responsible, for performing the 'instrumental' functions of the organization." And Curtis further concludes that more recently "...the superintendence not only has become more 'instrumental' but more 'adaptive" — in other words; more concerned with external-instrumental activity than with internal-instrumental, but in any case not much concerned with what Parsons has called "consummatory" (ends) functions. This reinforces the writers' view that decision analysis must focus on those socio-cultural forces that deter from the school's purpose; needless to say, purpose analysis is itself essential.

Leadership is not best understood by asking the question, who can best lead? In the first place this question does not distinguish between the skills necessary to become a leader and those necessary to lead once the position has been acquired. However, besides this theoretical inadequacy, the approach deflects attention from the underlying sociological conditions which influence leadership. The problem posed here is, under what conditions can the leader best lead? These conditions which influence leader behaviour involve such structural and cultural limitations as mobility patterns, vacancies, crises, organizational size, security of position, and the leader's 'cognizance of his social position and the institutional purpose that his organization was designed to fulfil. Although it is often more difficult to alter the organizational and cultural setting than to sift out personalities, the approach will clearly have implications for organizational alterations.

It is clear that when decisions are based exclusively on organizational welfare, they may violate ideologies of "individual interest" on the one hand, and broader institutional values on the other. Here is where the institutional leader clearly stands apart from the organizational leader in terms of his courage to face the problems of leadership. But if the conditions for staying in power are corrupting, as in the case of some labour union leadership and urban political positions. the demands of the job can erode the good intentions of the most idealistic of leaders. The sociological approach to leadership may eventually call for a major reorganization of school administration itself.

Implicit in any conceptualization of leadership is an assumption of super-ordinate-subordinate relations even though (as with small, informal groups) it may not be clearly visible. With formal organizations, however, leaders are usually charged with the responsibility of appraising the efforts of subordinates and this inevitably affects morale.

7

Officials' Role

School systems have a bureaucratic organization. Bureaucracy refers to a method of organizing administrative functions. The method consists or essentially two principles, co-ordination and specialization. Specialization, the process of breaking work down into standard components, is accomplished through a hierarchy of offices which establish spheres of delegated responsibility. Officials are appointed, rather than elected to office, and they should qualify on the basis of skill rather than personality characteristics alone. Thus, the basis of official superiority is supposed to rest on competence and knowledge. Specialization permits the economy of training skilled experts in a relatively short period, thus cutting personnel training costs and raising work standards. Spheres of jurisdiction are prescribed to offices, and duties of office should be performed by dedicated workers for whom the job constitutes a career.

Since work constitutes only one of the employee's interests, bureaucratic principles are contrived to (1) secure personal, long-term attachment to the organization, and (2) assure compliance with the requirements of office. The first problem is met by guarantees of security in the career in the form of advancement opportunities, pensions, and seniority. The second problem is handled through penalties set for deviation, by principles intended to exclude the total personality from the work situation, and by in-service training.

Specialization sets in motion a counter-process, coordination.

The work is coordinated from central offices responsible for reintegrating specialized activities into a consistent whole. Central offices are rooted in three principles: centralized graded authority, a system of rules, and impersonality.

Power Centre

Centralization gives bureaucracy its rational character. For in the central office resides ultimate authority for final decisions concerning the ends of the organization, decisions of the functions of each speciality, responsibility for delegated duties, the formulation of policy, and the regulation of affairs of subordinate officers. Every official is accountable to his superior for discharging the special duties of his office, a condition which is often referred to as "the chain of command"—an elaborate rural designed to maintain consistency among well-defined spheres, of competence. Referring a problem to a responsible department helps prevent inconsistent decisions between interdependent parts of the organization.

Important Regulations

Rules represent the extension of central authority into the routine work situation. Much of the administrator's daily routine consists of applying rules to particular cases. This persistent reference to rules routinizes even the most dramatic work problems which confront the organization by classifying them and prescribing standard solutions. An irate parent who approaches the superintendent of schools with a problem which seems uniquely tragic (as, for example, her child's failure in a subject) may resent the routine detached way she is treated by the superintendent's office. Nevertheless, at the same time it is precisely this ability to scrutinize problems—whether problems of illness in the hospital, death in the morgue, or failure in school—which increases the public's confidence in the professional bureaucrat. As a matter of fact, the parent would have little confidence in a superintendent who did not see something of the routine even in the tragic: it permits rationality to rule emotion-ridden situations.

However, what appears rational for the individual specialist may violate the rationality of the organization. For example, although a teacher may find a seventy-minute class period is the most efficient working time for her classes extending her class periods would, of course, disrupt the coordination of the entire school and consequently reduce rather than increase its overall efficiency. In this way, rules objectionable though they may seem in particular cases, are ideally patterned after a model of overall organizational rationality.

The principle of impersonality promotes discipline by separating office from person, thus, minimizing the significance of the total personality while illuminating the job requirements. The broad outlines of job performance are standardized, and office, holders are expected to divorce their personal preferences, property and friendships from the performance of their duties. Thus, official relationships among offices and clients are impersonal and contractual. This is particularly important since organizations normally recruit personnel with a variety of interests, training, and background who are frequently political enemies. By suppressing external distinctions, organizations attempt to build reliance on their own systems of evaluation. The "democratic" atmosphere is thus only an unintended consequence of minimizing social class, ethnic, family, and other social distinctions for purposes of efficiency.

The impersonal character of bureaucracy is protected by (1) elaborate record-keeping procedures and (2) handbooks which make knowledge the property of the organization rather than of particular persons, thereby rendering individuals expendable to the organization. Record files constitute the organization's memory, just as rules establish its division of labour. It is such principles which also permit personnel turnover without seriously disrupting the work routine.

School bureaucracy often violates the usual elaborate record-keeping of bureaucracy. Knowledge in the form of teacher-made curriculum materials, work-sheets, and study guides often remain the exclusive property of the teacher. Most higher echelon school bureaucrats, however, actively sleek to control teacher-made materials. Handbooks set forth certain principles, often stated as rules, regulations, and policies for personnel to follow. The handbook is impersonal; all personnel are treated as though they were alike. However, it is less threatening to receive a handbook with rules and regulations laid out for everyone than it is to be told individually what must be done, and it creates less personal resentment. The reader of the handbook may not personally care for some or all of the regulations, but he is comforted by the fact that he has not been singled out for special attention. The handbook tells him, in effect, that he can expect to be treated the same as everyone else.

It is curious that while the threat of possible penalty is usually inferred, most of the time no special penalties are listed if the teacher fails to follow the rules. For instance, it would be interesting to speculate what the penalty would be if a teacher failed to empty his mailbox as specified in the sample pages of a teacher's handbook as follows:

Teachers' Responsibility

All teachers are to be in their rooms by 8:20 A.M. and no later than five minutes before the homeroom takes up at 1:32 P.M. All are requested to remain after dismissal until after 4.30 P.M. Teachers should plan to be available for student and parent conferences within those time limits. Your being in the building someplace will not serve this purpose if you cannot be found. Develop the habit of encouraging students to visit you before school as well as after school. If it is necessary to leave earlier than 4.30 P.M., please obtain permission from the principal.

It is the common responsibility of each member of the faculty to control the movements and the behaviour of the students at all times throughout the day. Each teacher is expected to be on duty outside the classroom door after 8.30 A.M. and when classes are passing Men teachers should assume the responsibility for the supervision of the boys' restrooms; the ladies the same responsibility for the girls' restrooms.

Any and all material for the Daily Bulletin must be turned into the office of the Principal by 4.30 P.M. of the previous day. All materials must be approved by the principal. The Daily Bulletin will be in each teacher's box by 8 A.M. each day and must be read at the beginning of the first period.

Only in cases of extreme emergency will special bulletins or verbal announcements be sent to rooms, and these only with the approval of the principal.

The Time Table

Each Friday a calendar for the next week will be prepared and placed in your mailbox on Monday morning. This calendar will include as nearly as possible the scheduled' events of the week. Each Thursday all sponsors are asked to hand into the office the information about any special meeting planned for the next week such as the place, Jay, hour, and purpose.

Each teacher has a mailbox in the principal's office and should come in before school in the morning and during the noon hour to receive any letters, communications, or bulletins which may have been placed there. Teachers must not allow things to accumulate in the mailboxes. They should be emptied daily.

The Outcome

Thus, these two principles —specialization of work and the coordination of tasks and their derivatives (hierarchy of offices, delegation of authority, professional career, centralized authority, a system of rules, impersonality and files)-constitute the division of labor which is bureaucracy. Specialization and coordination present a picture of bureaucracy as a simultaneous expansion and contraction of responsibility, a constant process of delegation and recentralization. In general, the greater the specialization, the greater will be the centralizing tendencies since greater specialization demands greater coordination.

The socially significant consequences of modern bureaucracy are the centralization of control and standardization of work performance. The former permits rationality but, significantly, does so by removing the decisions from the individual worker and the local community. The latter provides the foundation of the regularity of our society as well as increasing its efficiency but at the same time imposes on the individual rigid work routine and pressures to confirm to the organization, reducing opportunity for self-expression or deviation.

This constitutes a very brief description of the ideal conception of bureaucracy as it has been imagined by theorists of our time. This is the conceptualization. implicit in descriptions of school systems found in traditional administration textbooks. While the term "bureaucracy" is often used in a derogatory sense by the layman, it is, as a matter of technical usage described above, simply a style of organization. There is no question that school systems are bureaucracies. The questions that ought to be raised, however, pertain to the extent that the school bureaucracies function in the ideal terms often used to describe its organization. These questions will be explored subsequently and in the chapters which follow.

The Measurement

The foregoing statements are typical of descriptions of modern large-scale organization. Most statements of this kind are directly or indirectly derived from the ideas of Max Weber and his followers. Because of his overwhelming influence on the development of ideal-type descriptions, the work of Weber and the assumptions implicit in derivative discretions of large-scale organizations deserve closer attention.

Weber's work owes a great debt to the ideal type, a tool which was originally used to lend precision to cross-cultural comparisons. The ideal type is not an average of existing attributes—that is, it is not an empirical generalization based on observations—but rather it is a "pure" type derived by abstracting the mast logically characteristic aspects implicit in a concept. Its purpose is not to describe reality. Far from it, it specifies a general perspective to evaluate specific factors observed. It alerts the observer of bureaucratic organizations to certain characteristics —their rules, hierarchy, specialization, and so on. The ideal type, in itself, is not to be compared with reality; rather it provides the criteria by which to compare different parts of the real world. Consequently, while it is a guide to research, it is not a substitute for it. Whether bureaucracies actually exist in the form specified by the ideal type is to be decided by empirical investigation, not by referring to Weber or other theorists.

However, scholars following Weber's leads have chosen to ignore their historical antecedents. Some investigators have interpreted ideal characterizations of organizations as empirical descriptions of bureaucracies, with resulting misconceptions about their nature. Others, who have found empirical situations out of harmony with the ideal description, became unnecessarily disillusioned.

Weber's own use of the ideal type also contributes to the confusion. While he objected to the notion that ideal types are empirical laws or hypotheses, his bureaucracy is in fact not simply a conceptual scheme, but a series of hypotheses as well. For example, Weber states, "...it is held that the members of the corporate group, insofar as they obey a person in authority, do not owe this obedience to him as an individual, but to the impersonal order. Hence, it follows that there is an obligation to obedience only within the sphere of the rationally delimited authority. Whether a subordinate may in fact be "obligated" to perform personal services for superiors is a matter for investigation. And if investigated, the statement as a hypothesis would undoubtedly be rejected in many instances.

Francis and Stone find three meanings of bureaucracy as Weber uses it, two of which are relevant for this discussion. One is for the purpose of making cross-cultural comparisons. In this connection, bureaucracy is a fixed jurisdiction, a graded system of authority, a system of central files, a set of special, skills called office management, official activities which demand the full time of personnel, systematic and general rules which specify procedure. This set of criteria permits the classification of particular organizations as bureaucratic or non-bureaucratic. Another meaning of bureaucracy is found in Weber's ideal type analyses, which are statements about the nature of organization, in contrast to historical comparison. The three major characteristics of this meaning, according to Francis and Stone, are rationality, impersonality, and routinization. (Weber has also used the term as embodying a set of testable hypotheses rather than as a type.)

A major disadvantage of the use of the ideal type is that it seems to stress the extreme situation. It thus shifts attention from variability to the polar conditions. Weber's stress on rationality, for example, tends to obscure the facts of irrationality; the emphasis on rules directs the observations away from conflict: the emphasis on the public goals of efficiency has led to the assumption that efficiency is the only goal of bureaucracy; and prophecies about the inevitable "bureaucratization," or rationalization of the modern world persuades observers to ignore conditions of the modern world which prevent bureaucratization. For these reasons, widespread use of the ideal type has fostered a number of myths about organization.

High Officials

It must be concluded that the popularity of ideal type descriptions of bureaucracy which are found in much of the literature of educational administration may easily lead the student to misconceptions of existing administrative situations.

The persistent reliance of administrators on the ideal conception of organization is most evident in the widespread use of organization charts. When asked to describe his organization, the administrator will invariably point to his organization chart. A notable treed away from dogmatic reliance upon ideal organizational charts and prescriptive lists of administrative duties can be noted in the texts written in 1940. In that year Moehlman in his standard work in the field. School administration, recommended that the autocratic, inflexible school organizations of that time be replaced by flexible democratic organizations, a popular theme of the period. Nonetheless, even Moehlman accompanied his appeal for improvement in current practice with an idealized table of organization and prescriptive lists of duties, which were certain to maintain the status quo he disliked.

Deciding Bureaucrats

Part of the confusion between ideal and actual conceptions of bureaucracy stems from a tendency to confuse power with authority. Power is the capacity to use force, and authority is the legitimate right to power. But neither power nor authority imply the actual demonstration of force; they refer to its potential. For this reason the right to use force does not imply that it can always be used. For example, the high school principal may be authorized by the community and its board to require the teachers to take on "extracurricular activities" as a condition of employment. But if their union resists, his power is severely curtailed, his official obligation to retain his teaching staff significantly reduces the available alternatives. At the same time, as the illustration suggests, subordinates are exercising power without necessarily having the authority to do so. Similarly, a superintendent or school board member may use unauthorized power to have teachers fired for personal reasons

These disparities between power and authority constitute one of the major dilemmas of modern organization. Indeed, the relationship between power and authority itself is somewhat of a dilemma. Although power is directly dependent on the number of available alternatives, the conditions of legitimacy may impose such restraint on the use of power that it is severely reduced.

While authority remains an exclusive property of the office, power is neither a property of office nor is it exclusively a personality characteristic. Rather, power is created out of certain situations and is available to persons favourably situated who have access to, the conditions which generate power. These specific situations are found in the official and unofficial characteristics of the organization itself. The official organization makes power more accessible to some personnel than to others. For example, the secretary of a superintendent in a large school system sometimes controls the mailing list. This duty potentially provides her with power to control dissemination of certain kinds of information to certain teachers. In fact, because it affords direct contract with the chief executive, the position of secretary can be a very powerful position with its thorough access to the chief executive's personal correspondence and its other opportunities to gain his personal confidence.

One analysis suggests that any organizational "status" located in a managerial structure which provides strategic access to the control, or influence upon the control of information, assumes significant dimensions of potential power. Hence, under some conditions, even a janitor may capture a position of power. Waller tells of a janitor to whom the superintendent often came for advice on major policy decisions. Not only may such a worker interest with most of the school personnel, but if he has been in the system longer than many of the faculty, or if he is a long-time resident of a small community, he may have an important influence on public opinion.

Power may be used for either "good" or "bad" purposes. Power, like money, is simply a medium of exchange. Its utility is measured by what it will enable the person to achieve that could not be achieved without it. And its value must be assessed in terms of the purpose for which it is used. Of course, like money, power is sometime desired for itself but, also like money, only in exceptional cases.

From a democratic point of view, perhaps the ultimate basis of authority is the agreement which citizens have reached on the assignment of certain powers to particular offices. Considering this democratic ideal almost exclusively, one author proposes that the authority of an order is determined by whether or not it is accepted by members of the organization. This, for instance, might mean that the superintendent has a right to judge teaching competence and discharge poor teachers only so long as other members of the community and/ or the organization agree. The consensus of organizational members seems to clearly imply authorization and conversely, the resistance of subordinates seems to challenge the right to perform these functions. It is to this condition that Jaques has devoted some rigorous analysis and to which he refers as "the sanctioning of authority."

Authorization from the majority of subordinates, in effect, permits the administrator access not only to existing rules but also, more important, some influence over the rule-making machinery. Thus power evolves from this control over rules. Merely by applying or withholding application of rules tends to encourage those conformity behaviours which affect consensus. Through such a process, one comes to understand the structural bases behind the cliche that "power begets power."

But however democratic, it cannot be presumed that authorization is the exclusive prerogative of the members of the organization or of the local community. In the first place, the members may disagree among themselves, in which case some other party will assume the right to grant or withhold authority. Also, even if counted, every person's opinion is not counted equally is the opinion of the principal equivalent to that of the janitor or the teacher? Another reservation arises from the fact that organizations themselves may rest on other than representative bases, they may be authoritarian. But there is a major restriction of the democratic concept of authority. If the distinguishing feature of authority is a sense of legitimacy, this legitimacy may be derived from sources outside the organization. Social traditions and other agencies, such as the legislature, religious bodies, professional organizations, local school boards, and the State Department of Education, can bestow legitimacy on the functions of an office even when subordinates within the organization or residents of a particular community object.

In fact, it is characteristic of an administrative society that authority is bestowed by outside agencies. A good example of this occurs in many communities in relation to civil defense. The writers know of two cases where either the school system or an administrator in the school system was authorized by agencies outside of the system to assume civil defense functions. In the first case, the city council decided that since the school system had the only shelter facilities in the city, the school board was the logical agency to assume the responsibilities for civil defense. The local newspaper carried the story and several service organizations in the community backed the idea before the board of education had been contacted. At a special meeting the board issued a statement in which it said that the school system would cooperate with civil defense officials in whatever way it could, but that civil defense was a community problem rather than a school problem. They raised serious questions about the use of school buildings for shelters. They also pointed out that as new buildings were constructed any additional construction for shelter purpose would increase building costs, and they protested any attempt to make the school district assume financial obligations beyond that of providing personnel and facilities for teaching. Nevertheless, the political pressure was such that the superintendent of schools became the local director of civil defense, a job he did not want. His authority rested on the community power structure rather than the consensus of subordinates. Largely because the school system refused to provided for shelter space in the new building, a vote on a bond issue was defeated.

In a second case the superintendent of schools was approached by a committee to take on the responsibility of educational director for civil defense in a medium-sized city. He suggested to the committee that they approach a top-notch young junior high school principal for the job. The young principal conferred with the superintendent and took the job. He had two interesting experiences. The first experience occurred while he was in the process of organizing a plan for the evacuation of children in the public school system. He had no problem with the junior high school teachers who saw him as their principal, but when he met with the elementary and senior high school teachers to explain the plan and elicit their support, he found that they would not coöperate with him, He finally accomplished the job by working through the superintendent and "borrowing the colonel's eagles." In other words, he had to borrow the prestige power and authority of the superintendent of schools. The staffs of the elementary senior high schools accepted him one basis of authority—that bestowed as an agent of the superintendent but not on the other as junior high school principal. To ask whether he had "authority" is to miss the point, he had several types of authority—bestowed by subordinates and super-ordinates—which had differential value before different audiences.

Because of the variety of authorities that can he appealed to in modern society, there is a persistent tendency for dissent to arise among groups bestowing various sources of authority. Power is always in the process of becoming authorized, and persons who are authorized to use power persistently tend to overstep their offices and use it in more questionable ways. Consequently, in practice it is often difficult to distinguish between power and authority—that is, to know when power is being utilized legitimately. Under these conditions the legitimacy of official acts is difficult to establish. For example, does a principal have the authority to withhold a student's grades because he is in trouble with the law? In cases where there is dissent among the public it is often not even clear who has the right to decide the issues. It is power itself that looms large in the solution of these conflicts. For whenever two groups support different conceptions of what is proper, they each attempt to accumulate enough power to have their point of view accepted, This was true of the Crusades and continues to stimulate the zeal behind missionary work. It is true on a lesser scale of most differences of opinion. In such cases, the establishment of authority itself often represents the outcome of a power struggle. Just as the North's authority to make federal laws which the South opposed was decided by the Civil War, so the question of whether the public or the professional teacher has the ultimate authority to pass judgment on the selection of textbooks will be decided by the outcome of that struggle.

In short, the problem of authority is regressively based on power, curiously, in marginal situations the right to use power may be bestowed only by those who have the power to bestow it.

When desparities do arise between power and authority, the dissent threatens the "we" aspect of the organization. But they typically do not occur in the daily routine of activities. There are, according to Barnard, several reasons why authority is seldom challenged by subordinates. First, most administrators take care to issue only those orders which they know will be obeyed. For the same reason, many rules which are resisted are not enforced in practice. Second, most persons are indifferent to the legitimacy of most orders. Most orders are irrelevant either to their moral codes or to their way of life. It seems to make little difference to many teachers whether they drive on the right-hand or the left-hand side of the road, or whether one text or another is used. Constant concern with such questions leads to "moral exhaustion". In fact, persons are disposed to grant authority rather than question it precisely because they are unwilling to take the time, effort, and abuse necessary to resist it. Finally, organizations often develop a sense of community which discourages outright dispute of authority. In these situations, the violation of an order by an individual seems to constitute an attack on the entire organization, including one's co-workers whose positions or very job may be threatened when their colleague "stirs up trouble."

It is, however, a mistake to judge the importance of an event by its infrequency of occurrence. A single unauthorized act of power can create an organizational crisis which becomes the source of deep-seated organizational tensions which in turn have the capacity to modify the total character of the organization. The sources of the disjunction between power and authority, when they occur, can often be traced to the nature of organization itself.

There are several reasons why the organization generates many of its own dilemmas. The first of these reasons is related to the fact that specialization tends to develop beyond official limits. An official will tend to devote most of his time and energy selectively to a few of a complex of duties which constitute his office. For example, the vice-principal in a school system may specialize in purchasing because he knows how to calculate the percentage of waste and breakage, knows how to estimate needs, knows the "right people" to buy from and where to get a "good deal"; he may find himself buying increasingly more for the entire system, even though he is not specifically authorized to do so. The very fact that he may know more about the details of the job than anyone else further enhances his control over the job.

As another example, the school typist is not ordinarily authorized to command teachers, but in fact she may have power over them because she can control the work schedule. While she cannot refuse to type authorized work, the teacher who does not treat the typist properly may find that her work is finished later than she had wished, and only the typist knows whether the time taken was reasonable.

Second, the tendency for delegation to develop beyond official limits separates power and authority. The duties of an official may be sloughed off or assumed by subordinates. In this way, the "dirty work" of the higher rank is absorbed into the lower ranks, bestowing power in the process. The addition of duties from a higher rank tends to increase the subordinates relative power. For example, while the administrator concentrates on purchasing, the budget, or curriculum development, his secretary assumes more responsibility, for preparing reports to the State Department of Education which in turn gives her reason to gradually exercise control over principals and others by prescribing proper reporting form, establishing deadlines, specifying the number of copies required, and so on.

Third, organizations have only partial control over the assignment of power because a person's power is also directly associated with the number and importance of his contacts outside the school. Teachers who have the support of many influential parents are valuable to the school, and they are in a position to get their own way. For example, the principal may be reluctant to refuse a pay increase to a teacher who is a good friend of an influential school board member. Within the organization as well power in excess of authority can be gained from personal contacts, which in turn are more easily made in some positions than others. The principal's secretary may be showered with the good will of his teachers because of her ability to delay or modify their messages to her superior, and because she has the opportunity to pass along her personal report on the teacher as well.

There are still other reasons why the school cannot completely control power. The power of personnel is, for example, partially an independent function of their chief executive's authority and power: the superintendent's secretary tends to claim prestige over the high school secretaries. Similarly, teachers working for an influential principal might claim status over other teachers in the system. The official position also determines which members have access to information. High school students sometimes have jobs which allow them private access to records, which bestows on them a position of power over their peers. In short, discrepancies between power and authority may develop because the official position places persons in differential access to power.

Finally, power becomes disassociated from authority whenever areas of jurisdiction are not clearly prescribed. In any organization there are jobs which are "no one's" particular sphere of authority, and which anyone may claim as his if he performs them well or frequently. In the process of adding unclaimed jobs to a position, the sphere of control is expanded. While these may eventually become authorized functions of the position, the transition creates ambiguous discontinuities between power and authority and constitutes the kind of dynamic element that gives an organization its distinctive character. Moreover, the simple fact of having difficulty in communicating with some officials can result in subordinates affecting changes in the authority structure. For example, the custodian may be reminded repeatedly that he must channel his requests through the principal, but if the principal is frequently "tied up" it is much easier to merely call the Director of Buildings and Grounds. A pattern that is effective is difficult to change.

It is apparent, then, that power and authority diverge in practice. This divergence corresponds to the discrepancy between the official and unofficial structure. The official structure is safeguarded by authority, while the unofficial structure is largely a function of power and non-authorized relationships. The multiple bases of authority and the role of power help to stabilize organizations in the face of dissent. Consensus is only one of the characteristics which account for the organization's stability and is not a necessary condition. The role of power wielded by the informal organization in maintaining organizational stability has still not been completely assessed, but stabilization seems to be a fundamental function of power in modern organizations.

The Apparatus

Bureaucracy is, then, a means of organizing work which permits—even encourages—specialization of talent and effort. Specialization creates a need for condition, which is achieved in a hierarchy of graded authority regulated by rules and other standardizing, depersonalizing mechanisms. A net result is a highly specialized, standardized, and centralized set of offices bound by depersonalizing rules. From a purely personal view point, this system may at times appear as a solemn system of red tape managed by indifferent personnel whose primary skills seem to be the application of forbidding rules and "buck-passing." Such a characterization, however, even if it were true, does not describe bureaucracy, but rather characterizes its presumed consequences for the individual, bureaucracy is not designed for the pleasure of individuals so much as it is engineered to institutionalize work. There are other consequences, mainly the efficient and effective uses of specialists.

However, the logically derived portrayal or the pyramidal structure is partly mythical, rooted in stereotypes of blueprint organizations which have become traditional. While it portrays an ideal conceptualization of the authority system from the view point of management, it seldom if ever depicts the actual use of power in many facets of operation. So long as it is clearly understood that it reflects the ideal, the pyramidal image of the organization has some utility. However, the temptation to convertly fuse the ideal and descriptive leave it susceptible to subtle transformations, wherein the ideal is represented as fact. When this occurs, the pyramidal image, like other features of the blueprint organization and indeed every feature of the ideal type, contributes to a mythology of organizations which is clearly detrimental to the understanding of conduct in organizations.

8
The Authorities

The importance of leadership is generally conceded. The execution of palicies developed in the school superintendent's office has repercussions throughout the community; examples of how educational leadership with respect to consolidation or school building programs infect the life blood of the broader society. In this chapter the significance of mature leadership will be more systematically explored.

Administrative Setup

It is fashionable to discuss leadership as a separate topic, apart from the nature of organization itself. But this is a misleading, if not warped, perspective of the process. It is an inescapable fact that the nature of leadership is conditioned by the nature of organization and of the society. Educational leadership cannot be understood apart from its complex, bureaucratic context and the "power" environment. For although leaders deal directly with individuals, ultimately it is organizations—that is, group traditions, established relationships, and vested interest groups—which are their main concern. Clearly, the problems, dilemmas, and inconsistencies of the organization and of the society are the problems of the leader. They constitute the leadership setting.

Ambiguity is an important and common element of the leadership setting. The school executive in particular lives in a world that is frequently inconsistent. He must set school policy in the face of conflicting public demands and internal factions. As stated earlier, just as effective supervision constitutes the ability to compromise organizational inconsistencies in the course of day-to-day relationships with personnel, so effective leadership involves the ability to live with the ambiguities created by such compromises and to incorporate them at the level of policy formulation and implementation.

The ambiguous setting is created largely by the problems so far discussed. It is instructive to enumerate them again. First, there are problems dealing with the competing demands of the public and various pressure groups. Indeed, the contemporary importance of administrators is largely due to their strategic relationship with the public, rather than to the inherent worth of internal coordination. Second, there are a series of tensions generated by myths that organizations either are, or ideally should be, rational, impersonally commanded, rule-directed, and harmonious, with consensus on ends and means, and, above all, on overall policy. Though these standards are never completely fulfilled, the belief that they should be fulfilled creates official pangs of conscience when performance falls below the ideal. Third, innumerable problems are created from processes of delegation. The leader is expected to maintain control and at the same time delegate his authority. Questions concerning the amount of authority that should be granted to subordinates and the amount of autonomy that is expected from them are perennial. Fourth, a series of problems arise because of inconsistencies between official and societal demands of extreme importance is the dilemma of exercising authority in an egalitarian society. The leader must strategically regard men as means, which is ideologically taboo in a democratic society. Differences between official and social evaluations concerning sex, age, ethnic and social origins, level of education, religion, and income must also be considered. Fifth, there is a recurring tendency for means to displace goals. The leader encounters special problems of maintaining his own position against poachers and the intrigues of other departments, while at the same time contributing to the welfare of both his own organization and to the social institutions for which he is responsible. Maintenance of office often entails greater attention to techniques and details and to internal politics than can be logically justified — that is, securing internal and external support, pleasing superiors, public relations, and so on. Finally, the leader must initiate change while at the same time maintain organizational continuity and stability. Line-staff conflicts and cleavages between local and cosmopolitan oriented personnel are natural adjuncts of this struggle.

The normal strains created by environmental pressures, inconsistencies of internal principles, conflicts between, office and status, ends-means dilemmas, and change-stability questions can easily become inadvertently exaggerated by certain leadership policies. At the same time, however, initiative and creativity are sometimes stimulated by the tensions that arise from these conflicts.

Moral Problems

It is also apparent that the leader lives in a morally complex environment where he must not only choose between right and wrong, but between two or more "rights." Consequently, to be effective, leaders must be morally complex themselves. This does not mean that effective leaders lack a conscience, but rather that they need a flexible and temperate one, as well as a sense of justice that is not rigid and takes into consideration the rights of all parties concerned. Indeed, all that many subordinates expect of their leader is that he will, over the long run, give them a "fair shake," and earnestly try to do what is "right" in situations where there is little consensus.

From one study of school executives comes evidence that "strong" leaders have a more realistic conception of the difficulties of administrative choices than "weak" leaders. Neither the school men who naively denied the extent of difficulties, nor those who greatly exaggerated the difficulties involved, received high leadership ratings from their subordinates. Effective leadership requires a realistic perception of dilemmas and some ability to clarify issues. Another writer suggests that weak leaders are fearful of conflict situations and seek merely to avoid trouble. They hesitate to act without consulting their superiors and fall back on official rules when they encounter problems, whether the rules are adequate or not. In relying on rules rather than ingenuity, the weak hold leadership positions tenuously (with seniority and experience as their only justifications for their position). They are easily displaced as rules go out of date. On the other hand, effective leaders tolerate dilemmas and seek to turn them to their own advantage or to the advantage of their organization. They are least morally threatened by a compromise because they are aware of moral complexities. Indeed, it is these complexities which provide the leader with an enormous opportunity to be creative and to "lead."

Axis of Administration

The simultaneous existence of formal and informal modes of organization provides the leader with at least two bases of authority, popularity and respect. Respect may be derived from either technical competence to lead the group to its goals, or from customary respect for the office itself independent of the person who occupies it. At times the leader is forced to decide whether to be popular with subordinates (by subverting official principles in their favour), or to uphold his official duties at the expense of his popularity. Sometimes he can do no more than cater to the will of his subordinates in order to maintain their goodwill; but the leader is also in many ways a group "deviate" who exercises a latitude in obeying and carrying out group norms which other members do not have. In extreme cases, a strong leader will be willing to contradict the sentiment of his subordinates and take a morally courageous stand at the risk of losing popularity. While the leader may be justly concerned about his popularity it, must be remembered that there is another basis of authority; he may be able to win the respect of subordinates with whom he is not especially popular if they agree with the ideals that he is trying to uphold. Although the leader needs strong support, he does not need unanimous support. Courageous leaders risk criticism without necessarily sacrificing their effectiveness.

It is unfortunate that many people somehow assume that the human relations approach to management requires that the leader he "liked" by his subordinates. Research in the field of group dynamics disputes this; it has been shown repeatedly that persons who exert important influence are frequently "disliked. Bennis points out that the position of Psychoanalysis would tend to concur. He states that this position follows along these same lines, that productive work is partially a function of hostility to the leader."

Whether or not a leader has the "courage" to risk unpopularity for the sake of upholding official or moral principles depends partially on how secure the leader feels and how much investment he has in his office. It is difficult for a leader who is primarily concerned about maintaining his position to jeopardize it for the sake of his ideas. Conversely, the courageous leader is probably among those whose involvement with principles it some point exceeds his personal commitment to his office. Commitment to office probably increases with age, marital status, property ownerhip, parenthood, and aspiration to succeed, and it probably declines with the existence of alternative career lines, outside income, and outside support.

The leader is in effect, a middle man between conflicting interests and values. He is a representative of third parties mediating bargaining process. In this compromising setting no party will be completely satisfied with any action. Therefore, the leader often finds himself in the position where any choice will detract from some of the organization's major goals and will meet with some disapproval; his problem is to make concessions which least deflect the organization from its overall goals. Consequently, the administrator must have more than technical skills, or even "human relations skills" designed to enhance his popularity. It requires the ability to anticipate the effects of alternative decisions on the organization's future course of action and the courage to deal with cultural and organizational dilemmas in the face of criticism.

Various Angles

The conceptualization of leadership, the skills that it requires, and its explanation apparently depends on an understanding of the forces within the leadership setting. Four views of leadership will be reviewed with respect to their relevance to the organizational context as outlined thus far: leadership as personality traits, as a set of functions, as social relations, and as a social process.

Administration at Work

People are inclined to explain leadership in terms of the leader themselves that is their personal traits independent of their cultural, social, and situational context. One writer suggests that explanations of leadership in terms of personalities is so tempting to administrators because they conveniently seem to imply that administrators are personally superior. Certainly the picture of workers as irrational beings, moved by sentiment and tradition and utilized as means to official ends, provides a convenient contrast to the image of administrators as rational, creative, free-willed decision makers. The overemphasis on the conformity of subordinates is swelled only the distorted stress placed on the personal, individualistic qulities of leaders.

There are several reasons for discounting the role of personality in leadership. First, it is not the leader's personality which makes him important. The administrator is important because of his job, his coordinating public relations, policy formulation, and representative functions. Second, there is not one but a range of leadership personalities. Probably most people with sufficient motivation and of average intelligence and experience could learn to be adequate administrators. The number of qualified persons tends to outnumber the jobs available at every level of employment. There is little reason to assume that the personal traits and abilities of administrators are more significant factors in their achievement than are their loyalties: aspirations, connections, and the chances of vacancies occurring at a crucial time in their career. In fact, leadership is so important that its fulfilment could scarcely be left to the chance that particular individuals with unique personalities will appear at the proper times. Also, except for gross estimations gleaned from interviews of brief contracts between subordinates and superiors, the leadership traits of promotables may not even be systematically or directly assessed before they assume important positions. Moreover, whatever minimum personality traits that are demanded for a particular job may very well develop after the leadership position has been assumed; the often noticeably altered attitudes of the worker who becomes boss, the student who becomes a teacher, or in fact the pedestrian who becomes a driver, are notable examples of the effects of status change on personality. Finally, whatever leadership traits which leaders may be observed to have in common may reflect the traits that are required to achieve positions of leadership rather than the traits necessary for actual leadership.

The above statements are not intended to completely deny the relevance of personality to leadership, but to place personality in its proper perspective. Generally, extreme personality traits may set the minimum limits for effective leadership. Extreme personality types are disqualified. Completely insane persons sometimes cannot lead effectively, although some psychopathic types, such as Hitler, have been effective leaders; and persons who are filled with hatred for their subordinates or extreme self-doubt and withdrawal probably do not make good leaders. But it is generally easier to identify the persons who do not make good leaders in these terms than those who do.

Objective Conclusions

Empirically speaking, the search for the ideal personality of "born leaders" has proved fruitless. Bird's review of the literature revealed that only five percent of the purported traits were common to four or more empirical investigations of leadership. Stogdill's review of the trait studies seems to justify a pessimistic appraisal. For example, six studies on the importance of age find that better leaders are younger, but tea studies also report that they are older, and seventeen report that it "differs with the situation." Similarly inconsistent results are typical of studies on height, weight, energy, health, emotional stability, appearance, I.Q., and self-confidence; although it is commonly purported that leaders have "insight," it is by no means apparent what that is.

On the other hand, personal attributes that involve social skill, ambition, and social direction seem to be important. Stogdill reports that effective leadership was found to be consistently related to "social skills," such as language fluency, humor, sociability, diplomacy, tact, and popularity. Leaders also seem to be highly motivated. Henry has found that American business leaders express strong mobility drives-achievement desire, respect for superiors, decisiveness, and somewhat severed obligations from parents. These may be the very traits which help a leader to deal with the frequently ambiguous social situation that he will encounter in a morally complex environment. Language skills, ambition, and decisiveness, the ability to maintain poise in potentially embarrassing situations, to act diplomatically and with tact under pressure, are all useful skills in complex situations. However, even such qualities are not necessarily generalized, inherent qualities of personality. Persons who can tolerate ambiguity in some situations may be completely overwhelmed in others, and even "ambitious" persons are not necessarily ambitious in every undertaking. In fact, whenever such traits as self-confidence and ambition do carry over between situations, it may be because of similarity between the situations.

Leadership can be understood better in terms of what the leader does rather than who the leader is, several functions, common to leaders will be outlined below.

Policy Formulation. In formulating policy, the leader must squarely face decisions about means, aims, and values, in this respect leadership is ultimately a moral concern. However, while all leaders are responsible for policy, the influence which a particular leader has over the policy of his organization varies. The leader is charged with the responsibility for both establishing the abstract goals of the organization and specifying the more specific working policies that guide the organization in its daily operations. While these two elements of policy are supposed to be logically related, there is a tendency for operating policy to become distinct from the abstract goals. Because many of these problems are fundamental concerns to persons who do not agree among themselves, the leader must endure much criticism.

Implementation. Once the policies have been formulated, they need to be put into effect by means of specific plans of operation. This involves making everyday, routine decisions which will help to achieve the goals. Needless to say, while the chief administrator is responsible for seeing that decisions are made, he normally does not make them himself. If he were the only person deciding these matters, his job would be much simpler than it is. His role is to see that someone assumes the responsibility to make decisions.

In the course of daily pressures and disagreements among the staff who have these decisions-making powers, the leader is often not in a position to follow the course of action that he would personally prefer.

Often the leader's only function is to prevent certain decisions which deviate too far from overall policy. For example, the superintendent may give his new secondary school principal complete responsibility for developing a sound in-service program in the high school, but when the superintendent hears that the principal plans to dismiss children early twice a month for faculty meetings, the superintendent may be inclined to intercede in order to clarify the school's policy by specifying the conditions under which the children may be dismissed; dismissal time is usually closely tied to policies, rules, and regulation regarding transportation and bus drivers even to statues. Weekly meetings of principal and central administrators are partly aimed at preventing decisions which deviate too far from overall policy.

Maintenance of Functional Autonomy. In policy formulation and decision-making, the leader has a dual responsibility—responsibility to the public and responsibility for the welfare of the internal operations. This somewhat jaundiced aspect of leadership is a source of considerable strain. For maintenance of the internal organization frequently requires some sacrifice to outside pressure groups, while external demands ordinarily deflect much of the leader's attention from the organization's long-range course of action. The leader must decide on the amount of internal control over policy and procedures which will be sacrificed for external and internal support.

The fact that leaders represent the interests of the organization to the external environment is often ignored. However, one writer divided twenty-three principals into two major groups: one group was high on both "consideration" and "initiation," and the other was low on both dimensions. Each major group was further divided into two sub-categories: those who were high in both "procurement" functions (acquisition of support for the school) and "disposal" functions (marketing of the product), and those who were low on both dimensions. These dimensions concerned the leader's ability to obtain for the school what it needs from outside sources and to protect the staff from outside interference. For each of the major groups, those who ranked high on procurement on disposal received higher effectiveness ratings from the staff; teachers' job satisfaction was higher and they expressed more confidence in the principal's leadership.

Besides guarding the organization's welfare, a leader is also responsible for coordinating the ends of the organization with the institutional values of the broader society. This is normally difficult, particularly in cases where upholding institutional values means jeopardizing the organization's prestige, as in cases when some schools must be discontinued in order to consolidate for the sake of improving education.

The Strategies

Viewed as interaction, effective leadership is partly dependent upon the leader's skill at (1) maintaining his position (position maintenance), (2) initiating ideas and commands (initiation), and (3) supporting the interests of his subordinates (consideration). Below are some general tactical approaches to the first and last of these problems. Initiation is related to the decision-making process.

The Status Quo

Holding a position of leadership does not insure the power to lead. For example, nothing can be so corrupting to a new leader's authority as his attempt to radically alter established ways before he first guarantees his own position. Consequently, much of the strong leader's time is devoted to the tactics of position maintenance—concerns which are often labelled "political." The fact that leaders must "play politics" probably discourages some otherwise promising persons who dislike using personal power and contacts and other political tactics to achieve leadership positions. It is also conceivable that persons who do achieve and maintain their positions of responsibility sometimes do so almost exclusively because of political skills, which is no assurance of their wisdom in policy formulation. Undoubtedly, some people who hold responsible positions in education go to great lengths to secure their positions—ranging from bribery and forged academic degrees to a career of hand-shaking at national conventions and impression management before important audiences. The relationships between achieving leadership positions, ability to lead, and devotion to institutional values poses crucial problem for understanding the nature of leadership.

With Respect to Superiors. When a leader senses that his position is threatened by other departments or by his own subordinates, there are several devices that he can adopt. The first tactic seems to be more effective when there is one powerful superior (for example, a strong superintendent or a strong school board member) who can protect and support the leader. However, if there are cleavages among the top leadership, pleasing one of them may simply incur for the leader the displeasure of his superior's own enemies. Also, since it is usually easiest to please persons who are weakest among the top leadership group, the support that he receives is likely to be from the least influential superior, or from one who will be reluctant to publicly risk his own insecure position in defense of a subordinate. Where many people hold power, the subordinate may attempt to please several of the top leaders, but if this requires him to adopt inconsistent "faces," that may also be dangerous.

On the other hand, the leader may enhance his position by stressing his competence; he may seek election to a state or national professional office, publish in trade journals, or increase his efficiency by cutting costs or by winning an important bond issue. Since "competence" can be easily advertised to other organizations, this approach has an added advantage; for nothing is so enhancing to the leader's current position as public knowledge that another organization wants him.

With Respect to Subordinates. The principal or superintendent who spends all of his time worrying about what his superiors think of him is inclined to ignore the influence that his teachers and students can have on his fate. "Neutral" subordinates are especially crucial, because their reaction is least predictable. Neutrals may sometimes be "won over" by raising their salaries, offering them personal considerations (such as a little time off, a new desk), or by paying them personal attention (such as going to their office rather than requesting them to come to his). Opponents are also obviously important. Their power can be weakened by transferring them to other departments, by offering them promotion or otherwise breaking down their solidarity. In general, the strong leader will support the position of some of his subordinates and simultaneously attempt to weaken the position of his adversaries.

The skilled leader uses a variety of tactics to maintain his position against the opposition of subordinates. Tactics that prevent their becoming united are crucial. Henry suggests that by using a common classroom technique, teachers are able to dissipate any unified resistance from students. He maintains that teachers encourage children to destructively criticize another child who differs in opinion from the teacher; this renders them "docile," that is, more concerned about finding the answer which the teacher wants, and giving it to her, than about expressing idea and interpretations that oppose hers.

Lower Categories

Communication. Subordinates tend to support superiors who confide in them. A principal is likely to support a superintendent who at least informs him of the decisions as soon as they are made. Nothing undermines a principal's authority so much as when his superintendent or some member of his school board fails to consult him before issuing a statement to his teachers. In addition to consulting his direct subordinates, the superintendent must give them information for them to function effectively. If a principal must consult his own superiors about policy every time someone on the faculty or in the public has a question, he jeopardizes his own authority and embarrasses the organization.

Likert compared groups of workers in industry which expressed favourable and unfavourable attitudes towards their official leaders. Nearly half of those who were favourable said that their superiors informed the men what was happening in the company and how well they were doing; less than thirteen per cent who were unfavourable to their supervisors gave that description. Nearly two-thirds of those who were favourable said that their supervisor hears complaints and grievances compared to less than one-third of those who were unfavourable to their supervisors. The favourable group reported virtually unanimously that they felt free to discuss important things about the job with their supervisor and that it does some good to discuss them, while only six in ten or less of the unfavourable group reported the same. Two-way communication, it appears, is crucial for effective leadership because it helps to maintain the subordinate's position (even when it is not logically essential for him to accomplish his task).

However, the fact that top executives need some freedom to be flexible and to compromise as situations arise imposes limits on the amount of policy-making, which superintendents can pass on to principals, for it is often strategically unwise to make any more policy statements than immediately necessary.

Praise and Blame. Another way the leader can influence the security of his subordinates is through his use of praise and blame. Homans asserts that the leader will neither blame nor praise a member of his group before other members. Blaming individuals in public creates a threatening situation for the other members as well, who have engaged in the practice and who fear similar reprisals.

Generally leaders will not place their position in jeopardy more often so. Oddly enough, this principle applies to the use of praise too. For in publicizing praise, the leader unnecessarily runs the risk that his opinions will not be shared by his subordinates or by the public, the subordinates often have more information than he does. This is one of the daily hazards that confront teachers whose evaluation of pupils often does not correspond with peer group and parental evaluations.

Leaders can show personal consideration only to the extent that they are legitimately aware of their subordinate's interests and problems. However, a leader has two handicaps. First, because his position is threatening to his subordinates, a leader's efforts to learn about their activities are resisted. This tempts him to use unofficial, informal, even unethical procedures to obtain information, such as spy systems. But if the spies are discovered by subordinates, it clearly signifies a state of open "warfare" between the leader and his followers. Second, the leader can officially acknowledge that he has only that information which he should "legitimately" know. This condition restricts the amount of interest he can officially display in a personal problem of a subordinate which he earned about informally.

Unofficial channels provide one means of learning about subordinates. Personal interests are frequentiy revealed in the gossip of informal gatherings. In fact, the "office party" offers one of the few occasions where people can step out of their official roles and properties and speak their minds. Both social status and personality differences are obscured in the party for the sake of maintaining the situation itself. A person can speak his mind at a party precisely because it is intended to be a depersonalized and egalitarian situation. The leader who remains inconspicuously present may sense a great deal, provided that his presence does not dampen the party with an air of officiousness. However, there is always a danger that when an administrator abandons his official rank in order to be taken into the confidence of his subordinates in such gatherings, he will jeopardize his official leadership role later in the formal setting. This dilemma between "officiousness" (or initiation) and informal interaction with subordinates (or consideration) may be partially resolved if informal interaction with subordinates is confined to private places and small groups. The ways which particular leaders compromise their official and informal interaction habits underly a variety of personal leadership patterns.

Beyond Formality

The informal organization of subordinates can be strategically utilized by leaders to support their own position. Many times, for example, the informal organization may be entrusted to handle discipline problems. There are usually compelling reasons why subordinates disobey, often inherent in the organizational structure itself, and subordinates may have a better sense of these reasons and causes for undisciplined behaviour than the superior.

The leader can gain the support of subordinates by supporting their leaders. For example, there is evidence that leaders of inmates in prisons have more favourable attitudes than non-leaders toward authority in their prison camp, are less likely to escape, and are less likely to request transfer or to be transferred for "maladjustment." These cooperative and sympathetic attitudes of the leaders of prisoners toward the administration were due largely to the support which the administration gave to the informal leaders. The latter were generally more concerned about the inmates who were after their positions than about the shortcomings of the administration or prison guards. The administration gave the informal leaders of inmates more desirable jobs on labour gangs, and they were more likely to receive high status bottom bunks despite official "random" assignment procedures. In return, inmate leaders promoted administrative goals.

This kind of cooperative arrangement which can develop between officials and the informal leaders of subordinates suggests that informal teacher and student groups can be enticed to support the administration by recognizing and promoting their leaders.

Carlson reports that new superintendents were able to counteract long-standing informal resistance by (1) stopping their social contacts with the adversary (that is, increasing social distance), (2) bringing in an outside agency to conduct a survey and confirm the need for change, and (3) promoting the leadership of the advisory group (that is, a teachers' union) to a position of administrative responsibility where it can be co-opted. The first principle was used by an inside successor who had a history of personal relations with the adversary, and the third principle was used by a successor from the outside who was unencumbered by personal relations. Teachers often utilize this third principle of cooptation, when student leaders are invited to "sit in" on faculty meetings and to have representatives at important committee meetings which affect the lives of the students. The fact that student leaders are recognized by the system develops in them a sense of commitment to that system.

A leader's position is enhanced to the extent he can maintain a wide range of external as well as internal "contacts" which provide him with information and potential support. He may establish a personal following among the students or parents which makes it difficult for the school board to fire him, or he may attempt to establish cooperative relationships with community influential. For example, a school milk contract may be awarded to the company which will return the greatest support for the school's forthcoming bond issue, rather than to the low bidder. While "fixing" of school contracts is in itself unethical, it often occurs within the context of an exchange of favour which is essential to the existence and effectiveness of the organization.

9

Trends in Administration

Our objective is simpler and, in one sense, more fundamental, to determine the relationship between the superintendent's own perception of how he behaves on the Initiating Structure and Consideration dimensions, as contrasted with the board and staff perception; and, furthermore, to discover the corresponding relationship between his the board's, and the staff's beliefs concerning how he should behave as a leader. This, of course, implies several additional questions. To what extent do board members agree in their descriptions of the superintendent's leader behaviour? Is there greater agreement about how he should behave than about how he does behave? These are the major questions that we shall examine in this study.

The superintendent, as the officially designated leader in charge of the school organization, is confronted by two major sets of responsibilities. He is responsible to the board of education, but he also must be responsive to the members of his own professional staff. Both reference groups, the board and the staff, impose upon him importations of how he should behave as a leader. When these expectations are essentially similar, he probably encounters no difficulty in orienting his behaviour to them. But to the extent that they are incompatible, he is placed in a position of potential role conflict. How should he behave as the leader? Should he respond principally to the expectations of his board or to those of his staff? Or should he "be his own man' and persist in his own style of leadership irrespective of what either board or staff may wish? These practical questions plague most school administrators and are of equal concern to those responsible for their pre-service and in-service training.

This investigation is closely related to the whole question of evaluating the performance of school superintendents. Objective measures of the superintendent's job performance or of the effectiveness of his leadership are extremely rare, for the development of such measures is a sorely neglected area of research. Evaluations of the superintendent's job performance customarily take the form of subjective ratings of his effectiveness. These ratings are seldom made with the help of a well-constructed rating schedule that elicits evaluations of his performance in specified areas of his job; instead, they usually entail little more than global judgments of whether the superintendent's performance is "good" or "bad." This is not the place to explore the ramifications of the criterion problem in educational administration. But one troublesome question must be raised. If we discover an appreciable lack of relationship between the descriptions of the superintendent behaviour given by his board members and by his staff, and also find that the agreement among board members about how the superintendent behaves is far less than perfect, with what degree of confidence can we then accept, as a dependable criterion of the superintendent's performance, an evaluation of his behaviour given by a single board member?

Accurate and judicious evaluation of an individual's performance admittedly involves a more complex process than a straight forward description of what he does – of how he behaves. A valid criterion of ideal behaviour should provide the foundation for whatever evaluation is made of the effectiveness of the behaviour of a particular individual. Hence, to such extent that a given rater's information about how a person does behave is unreliable, his evaluation of the effectiveness of that behaviour is suspect. In short, if board members do not possess sufficient information about how the superintendent actually behaves to permit them to describe his behaviour consistently among themselves and in reasonable agreement with the consensus of staff members, then a serious question can be raised about using board members' evaluations of the superintendent as the sole criterion of how effectively he performs his job. There is need for empirical research designed to explore this aspect of the criterion problem. Obviously, the present investigation provides no final answer on this score. Nevertheless, we shall examine the findings in terms of the question. What are the implications of these results for improving our present methods of evaluating the job performance of superintendents?

This study of the leadership behaviour of 50 Ohio school superintendents deals again with the same dimensions of leader behaviour: Initiating Structure and Consideration. The superintendents' behaviour in respect to these two dimensions of behaviour has been measured with the LBDQ-Real on which the staff and board respondents and the superintendents themselves indicate the frequency with which the superintendent engages in specific forms of leader behaviour. The leadership ideology of the members of these same three respondent groups was measured by having each respondent indicate LBDQ-Ideal how he believed an ideal superintendent should behave. The items on the LBDQ-Real and the LBDQ-Ideal are identical.

The LBDQ's were administered in each community by a member of the research team. The meetings with the staff and the board were held separately but not necessarily on the same day. Each team member assured the participants that the anonymity of their answers would be protected. Although the general purpose of the study was explained to all participants, no reference whatever was made to the concepts of Initiating Structure and Consideration as dimensions of leader behaviour.

The raw data consisted of the responses on 1274 questionnaires divided equally between LBDQ-Real and LBDQ-Ideal. Each questionnaire was scored on the Initiating Structure and Consideration dimensions. The LBDQ-Self scores, both Real and Ideal, were secured directly from the superintendents themselves. Each of the fifty superintendents received an Initiating Structure score and a consideration score that expressed his description of his own behaviour in respect to these two dimensions. Similarly, his two LBDQ-Ideal scores indicated what he believed his behaviour should be on these dimensions. The staff scores were obtained by having seven members of each superintendent's staff (that is, members of the work-group that reported directly to him) describe his leader behaviour. The average of the seven scores by which his staff members described is Initiating Structure behaviour was designated as his LBDQ-Real staff score on Initiating Structure. Likewise, an LBDQ-Real staff Consideration score was computed for each superintendent. The corresponding LBDQ-Ideal staff scores were determined in the same way. Scores for the board's descriptions of the superintendents' behaviour (LBDQ-Real, board) and scores that expressed their leadership ideology (LBDQ-Ideal, board) were computed by an analogous procedure. On the average, five-board member descriptions were obtained for each superintendent.

By this procedure the responses from the 1274 questionnaires were reduced to 600 scores, with 12 scores for each of the 50 superintendents:

1. LBDQ-Real, Self — Initiating Structure
2. LBDQ-Real, Self — Consideration
3. LBDQ-Real, Staff — Initiating Structure
4. LBDQ-Real, Staff — Consideration
5. LBDQ-Real, Board — Initiating Structure
6. LBDQ-Real, Board — Consideration
7. LBDQ-Ideal, Self — Initiating Structure
8. LBDQ-Ideal, Self — Consideration
9. LBDQ-Ideal, Staff — Initiating Structure
10. LBDQ-Ideal, Staff — Consideration
11. LBDQ-Ideal, Board — Initiating Structure
12. LBDQ-Ideal, Board — Consideration

The data were then analyzed in respect to these 12 scores. The findings can be summarized as follows:

1. On each leader behaviour dimension, the staff respondents tend to agree in the description of their respective superintendents. Likewise, the board respondents tend to agree the description of their respective superintendents. Although the staff and the board members each agree among themselves as a group in their description of the superintendent's leadership behaviour, the two groups do not agree with each other. Thus knowledge of the superintendent's leadership behaviour as perceived by his board does not permit us to predict with greater than chance accuracy how these same aspects of the superintendent's behavior will be perceived by the members of his immediate staff. Hence, if we intend to use descriptions of the superintendent's leadership behaviour as a criterion of performance, we need to take into full account the source of the description. It is evident that such descriptions should be secured from both board and staff. Neither source by itself provides a complete description of the superintendent's behaviour. We conclude from these findings that the superintendents tend to adopt different behavioural roles in dealing with the members of staff and board groups.

2. Although the boards, on the whole show statistically significant agreement among their members in their descriptions of their superintendents' leadership behaviour, this agreement is far from perfect. The unbiased correlation ratio is .52 for Initiating Structure and 63 for Consideration. This finding raises a provocative question: if board member agreement in describing the leadership behaviour of superintendents is no greater than these correlations indicate, then how much confidence can we place in an evaluation of the superintendents effectiveness based upon board members' ratings? The same argument applies to staff member descriptions of the superintendent's behaviour. Here again, the unbiased correlation ratio (.44 for each dimension), though statistically significant, reflects far less than perfect agreement.

3. In respect to Consideration, consistency in the superintendent's role behaviour in dealing with the several members of his board shows only a chance association with the consistency the superintendent displays in dealing with the several members of his staff. In short, the superintendent may reveal a consistent "front" of Consideration to all members of his board, but it does not follow from this that he displays a similarly consistent "front" of Consideration to all members of his staff.

4. In respect to Consideration, the superintendents do not see themselves as either their staffs or boards see them. The staffs see the superintendents as showing less Consideration than they are described as showing either by the boards or by the superintendents themselves.

5. There is significant but low correlation (.44) between the superintendents' self-descriptions and the staff members' descriptions of their Initiating Structure behaviour.

6. The boards describe the superintendents as Initiating Structure to a greater extent than they are perceived as doing by either the staffs or the superintendents themselves.

7. On both dimensions, the board descriptions show only chance relationship with both the staff and the self-descriptions. The boards tend to describe the superintendents as higher on both Consideration and Initiating Structure than they are described by the staffs and in this sense show greater inclination than the staffs to view their superintendents as effective leaders. This suggests that the superintendents "play up to the boards" - behave, in fact, more effectively as leaders in dealing with their boards than in working with their own staffs. Even though the superintendent may possess good leadership skills as evidenced in his relationship with his board, he seems inclined to "let down a little" in his dealings with his staff.

8. The boards do not differ significantly from school to school

in their expectation of how the superintendent should behave on either dimension.

9. There are significant differences between boards and staff in the extent of their agreement about how the superintendent should behave on Consideration. But in respect to Initiating Structure, the within-group agreement for boards and for staffs is approximately the same for all staffs and all boards.

10. The staffs do not differ significantly from school to school in their expectation of how much Consideration the superintendent should show, but there is a slight difference in their expectation of how much Structure he should Initiate.

11. For the most part, staff and board conceptions of how an Ideal superintendent should behave do not differ from school to school. These conceptions constitute general norms of how staffs, boards, and superintendents believe a superintendent should behave. All three groups of respondents characterize an Ideal superintendent as one who scores high on both Consideration and Initiating Structure.

12. The superintendents set for themselves higher standards of Consideration than either the staffs or the boards set for them. The boards, in fact, expect the superintendents to show greater Consideration to their staffs than the staffs themselves posit as Ideal.

13. The boards believe that a superintendent should be very strong in Initiating Structure. The superintendents themselves and the staffs both believe that the superintendents should Initiate far less Structure than the boards expect. The staffs, in turn, prefer less Structure than the superintendents believe they should Initiate.

14. The perceived leadership behaviour of the fifty superintendents differs significantly from the ideal behaviour of a superintendent as conceived by all three

respondents groups. Whereas only 19 superintendents are described by their staffs in the "high-high" quadrant 48 out of 50 of these staffs believe that this quadrant characterizes the leadership behaviour of an Ideal superintendent. Conversely, though eight of the superintendents are described in the "low-low" quadrant, the staffs unanimously agree than an Ideal superintendent would not behave in this fashion. Similar differences between the Real and the Ideal distributions by quadrant occur for both other respondent groups.

15. An analysis was made of the number of superintendents classified in the two quadrants on the main diagonal according to the descriptions of their behaviour given by both their boards and their staffs. Eleven of the '0 superintendents (22 per cent of the sample) were described as effective leaders by both their staffs and their boards-that is, were described as scoring high on both Consideration and Initiating Structure. On the other hand, only two of 50 superintendents were described by both their staffs and their boards as ineffective leaders—that is, low on both dimensions. This quadrant analysis technique provides a useful way of evaluating the leadership effectiveness of superintendents and appears especially applicable in those instances where the description of the superintendent's leadership behaviour by both his staff and his board indicates that he can be classified in either the "high-high" or the "low-low" quadrants.

The Theory

The leadership ideology of board and staff members, and of the superintendents themselves, is essentially the same. Effective or desirable leadership behaviour is characterized by high scores on both Initiating Structure and Consideration. Conversely, ineffective or undesirable leadership behaviour is marked by low scores on both dimensions. These findings on the leadership ideology of superintendents, staff members, and board members agree with the results of the earlier Air Force study in which it was found that aircraft commanders rated effective both by superiors and crew score high on both leader behaviour dimensions. These results are also consisted with Hemphill's findings that college departments with a campus reputation for being well administered are directed by chairman who score high on both leader behaviour dimensions. In short, the effective leader is one who delineates clearly the relationship between himself and the members of the group and establishes well-defined patterns of organization, channels of communication, and way of getting the job done. At the same time, his behaviour reflects friendship, mutual trust, respect, and warmth in the relationship between himself and the members of the group.

The findings indicate that the superintendents differentiate their role behaviour. In dealing with their boards they tend to be effective as leaders, but they are inclined to be less effective in working with their staffs. Even when superintendents possess sufficient skill to be highly effective as leaders, they often "Jet down" a little in dealing with their staffs. Here it is important to note that the superintendent has less frequent direct contacts with his board than with his staff. This affords him more time for planning the strategy of his behaviour in working with the board. Because the board is in a stronger power position than the staff, the superintendent evidently puts this time to good use. In his relationship with his staff, on the other hand, the superintendent is frequently forced to meet exigencies, with the result that he may not have sufficient time to apply to each new problem his full potentiality for leadership.

It is difficult, but not impossible, to overcome the pressure of events. To avoid being crowded by time, many executives delegate to associates a large share of authority and responsibil·ty. This transfer of authority is in itself, of course, an essential aspect of Initiating Structure in the interaction of group members. Hence the present findings confirm our subjective impression that far too many superintendents allow their principal responsibilities to become obscured by trivia, with the result that they abdicate their leadership role and allow themselves to degenerate into mere functionaries. Routine and perfunctory activities have a specious attractiveness because they often allay anxieties that are inherent in the superintendent's leadership role. But we must avoid the mistake of confusing sheer routine activity with the productivity and creativity required for effective leadership.

The superintendent's tendency to play different roles with board and staff is revealed by the lack of relationship between the board and staff descriptions of the superintendent's leader behaviour. Although the members of each of these two reference groups show statistically significant agreement in their perceptions of the superintendent's behaviour, the agreement is far from perfect. This finding has important implications for research on the effectiveness of the superintendent's job performance. The salient implication concerns the use of board member rating as the criterion of leadership effectiveness. Our findings have provided two cogent arguments against this practice. First, we have noted that the board members show considerably less than perfect agreement simply describing how the superintendent behaves, a finding which casts serious doubt upon how much board member agreement we can expect to find among independent evaluations of the superintendent's leadership effectiveness. This criticism applies especially to global judgments made without the benefit of a carefully constructed rating schedule of known reliability. Second, in evaluating the superintendent, we must take into account information from all relevant reference groups. When the descriptions of the superintendent's behaviour emanating from two relevant reference groups such as the board and staff are not significantly correlated, it is all the more imperative that data from both sources be examined as potential criteria. In the present study, we have not exhausted the reference groups that can furnish independent and pertinent criterion information on the superintendent's performance. We have confined our inquiry to reference groups focal to the superintendent's efforts in the internal administration of the Schools. Similar studies could be developed to examine the superintendent's behaviour in external administration-that is, in community and public relations activities.

Our findings point out the need for a multiple-criteria approach to the study of the leadership effectiveness of school superintendents. This means that we must first establish several independent, objective criteria of the superintendent's effectiveness and then determine the relationship between (1) these criteria and selected predictor variables and (2) the criteria themselves. Predictor variables can be posited readily enough. What we lack are dependable, objective criteria of effective school administration. Criteria, by definition, entail value-judgments. For this reason, whenever we are confronted by several criteria that do not have a high correlation with each other, a further value-judgment may be required to rank the relevance of the separate criteria. The responsibility for a judgment of this kind should rest with the board of education as the official body representing the community in matters of public education. The social scientist, as a scientist, is not required to make these value-decisions, but he can make an equally, important and perhaps even more fundamental, contribution. He can demonstrate to what extent the various criteria proposed are dependable and whether they are in any way incompatible with each other. He can show, for example, that Leadership Style A is effective in terms of Criterion A, and Leadership Style B is effective in respect to Criterion B. He may also note, however, that Leadership Styles A and B are incompatible, perhaps even antithetical. For instance, the superintendent who must spend a lot of time "politicking" in the community in order to put through a salary raise for his teachers may be forced to spend so little time with his teachers that they characterize his behaviour as low in consideration. If the board or the staff should insist that the superintendent be active in securing better salaries for teachers (Criterion A), and also that he be perceived by his staff as Considerate (Criterion B), then the superintendent may be faced by a real dilemma. For if he is to be perceived as considerate by the staff he must devote time to personal interaction with individual staff members. If this same time is demanded for community contacts to gain support for a salary increase for teachers, the superintendent has to make a choice. There are only 24 hours in a day, and the superintendent, like every executive, must choose how he can best allocate the time at his disposal. Under such circumstances as these, if the board demands that the superintendent satisfy both Criterion (A) and Criterion (B) they may impose upon him an intolerable burden of role-conflict. On this point Seeman has provided an illuminating discussion of role-conflict and ambivalence in the leadership behaviour of school superintendents. As we have said, the choice of the criteria of effective administration is a prerogative of the local community, but it should be an informed choice in which conflicting or incompatible demands upon the administrator are clearly recognized as such. It is here that research can make a trenchant contribution by furnishing dependable, objective data that will permit communities to make wiser and better-informed decisions in establishing criteria for evaluating the performance of their school superintendents.

The fact that the superintendents play a different role with their boards from that which they assume with their staffs does not necessarily imply that they are confronted by role-conflict. Some administrators undoubtedly compartmentalize their behaviour, and in doing so minimize the likelihood of role-conflict. Others, however, may find themselves torn by what they perceive as differential expectations imposed upon them by board and staff. In the present study we have not attempted to explore the dynamics of the superintendent's behaviour in the matter of role differentiation. To do this would require a clinical, case-study approach similar to that employed by Seeman. As he has clearly demonstrated, this is an important area for further research in educational administration, and one in which the methods of the present study can be used in conjunction with straightforward case-study techniques.

Until such time as we are sure of the ultimate criteria we seek, we may be wise to settle for "intermediate" criteria that have strong presumptive evidence in their favour. The LBDQ-Real scores may be construed as an intermediate criterion of this kind. In as much as we lack suitable objective criteria of the effectiveness of school executives at this time, we may assume tentatively that the relationship between leader behaviour dimensions scores and effectiveness which has been found in the Air Force and in higher education studies we have cited applies with equal force to school superintendents. Our present findings on leadership ideology support this assumption. If we are willing to accept it, then we may use LBDQ-Real scores secured from board and staff as an intermediate criterion for evaluating the effectiveness of the superintendent's behaviour. Obviously it is a rough measure, but it does provide a first approach to the objective appraisal of leadership effectiveness. We would suggest that those who are interested in experimenting with this approach use the quadrant analysis technique that we have described.

Although the three respondents groups of the present study all agree on the Ideal, the behaviour of this sample of 50 superintendents—as described by the boards, the staffs, and the superintendents themselves falls significantly short of the ideal. This discrepancy should not necessarily be conceived as an indictment of these superintendents; for ideals, by definition, are objectives difficult to attain. It is heartening to find that approximately one-fifth of the superintendents in the sample approach the ideal in the eyes of their boards and staffs. At the opposite end of the scale, only 4 per cent of these superintendents are categorized, both by their boards and staffs, as ineffective leaders.

In what way do the superintendents tend to fall short of the Ideal? On the one hand, these administrators demonstrate good leader behaviour in their high Consideration for members of their staffs; on the other, they fail to Initiate Structure to as great an extent as is probably desirable. As a group, they appear somewhat disinclined to Initiate Structure in their interaction with group members. One may Speculate about possible reasons for this. In some of our discussions with administrators we have encountered a tendency to view Consideration and Initiating Structure as incompatible forms of leader behaviour. Some administrators act as if they were forced to emphasize one form of behaviour at the expense of the other. Yet the correlation between the LBDQ-Real dimension scores for this sample is .23 (not significant) for the staff descriptions and .61 (significant at the .01 level) for board descriptions. Hence there is nothing negative or antithetical in this inter-dimensional relationship. The fact that the inter-dimension correlation for the board's descriptions is higher than the corresponding correlation for staff descriptions suggests that the superintendents can stress both dimensions of behaviour when they believe that this is sufficiently worth their effort—especially in dealing with members of the board.

Why, then, the apparent disinclination to place similar stress upon both aspects of behaviour in dealing with the staff? This reluctance may be a reflection of some of the current emphasis in education upon "human relations." The human relations approach and the burgeoning interest in group dynamics have developed in part as a protest against reactionary and even authoritarian leadership styles that have prevailed in far too many school situations. But in our enthusiasm for the new approach, have we perhaps swung the pendulum too far?

In applying the human relations approach it is important that we do not overlook the responsibility imposed upon every official leader by the institutional realities of the formal organization of which he is a part. The official leader has a responsibility and, in fact, a contractual obligation to accomplish a specified mission, and certain aspect of this mission may be beyond the purview of decision by the immediate work group. It therefore is imperative for us to re-examine our ideas about the proper balance between human relations — that is, Consideration—and Initiating Structure behaviour within formal organization, and to become more critical about applying generalizations adduced from experience with informal groups to groups embedded within formal hierarchical organizations. Some principles may apply to both kinds of groups, but there is insufficient research evidence to permit us to assume a priori that leadership style that succeed in informal, autonomous groups will be equally effective in formally organized work groups.

The swing of the pendulum seems also to be associated with a tendency to judge the Initiation of Structure as being non-democratic. This point of view is ill-founded, for there is no necessary negative relationship between democratic leadership and the Initiating of Structure. In fact, it is our impression—and here we are speculating that what ordinarily is referred to as democratic administration or, democratic leadership is precisely what we have defined "operationally" as leadership behaviour characterized by high Initiation of Structure and high Consideration. This we have evaluated as effective leadership.

Where the Initiation of Structure is weak, however, it is doubtful that there exists sufficient leadership – whether democratic or non-democratic – to be dignified by the name. Democratic leadership is highly desirable, but, for a leader's behaviour to earn this description, it is not sufficient for the leader to be democratic – he must also demonstrate definite acts of leadership.

Having diagnosed the superintendent's leadership skills, what can we do to help him improve these skills? It is regrettable that there is no pat answer; we must read the notes as well as we can and let our own psychological insights suggest the tune. Role-playing can help, and professional counselling can accomplish a great deal. Practice in situational analysis and case-study methods are often useful. But the training task is formidable; nor are we always sure that the training methods achieve what was intended in the first place. Yet the situation is not entirely hopeless; on the basis of present knowledge, we can avoid several false starts. For example, a glib prescription for men low on Consideration is to "give them a course on Consideration." I do not believe this will work, for we can not make men more considerate by teaching them these skills directly; the necessary changes need to be induced through a therapeutic relationship.

Industrial consultant organizations have devised ingenious ways for improving executive skills. These methods often include a professional counselling relationship between the executive and the consultant. It may be time for us to examine similar possibilities in education-and this does not mean that we must install a psychoanalyst's couch in each superintendent's office! Furthermore, we are at a point where we can start some important basic research on better training procedures for school administrators. Increasingly, however, we have learned that how-to-do-it recipes are not enough; that we shall have to pay greater attention to administrative theory.

The LBDQ technique provides one method for evaluating certain aspects of the superintendent's effectiveness as a leader. The project on effectiveness criteria for elementary principals has developed important techniques for evaluating principals. Several additional evaluation procedures are being devised at other universities. The question now is whether school administrators do, in fact, want to have their own effectiveness evaluated.

Effects and Outcome

Our findings have clear implications for the training of educational administrators to the extent that we can describe those forms of leadership behaviour which the board, the staff members, and the superintendents themselves consider most desirable, and which also are the most effective. Furthermore, we can specify the character of the role differentiation used by the superintendents vis-a-vis their boards and their staffs. But at this point, about all that we can say to the trainee or to the superintendent in service is. "This is how we believe you should behave." The chief shortcoming to be found with this is that exhortation is a notoriously poor training method. Little is accomplished by merely telling trainees how they should behave; we must also establish conditions in the training situation itself that will be conducive to behavioural change in the desired direction. Training in administrative skill involves many subtleties and is a complex process. We cannot inoculate a trainee with high Consideration and high skill in Initiating Structure in the same way that we inoculate a child with the virus of the Salk vaccine. The required leadership skills must be learned, and, as with all learning, ample opportunity for practice must be provided.

In leadership training we must examine our assumptions very cautiously. It has been theorized, for example, that human relations training will increase the Consideration that trainees show their work-group members. But Fleishmen, in a study for the International Harvester Company, has demonstrated that the success of human relations training depends upon a variety of factors, not the least of which is the "social climate" in which the trainee functions in performing his job. An orthodox human relations training program can, under some circumstances, not only fail to achieve its stated purpose, but even boomerang upon its initiators by instilling in trainees apathetic, and often negative, attitudes toward human relations objectives. In short, we cannot assume on faith that the training we conduct will achieve the purposes we have in mind. Nor can we measure the effectiveness of training by the good intentions our trainees profess. The ultimate test of the success or failure of training lies in the changes that take place in the trainees' behaviour.

Evidence from this inquiry and findings from an earlier Air Force study show that the leader's description of his own leadership behaviour and his concept of what his behaviour should be have little relationship to others' perceptions of his behaviour that others have. In the case of the superintendents, this is especially true in respect to Consideration. For this reason, we must be extremely wary about using statements made by the trainees as an index of the success of training. What a man says about himself is not the most dependable measure of changes that have assertedly taken place in his behaviour. On the other hand, changes which his direct associates perceive in his behaviour would appear to constitute a suitable index of results of training. Our present evidence indicates that the LBDQ-Real is well adapted to this purpose and can provide a reliable gauge of the superintendent's leadership behaviour in respect to the Initiating Structure and Consideration dimensions. It should be possible to conduct training experiments in which the difference between the LBDQ pre-training scores and the LBDQ post-training scores is used as an indicator of change by which we can evaluate the effectiveness of the training program. This technique, however, cannot be used for pre-service training of school administrators because a dependable pre-training LBDQ measure is unobtainable. But for the in-service training of men currently employed as administrators, such a method of evaluating training should prove quite valuable. It can even provide a means for comparing the relative effectiveness of various training procedures.

The evidence from these enquiries shows that effective leadership is characterized by high Initiation of Structure and high Consideration. These two dimensions of leader behaviour represent fundamental and pertinent aspects of leadership skill. The LBDQ-Real provides an objective and reliable method of describing the leader's behaviour on these two dimensions. It should be possible to train leaders in the skills that compose these dimensions, but the methods for accomplishing this training have yet to be developed. We have noted two practical applications of the present approach: (1) the use of LBDQ-Real scores as an intermediate criterion of the leadership effectiveness of superintendents and (2) the use of differences between pre-training and post-training LBDQ-Real scores as an index of changes in behaviour attributable to specific training programs.

The dimensions of leadership behaviour we have delineated obviously do not exhaust the field. It would be famous to imply that these dimensions constitute the criterion of leadership effectiveness. They do not. However, they probably do represent a criterion that should be taken into account in evaluating the leadership skills of superintendents. Ours is only one approach to the study of the leader's behaviour. Other investigators will, in turn, supplement our findings, and will take into account additional variables which we were not ready to include in the present series of studies.

We will greatly increase our understanding of leadership phenomena if we abandon the notion of leadership as a trait, and concentrate instead upon an analysis of "the behaviour of leaders."

The idea of leadership has been used in a variety of ways, most commonly in referring of the "leader" as an outstanding member of a class. Thus radio and TV commercials proclaim that a certain brand of cigarettes is the leading one, and that a new movie star is the leader of the current covey of actresses. Because of our American predilection for bigness, in no matter what sphere, the leader in this sense refers to the most popular product—or more specifically, to that item with the greatest sales-market potential. Similarly in education, we often confuse leadership with sheer bigness. But this use of the term applies equally to either things or people, and fails to take into account the central psychological characteristic of leader behaviour: that this is the behaviour of a leader functioning vis-a-vis members of a group in an endeavour to facilitate the solution of group problems. The behaviour of the leader and the behaviour of group members are inextricably interwoven, and the behaviour of both is determined to a great degree by formal requirements imposed by the institution of which the group is a part. For example, Mary Noel, fourth-grade teacher, is the formally designated leader of the children in her class. How she behaves as a leader is influenced by the behaviour of the children (which includes their expectations of how a teacher should behave as a leader). Moreover, her behaviour is conditioned by the policies and regulations, both written and unwritten, of the particular school system in which she is employed. As a result of the year which they spend with her, the children in Mary's class are expected to show certain minimum changes in behaviour, especially in respect to scholastic achievement and skill in interpersonal relations. The accomplishment of these objectives is the salient group problem to which Mary must contribute her solution, and it is presumed that her contribution will be greater than that of any other group member in her fourth-grade class. This, of course, is why she was employed.

In accepting her assignment as teacher of the fourth grade, Mary assumes a role as leader of this group. This, however, tells us absolutely nothing about the effectiveness of her performance in this role—that is, how effectively she contributes to the solution of group problems. What, then, are we to mean by leadership? The assumption of a leader's role? The effectiveness with which this role is performed? Or the capacity of the individual to perform this role effectively? These cause a farther question to arise: By what criteria are we to judge effectiveness? For research on leader behaviour shows that effectiveness in respect to Criterion X is not necessarily correlated with effectiveness in regard to Criterion F. For example, the behaviour of a leader who is effective in maintaining high morale and good human relations within the group is not necessarily effective in accomplishing high reduction and goal-achievement.

The Problems

This dilemma of definition emerges from the fact that we have incorporated into the term "leadership" both descriptive and evaluative components, and have thus burdened this single word (and the concept it represents) with two connotations: one refers to a role and the behaviour of a person in this role, and the other is an evaluation of the individual's performance in the role. We have compounded this confusion even more by conceptualizing leadership as an essentially innate capacity of the individual manifested with equal facility, regardless of the situation in which the leader finds himself. Yet Stogdill has shown that the trait approach to leadership, as it has been used in most studies reported in the literature, has yielded negligible, and often contradictory, results. Sanford has aptly summarized the situation:

From all these studies of the leader we can conclude, with reasonable certainty, that:

(a) there are either no general leadership traits or, if they do exist, they are not to be described in any of our familiar psychological or common-sense terms,

(b) in a specific situation, leaders do have traits which set them apart from followers, but what traits set what leaders apart from what followers will vary from situation to situation.

In short, the behaviour of leaders varies widely from one leadership situation to another. In this connection, Hemphill, in an elaborate and careful study of approximately 500 assorted groups, has demonstrated empirically that variance in leader behaviour is significantly associated with situational variance. For example, let us consider the size of the group as a situational determinative. (Hemphill has analyzed in detail the relation between the leader's behaviour and the size of the group and has concluded that, as compared with small groups, large groups make more and different demands upon the leader. In general, the leader in a large group tends to be impersonal and is inclined to enforce rules and regulations firmly and impartially. In smaller groups, the leader pays a more personal role. He is more willing (and perhaps also more able) to make exceptions to rules and to treat each group member as an individual. Stated baldly, the evidence from these studies means that it is possible for Mary to function effectively as a leader in the fourth-grade class of East Clambake Elementary School, and yet operate quite ineffectively as a leader in the fourth grade class of West Clambake Elementary School. In brief, much depends on the situation.

However, we do not want to overemphasize the determinative effects of a given situation on a given leader. The question never is one of whether the results of a leader's efforts are determined either by the situation or by specific behaviours of the leader. Rather must we phrase our question in a different form: how much of the variance in group productivity is associated with variance in Situational Variable A? With variance in Situational Variance B? How much of the variance in productivity is associated with variance in, for example, the Consideration of the leaders? With variance in the leader's skill in Initating Structure in his interaction among group members?

We can understand the current status of leadership research better if we will first stop to analyze briefly the way in which knowledge is accumulated in any scientific area.

Historically, in most disciplines one discovers a tendency for new movements or emphasis to arise in revolt against the orthodoxies of a given period. These new movements later , tend to crystallize into the orthodoxies of the next period, and fresh counter-movements arise in turn. The final position we reach is usually one on middle ground between the original orthodoxy and the first reaction against it. Zig-zag movements of this kind are not uncommon in the progress of science. Leadership research is currently in the process of following this same developmental course. Early research was marked by a search for traits of leadership that would discriminate between leaders and non-leaders. The Situational emphasis which has characterized research during the past decade arose as a protest against the earlier trait approach, but in some respects this present emphasis may have been carried to excess. To say that leader behaviour is determined exclusively by situational factors is to deny to the leader freedom of choice and determination. This violates common sense and experience. Even now, within research circles, a gradual but growing counter-reaction is taking shape—a drawing away from the extreme situational position, with increasing recognition that the truth probably lies in an area of middle ground.

But now in appraising the trait approach anew, we will have the advantage of a fresh perspective. In the next decade, research workers may be less avid in seizing upon convenient phenotypic data as pertinent variables and may be more willing to explore the relevance of genotypic variables that are not as readily discernible as "givens." (In short, in the past we have tended to examine essentially peripheral traits and attributes. Although we have been guided by intuition about possible relationships between these attributes of leaders and other leadership phenomena, we have operated, for the most part, without the benefit of sufficient empirical information about leadership phenomena that would enable us to sharpen our definitions of the variables involved. Herein lies a major benefit of the period of situationally-oriented leadership research: this research has suggested new ways of constituting the more crucial variables that pertain to the individual as a leader. Eventually, it may be possible to define a few variables of genotypic order that will prove predictive of leader behaviour in a variety of situations. For example, McClelland's series of studies on the achievement motive may throw new light on leadership behaviour. Thus Hemphill and his co-workers have conducted a series of experiments on small groups in order to determine the relationship between (1) "need achievement and need affiliation," and (2) the frequency with which group members attempt leadership acts. With the accumulation of a fund of experimental evidence in this area, the new theories of leadership that are generated probably will incorporate ideas which, at least superficially, will resemble those that characterized the original trait approach. The difference in conceptual sophistication is likely, however, to be no less profound than that between pre-Einsteinian and post-Einsteinian physics. All this, of course, rests with the future. The point is made at this juncture simply to underscore one salient feature of good research strategy that it is sometimes wise to move backwards (or at least in a direction that appears to be backwards) in order to insure greater and more sure-footed strides into the future.

These, then, are the reasons why we prefer at this time to think in terms of leader behaviour rather than leadership. Our concept of leader behaviour sidesteps a few important issues. It limits us, for instance, to dealing with formal organizations, and focuses attention exclusively upon the "head men" within these organizations. Furthermore, the whole question of the distribution of leadership acts among members of the group is avoided. Nor are our formulations readily adaptable to certain aspects of leadership phenomena that can be observed within informal community groups. Our only defense of such limitations is that we have had to start somewhere. We chose to start with the officially designated leaders of formal organizations. This was a heuristic decision. As more information is gathered and as we gradually begin to build a systematic conceptual framework within which additional hypotheses about leader behaviour can be tested, we shall undoubtedly test these hypotheses in informal as well as formal organizations, and with group members other than those officially designated as leaders. The fact that we have not explored these other leadership phenomena implies no skepticism of their importance but is simply an admission that we have not yet found the time and the opportunity (and the funds) to investigate these equally challenging areas.

What, then, do we gain by shifting our emphasis from leadership to the analysis of the behaviour of leaders? There are two major methodological advantages. In the first place, we can deal directly with observable phenomena and need make no a priori assumptions about the identity or structure of whatever capacities may or may not undergird these phenomena. Secondly, this formulation keeps at the forefront of our thinking the importance of differentiating between the description of how leaders behave and evaluation of the effectiveness of their behaviour in respect to specified performance criteria.

The Streams

Evaluations of leadership, on the one hand, can be obtained readily enough by means of various rating schedules. On the other, the measurement of a group's description of its leader's behaviour is a less commonly med procedure. Because we can never measure all the behaviour of an individual. Any measurement procedure we adopt must entail some form of selection. We have chosen to measure two specific dimensions of leader behaviour: "Initiating Structure" and "Consideration." You will recall that Initiating Structure refers to the leader's behaviour in delineating the relationship between himself and members of the work-group, and in endeavouring to establish well-defined patterns of organization, channels of communication, and methods of procedure. Consideration refers to behaviour indicative of friendship, mutual trust, respect, and warmth in the relationship between the leader and the members of his staff.

It is important to note that this concept of Consideration does not include what can be best described as merely "spray-gun consideration." The latter behaviour is typified by the PTA smile, and by the oily affability dispensed by administrators at faculty picnics and office parties. Promiscuous Consideration defeats its purpose by its very promiscuity. Genuine Consideration must be focused upon the individual recipient and must be tuned to his requirements at a particular time and place.

There is nothing especially novel about these two dimensions of leader behaviour. The principles embodied in the concepts of Initiating Structure and Consideration probably have always been used by effective leaders in guiding their behaviour with group members, while the concepts themselves, with different labels perhaps, have been invoked frequently by philosophers and social scientists to explain leadership phenomena. Practical men know that the leader must lead—must initiate action and get things done. But because he must accomplish his purposes through other people, and without jeopardizing the intactness or integrity of the group, the skilled executive knows that he also must maintain good "human relations" if he is to succeed in furthering the purposes of the group. In short, if a leader—whether he be a school superintendent, an aircraft commander, or a business executive—is to be successful, he must contribute to both major group objectives of goal achievement and group maintenance. In Barnard's terms, he must facilitate cooperative group action that is both effective and efficient. According to the constructs that we have formulated, this means that the leader should be strong in Initiating Structure and should also show high Consideration for the members of his work-group.

These two kinds of behaviour are relatively independent but not necessarily incompatible. Cartwright and Zander, for examples have observed.

Any given behaviour in a group may have significance both for goal achievement and for maintenance. Both may be served simultaneously by the actions of a member, or one may be served at the expense of the other. Thus, a member who helps a group to work cooperatively on a difficult problem may quite inadvertently also help to develop solidarity. In another group, however, an eager member may spur the group on in such a way that frictions develop among the members; and even though the goal is achieved efficiently, the continued existence of the group is seriously endangered.

To measure leader behaviour and leadership ideology, we have used a Leader Behaviour Description Questionnaire devised by the Personnel Research Board at The Ohio State University. Hemphill and Coons constructed the original form of this questionnaire, and Halpin and Winer, in reporting the development of an Air Force adaptation of this instrument. identified Initiating Structure and Consideration as two fundamental dimensions of leader behaviour. These dimensions were identified on the basis of a factor analysis of the responses of 300 crew members who described the leader behaviour of their 52 aircraft commanders Initiating Structure and Consideration accounted for approximately 34 and 50 per cent, respectively, of the common variance.

On the basis of the factor analysis, keys were constructed for these two dimensions of leadership behaviour. The original Consideration key of 28 items has an estimated reliability (corrected by the Spearman-Brown formula) of .94. The corresponding estimate for the 29-item Initiating Structure key is .76. In the later, published form of the LBDQ there are only IS items on each of the keys. The estimated reliabilities are .93 and .86, respectively.

By measuring the behaviour of leaders on the Initiating Structure and the Consideration dimensions, we can determine by objective and reliable means how specific leaders differ in leadership style, and whether these differences are related significantly to independent criteria of the leader's effectiveness and efficiency. In sum, the Leader Behaviour Description Questionnaire offers a means of defining these leader behaviour dimensions operationally, making it possible for us to submit to empirical test additional specific hypotheses about leader and group behaviour.

The LBDQ is composed of a series of short, descriptive statements of ways in which leaders may behave. The members of a leader's group indicate the frequency with which he engages in each form of behaviour by checking one of five adverbs; always, often, occasionally, seldom, or never. Each of the keys to the dimensions contains 15 items, and each item is scored on a scale from 4 to 0. Consequently, the theoretical range of scores on each dimension is from 0 to 60. The 15 items which define each dimension follow:

Basic Structure

1. He makes his attitudes clear to the staff.
2. He tries out his new ideas with the staff.
3. He rules with an iron hand.
4. He criticizes poor work.
5. He speaks in a manner not to be questioned.
6. He assigns staff members to particular tasks.
7. He works without a plan.
8. He maintains definite standards of performance.
9. He emphasizes the meeting of deadlines.
10. He encourages the use of uniform procedures.
11. He makes sure that his part in the organization is understood by all members.
12. He asks that staff members follow standard rules and regulations.
13. He lets staff members know what is expected of them.
14. He sees to it that staff members are working up to capacity.
15. He sees to it that the work of staff members is coordinated.

Consideration

1. He does personal favours for staff members.
2. He does little things to make it pleasant to be a member of the staff.
3. He is easy to understand.
4. He finds time to listen to staff members.
5. He keeps to himself.
6. He looks out for the personal welfare of individual staff members.
7. He refuses to explain his actions.
8. He acts without consulting the staff.
9. He is slow to accept new ideas.
10. He treats all staff members as his equals.
11. He is willing to make changes.
12. He is friendly and approachable.
13. He makes staff members feel at ease when talking with them.
14. He puts suggestions made by the staff into operation.
15. He gets staff approval on important matters before going ahead.

The form on which the group members describe their leader's behaviour is referred to as the "LBDQ-Real, Staff." With modified instructions, this same instrument may be used to measure the leader's own leadership ideology. On this form each item is worded to indicate how a leader should behave, and the leaders answer the questionnaire accordingly. This form is designated as the "LBDQ-Ideal, Self." Similarly, we may ask the staff members to describe how they believe the leader should behave. Such scores are termed "LBDQ-Ideal, Staff."

Although group members differ in their perception of the leader's behaviour, analyses of variance in which the "between group" variance and the "within group" variance on these dimension scores were compared for several independent samples of leaders have yielded F ratios all significant at the .01 level of confidence. The leader's behaviour therefore can be described most succinctly by assigning to him, for each dimension, the mean of the LBDQ-Real scores by which his group members have described him. The correlations between these Consideration and Initiating Structure scores range-between 0.38 and 0.45.

The LBDQ can be adapted readily to different group requirements without altering the meaning of the items. For example, with Air Force personnel the term "crew" is used; with educational administrators, "staff" is substituted for "crew." Similarly, for industrial and other situations, minor changes in wording can be made in each item according to the nature of the groups with which the questionnaire is used.

Again, the leader behaviour dimensions of Initiating Structure and Consideration are not to be conceived as traits of leadership. They simply describe the behaviour of a leader as he operates in a given situation. Nothing in the research completed to date with the LBDQ contradicts this position. The questionnaire measures the leader's behaviour in a specified situation—for example, as the commander of an aircrew, or as an administrator in a public school—but does not purport to measure an intrinsic capacity for leadership. But whether individuals tend to employ the same style of leader behaviour in different situations is an empirical question that remains to be answered. However, certain organizational climates can coerce the man to change his leadership style simply to save his job, at no matter what cost in his loss of human dignity.

Academic Leaders

With this background on the theoretical predilections that provided the impetus for The Ohio State Leadership Studies, we now are ready to examine the substantive findings of a group of these studies in which the LBDQ was used.

Most of the developmental work on the Leader Behaviour Description Questionnaire was done in a series of studies of aircraft commanders.Related studies have also been conducted in industry and education. Since the industrial studies were concerned primarily with training, they are not directly pertinent to our present purposes. In this section, therefore, we shall first summarize five of the Air Force studies and one educational study; we then will describe in detail the findings of two other educational studies.

Air Crew Studies

1. LBDQ scores were obtained on 52 B-29 commanders during training in the fall of 1950, and 33 of these commanders were subsequently rated on their combat performance in flying over Korea during the summer of 1951. Twenty-nine of these 33 commanders were described again on the LBDQ by their combat crews. For 27 of the crews, a Crew Satisfaction Index was computed on the basis of the member's answer to the question: "If you could make up a crew from among the crew members in your squadron, whom would you choose for each position?" The ratio between the number of nominations an incumbent commander received and the number of nominations made for the aircraft commander position was used as an index of the crew's satisfaction with the incumbent's leadership. The LBDQ scores in training were correlated with this index and with superiors' ratings of the commanders' combat performance. Similarly, the LBDQ scores in the Far East Air Force were correlated with both the index and the ratings. Finally, in each situation—training and combat— partial correlations were computed for the relationship between each dimension and the ratings (or index) with the effect of the other dimension partialled out.

In both the training and combat situations, a trend was found toward negative correlations between the superiors' ratings and the Consideration scores, and positive correlations between these ratings and the Initiating Structure scores. Conversely, the correlations between the Crew Satisfaction Index and the Consideration scores were positive and high. The partial correlations served to accentuate this trend, which was more pronounced in combat than in training. Thus superiors and subordinates are inclined to evaluate oppositely the contribution of the leader behaviour dimensions to the effectiveness of leadership. This difference in evaluation would appear to confront the leader with conflicting role expectations.

2. Eighty-Seven B-29 aircraft commanders, flying combat missions over Korea, were the subjects of a study with a design similar to the one reported above. The commanders were rated by their superiors on seven characteristics (for example, "effectiveness in working with others," "attitude and motivation," "over-all effectiveness") and by their crews on three characteristics: "confidence and proficiency," "friendship and co-operation," and "morale." Furthermore, as in the earlier study, a Crew Satisfaction Index was computed. The Consideration and the Initiating Structure scores were correlated with the ratings by superiors and by crew members, and with the Crew Satisfaction Index

The ratings by superiors yielded significant correlations with the Initiating Structure scores, whereas none of the corresponding Consideration correlations was significant. The crew ratings, including the Index, correlated significantly with both leader behaviour dimensions but tended to be higher for the Consideration scores. Two of the Consideration correlations in particular should be noted: .75 with the Crew Satisfaction Index and .84 with the crew ratings of the commanders on "friendship and co-operation." Both correlations differ significantly from the corresponding correlations of .47 and .51 (in themselves significant at the .01 level) with the Initiating Structure scores.

One further hypothesis was tested in this study: that the commanders rated highest by their superiors would score above the mean on both leader behaviour dimensions whereas those commanders rated lowest by their superiors would score below the mean on both dimensions. The commanders had been rated on "over-all effectiveness in combat." Two groups of commanders were identified: 13 men in the upper 15 per cent of this rating distribution and 12 in the lower 15 per cent. For each group taken separately, the Consideration and the Initiating Structures scores were plotted into the four quadrants defined by co-ordinates corresponding to the means of the two leader behaviour dimensions. These two scatter-plots were then collapsed to construct the 2x2 classification.

The probability of occurrence of frequencies as deviant from the null hypothesis frequencies—or of greater deviance—is less than 3 in 100. This means that commanders who score above the average on both leader behaviour dimensions are evaluated by their superiors as high in over-all effectiveness, whereas those who score below the average on both dimensions are likely to be rated low in effectiveness. In short, the successful leader is the man who furthers both group maintenance and group achievement.

3. The members of 52 newly assembled B-29 crews at Combat Crew Training School described their commanders on the Leader Behaviour Description Questionnaire and rated each other and the crews as units on such items as "crew morale," "friendship," "proficiency," and "willingness to go into combat with each other." These measures of crew attitudes were obtained twice—at the beginning of the training period and towards the end of training. An average period of 10 days intervened between two administrations of the questionnaire. Correlations were computed between changes in attitude and the Initiating Structure and Consideration scores on the Leader Behaviour Description Questionnaire. It was found that the members of crews whose commanders were described as high on Consideration tended to increase their ratings of each other on such attitude items as "mutual confidence," and willingness to go into combat together, and that the members of crews whose commanders were described as high on Initiating Structure tended to increase their ratings of each other on "friendship" and "confidence." It was concluded that during this initial period of crew assembly the members of crews whose commanders scored high on both Consideration and Initiating Structure tended to develop more favourable crew attitudes than the members of those crews led by commanders who scored low on both leader behaviour dimensions. These findings indicate the influence of leadership style upon early group-learnirg experience.

4. Rush has reported the relationship between the Leader Behaviour Description Questionnaire scores of B-29 and B-50 aircraft commanders and "group dimension" measures of air crews drawn from three independent samples: Combat Crew training

School, Combat Crew Standardization School, and Far East Air Force:

For each sample crew means on the five dimensions of the Crew Dimension Questionnaire (CDQ) were correlated with mean scores for the two LBDQ dimensions. Results were highly consistent across samples and appeared meaningful in terms of the definitions of the various dimensions. Perhaps the best way to summarize the results of this analysis is to discuss the correlation for each of the CDQ dimensions as follows:

Control. Scores on this dimension were negatively related to Consideration in all three samples, while the correlations with Initiating Structure were not significant. One possible Interpretation of these results is that when crew members perceive the AC [that is, the aircraft commander] as a controlling agent, they construe his behaviour as not considerate.

Intimacy. Initiating Structure was not significantly related to this dimension but Consideration showed significant positive correlations. Crews which descrive themselves as more intimate tend to judge their AC's as being more considerate.

Harmony. Scores on this dimension correlated positively with Consideration while the correlations with Initiating Structure were not significant. This would seem to point to the influence of leader behaviour in establishing certain interpersonal relationships among crew members. The amount of effort he spends in organizing crew relations and defining the roles of crew members doesn't seem to make much difference in the harmony of the crew. However, the way in which he goes about his duties does appear to be a factor in the development of compatible relationships.

Procedural Clarity. This characteristic of crews, which refers to the way procedures and duties are defined for each crew member, was related to Initiating Structure in a positive direction. Correlations with Consideration were not significant. Thus the manner in which the leader acts toward crew members does not appear significant in establishing a well defined set of relationships among crew members. But the frequency with which he engages in acts construed as Initiating Structure is related to the clarity of duties and functions in the crew.

Stratification. Scores on this dimension were highly related to Consideration in a negative direction, while correlations with Initiating Structure were not significant. In other words, crews which describe their leader as relatively less considerate tend to be characterized by greater awareness of status hierarchies within their crew.

In general, these results point to the interaction between group dimensions and leader behaviour. It seems clear that if we are to understand the psychological characteristics of crews, we must deal not only with what the AC does, but also how he does it. In air crews, the actions of the AC may set the style, so to speak, for the interpersonal relations of crew members.

5. In a study of 132 B-29 and B-50 commanders, a comparison was made between commanders' ideologies of leadership behaviour and their crews' descriptions of their actual behaviour in relation to the two leader behaviour dimensions. The ideology scores were computed from the commanders' own responses to the LBDQ-Ideal. In expressing their leadership ideology, the commanders clearly recognized the desirability of scoring high on both dimensions of leader behaviour, but the correspondence between their statements of how they should behave and their behaviour as described by their crews was negligible. In the case of the Initiating Structure dimension, the correlation did not differ significantly from zero. Although the corresponding correlation of .14 for the Consideration dimension was significant at the .05 level of confidence, this represented only a low degree of association. The moderate reliability of the Initiating Structure and Consideration scales, and the fact that the distributions are not entirely normal, probably contribute to the low magnitude of the correlations obtained. Nevertheless, the evidence suggests that the aircraft commander's knowledge of how he should behave as a leader has little bearing upon how he is perceived as behaving by the members of his crew.

Academic Survey

The members of 18 departments in a liberal arts college described their department heads and indicated on the LBDQ-

Ideal how they believed a department head should behave. They also ranked the five departments in the college that had the general reputation on the campus of being best led or best administered and the five departments that were least well led or least well administered. In making these rankings, each respondent excluded his own department. The correlations between the reputation scores and the LBDQ-Real scores were .36 for Consideration and .48 for Initiating Structure, with .47 required for significance at the .05 level. When discrepancy scores – measuring the absolute difference between the Real and the Ideal scores on each of the leader behaviour dimensions – were correlated with the reputation scores, the obtained coefficients, –.52 and –.55, respectively, were both statistically significant. The greater the departure of the actual behaviour of the department head (on either leader behaviour dimension) from the norm of how ideal behaviour on this dimension was conceived by the members of his department, the poorer was the administrative reputation of the department.

A cutting score of 41 on Consideration and 36 on Initiating Structure for the split on one co-ordinate, and the median reputation score for the split on the other, were used to distribute the 18 cases into quadrants as illustrated in Table.

The Relationship Between the Reputation Achieved by College Departments and the Consideration and Initiating Structure Scores of Department Chairmen Taken Conjunctively (N =18)

Chairman's Leadership	*Number of Chairmen*	
	Below Median Reputation	*Above Median Reputation*
Score of 41 or large on Consideration and a score of 36 or More on Initiating Structure	1	8
Score of less than 41 on Consideration or less than 36 on Initiating Structure	8	1

Source: After John K. Hemphill, "Leadership Behaviour Associated with the Administrative Reputation of College Departments," The Journal of Education Psychology, 46, No. 7, November 1955, p. 396. Reprinted by permission of the Publisher.

The import of these data is clear: the departments with high reputation are those whose chairmen score high on both leader behaviour dimensions.

It is appropriate at this point to summarize five principal findings of this series of leader behaviour studies.

1. The evidence indicates that Initiating Structure and Consideration are fundamental dimensions of leader behaviour, and that the Leader Behaviour Description Questionnaire provides a practical and useful technique for measuring the behaviour of leaders on these two dimensions.
2. Effective leader behaviour is associated with high performance on both dimensions. The aircraft commanders rated highest by their superiors on "over-all effectiveness in combat" are like in being men who (a) define the role which they expect each member of the work-group to assume, and delineate patterns of organization and ways of getting the job done, and (b) establish a relationship of mutual trust and respect between the group members and themselves.
3. There is, however, some tendency for superiors and subordinates to evaluate oppositely the contribution of the leader behaviour dimensions to the effectiveness of leadership. Superiors are more concerned with the Initiating Structure aspects of the leader's behaviour, whereas subordinates are more concerned with (or "interested in") the Consideration the leader extends to them as group members. This difference in group attitude appears to impose upon the leader some measure of conflicting role-expectations.
4. Changes in the attitudes of group members toward each other, and group characteristics as harmony, intimacy, and procedural clarity, are significantly associated with the leadership style of the leader. High Initiating Structure combined with high Consideration is associated with

favourable group attitudes and with favourable changes in group attitude.

5. There is only a slight positive relationship between the leaders believe they should behave and the way in which their group members describe them as behaving. For this reason, those engaged in leadership training programs should be especially wary of accepting trainees' statements of how they should behave as evidence of parallel changes in their actual behaviour.

Having presented this background material on the LBDQ, we will now discuss two studies that deal directly with school superintendents. The first of these two compares superintendents and aircraft commanders.

It is presumed that every leader, irrespective of the institutional setting within which he operates, engages to some extent in both forms of leader behaviour - Initiating Structure and Consideration. Consequently, in comparing groups of leaders from different institutional settings we should expect to find some degree of overlap in leadership behaviour. But where the institutional settings differ markedly—as in the case of public education and the Air Force—we also should expect to discover significant differences between groups of leaders drawn from two such settings. The leaders whom we have studied—educational administrators and aircraft commanders-function within institutional settings that traditionally would appear to emphasize different aspects of leader behaviour. On the basis of predicated differences between these two settings, the following hypothesis was formulated: that educational administrators will demonstrate, in both leader behaviour and leadership ideology, more Consideration and less Initiation of Structure than aircraft commanders. Accordingly, the purpose of this study is to determine whether these two groups of leaders differ significantly in their leadership ideology and their leadership style.

The sample was composed of two groups of subjects: 64 educational administrators and 132 aircraft commanders.

The 64 educational administrators were drawn from two-sources. Thirteen of the group were participants in an interdisciplinary graduate seminar on "Leadership for Educational Administrators" conducted during the Winter Quarter, 1954, and sponsored by the School-Community Development Study at The Ohio State University. Eight of the 13 members were principals; the others, local superintendents and supervisors. The remaining 51 members of this sample were all superintendents of Ohio schools studied during the spring of 1954. Sixty-two of the sample were men, and two were women. These 64 administrators answered the LBDQ-Ideal, and also were described on the LBDQ-Real by 428 members of their respective staffs. The LBDQ-Real and the LBDQ-Ideal were administered by members of a research team with the guarantee that the anonymity of each respondent would be protected. On the average, 6.7 descriptions (a=.8) were secured for each administrator.

The 132 aircraft commanders were in charge of B-29 and B-50 crews. The two aircrafts are essentially similar, with an eleven-man crew on the B-29 and a ten-man crew on the B-50. Seventy-six of the commanders were studied in the Far East Air Force at the time they were flying combat missions over Korea. The other 56 were members of select Strategic Air Command crews undergoing evaluation in this country. These two groups of commanders did not differ significantly either in leadership ideology or in leader behaviour as measured here, and hence have been combined into a single sample. The 132 commanders answered the LBDQ-Ideal and were described on the LBDQ-Real by 1099 members of their respective crews. On the average, 8.3 descriptions (a=1.6) were secured for each commander.

For the combined sample, the primary data consist of the responses of 196 group leaders to the LBDQ-Ideal and descriptions of these leaders on the LBDQ-Real by the 1527 members of their respective groups.

The 1723 LBDQ's were scored on the Consideration and Initiating Structure dimensions. The leader's own scores on the Ideal form were used to represent his ideology in respect to the two dimensions. With the LBDQ-Real, it was appropriate to determine first how well group members agreed in describing their respective leaders. Accordingly, for each sample and separately by dimension, between-group versus within-group analyses of variance were made. The Fratio was significant at the .01 level of confidence in each instance. The extent of agreement among group members in describing their leaders may be expressed by the unbiased correlation ratio (epsilon). These ratios for the Consideration dimension are .49 and .61 for the administrators and commanders, respectively. The corresponding ratios for Initiating Structure are .49 and .44. For the LBDQ-Real, group-mean Initiating Structure scores were therefore used as indices of the leader's behaviour on these dimensions.

For each leader, and on each dimension, one score (the LBDQ-Ideal) expresses his own ideology, and another (the LBDQ-Real) describes his behaviour as perceived by the members of his own group. The comparisons of the leadership ideology and leader behaviour of the administrators and the commanders have been made exclusively in terms of group differences, and have been analyzed in two ways: first, by t ratios of the mean difference between the number of leaders from each group who scored either above or below the mean of the pooled samples on each (and both) of the dimensions; secondly, the differences in leadership styles have also been analyzed according to number and per cent of cases in each sample that fall into the quadrants.

Table presents a comparison of the mean LBDQ Real and the mean LBDQ-Ideal scores of the educational administrators and the aircraft commanders.

In Table are listed, by sample, the correlations between the leader behaviour dimension scores on the LBDQ-Real and the LBDQ-Ideal, and the correlations between the Real and the Ideal scores on each dimension.

The findings in table support the hypothesis that leaders who function within these two different institutional settings exhibit differences in their leadership ideology and differences in their style of leadership behaviour. Specifically, the administrators, in both leadership ideology and leader behaviour as measured by the LBDQ, show more Consideration and less Initiation of Structure than the commanders. These differences are all significant at the .001 level of confidence.

Product-Moment Correlations between Leader Behaviour Description Questionnaire Real and Ideal Scores

	Educational Administrators (N=64)	Aircraft Commanders (N=132)	t
Consideration— Real Consideration — Ideal	.09	17*	.53
Initiating Structure - Real Initiating Structure— Ideal	.34**	.14	1.37
Consideration — Real Initiating Structure -Real	.13	.45**	2.28*
Consideration — Ideal Initiating Structure— Ideal	.22	.29	.48

*Significant at the 05 level of confidence.
**Significant at the .01 level of confidence.

Source: From Andrew W. Halp n, " The Lender Behaviour and Leadership Ideology of Educational Administrator's and Aircraft Commanders, "Harvard Educational Review, 25. Winter 1955, p. 24.

The leaders in both samples indicate that they should show more Consideration and greater Initiation of Structure than their group members perceive them as doing. These differences, too, are significant at the .001 level of confidence. The differences between the two samples on the Ideal are in the same direction as those on the Real, so that the pattern of Ideal means corresponds to the pattern of Real means.

But this similarity in pattern of group means does not imply a necessary relationship between how individual leaders behave and how they believe they should behave. It has been noted previously that a leader's beliefs about his leadership behaviour are not highly associated with his leadership behaviour as described by his own group members. In general, this is confirmed by the present findings.

The commanders, both on the LBDQ-Real on the LBDQ-Ideal, show significant correlations between the Consideration and the Initiating Structure scores, whereas the administrators do not. Although the interdimension correlations do not differ significantly in the case of the Ideal, the difference between the interdimension correlations on the LBDQ-Real is statistically significant. This indicates that the administrators, to a greater extent than the commanders, treat the two dimensions as if they were independent.

The differences between the leadership styles of the administrators and the commanders may be analyzed also according to the number and per cent of cases in each sample that fall into each of four quadrants: (1) "above the mean on Consideration" and "above the mean on Initiating, structure," (2) "below the mean on Consideration" and "below the mean on Initiating Structure," (3) "above the mean on Consideration" but "below the mean on Initiating structure," and (4) "above the mean on Initiating Structure" but "below the mean on Consideration." The two means are based upon the pooled samples of administrators and commanders and may be constructed as coordinates which define these four quadrants.

Earlier findings with aircraft commanders have suggested that the most effective leaders are those represented in the upper right quadrant, and the least effective those in the lower left quadrant. The leaders represented in the other two quadrants may be conceived as falling within a middle range of effectiveness. In the one instance, represented by those leaders in the lower right quadrant, there is a tendency to show sufficient Consideration but not enough Initiation of Structure; in the other, the converse holds – the leaders are strong in Initiating Structure but fail to show enough Consideration for the members of the group.

The statistical significance of the difference between the number of administrators and the number of commanders who scored in each quadrant was determined by the chi-squared test. The x^2 values and corresponding p values are presented in Table.

x^2 And p Value*s for difference between the number of Educational Administrators and the number of Aircraft Commanders whose LBDQ-Real Scores Fall in Each Quadrant

Quadrant	x^2	p^2
Above Mean on Both Initiating Structure and Consideration	3.80	>.05
Below mean on both Initiating Structure and Consideration	2.54	>.05
Above Mean on Consideration but Below Mean on Initiating Structure	43.61	<.001
Above mean on Initiating Structure but Below Mean on Consideration	10.43	<.01

With 1 df, require 3.84 at p=.05, 6.64 at p=.01 and 10.83 at p=.001.

Source: From Andrew W. Halpin. "The Leader Behaviour and Leadership Ideology of Educational Administrator and Aircraft Commanders," Harvard Educational Review. 25, Winter 1955. p. 26.

At the .05 level of confidence, the two groups of leaders do not differ significantly in respect to either the number of highly effective or highly ineffective leaders. It should be noted, however, that the x^2 value in the upper right quadrant (3.80) does approach the value required (3.84) for significance at the .05 level of confidence. This suggests that according to the posited criterion of effectiveness the commanders show a greater tendency toward effective leadership than is demonstrated by the administrators.

The principles differences between the two groups of leaders are found in the off-quadrants. Those leaders among the administrators who score in neither the highly effective nor the highly in- effective quadrant tend to cluster in the lower right quadrant and are characterized by high Consideration but low Initiation of Structure. Conversely, those leaders among the commanders who score in neither the highly effective nor the highly ineffective quadrant tend to cluster in the upper left quadrant, and are characterized by high Initiation of Structure and low Consideration. In both instances, the differences are highly significant. In short, these findings suggest that the leaders in these two groups who are not effective differ systematically in the nature of their shortcomings. The aircraft commanders are inclined to show less Consideration than is desirable, whereas the educational administrators tend to be remiss is not initiating sufficient structure.

x^2 And p Valves for Difference between the Number of Educational Administrators and the Number of Aircraft Commanders Whose LBDQ-Ideal Scores Fall in Each Quadrant

Quadrant	x^2	p^2
Above Mean on Both Initiating Structure and Consideration	8.32	< .01
Below Mean on Both Initiating Structure and Consideration	.50	> .05
Above mean on Consideration but Below Mean on Initiating Structure	65.46	< .001
Above Mean on Initiating Structure but Below Mean on Consideration	18.46	< .001

With 1 df, require 3.84 at p = .05, 6.64 at p=.01, and 10.83 at p=.001.

Source: From Andrew W. Hal pin, "The Leader Behaviour and Leadership Ideology of Educational Administrators and Aircraft Commanders," Harvard Educational Review, 25, Winter 1955, p. 27.

Finally, instead of comparing the two groups of leaders by this quadrant method we may simply note the per cent of each group that scores above the mean of both samples on each leader behaviour dimension, both Real and Ideal. The juxtaposition of the data for this purpose, as given in Table highlights the fact that an essentially similar pattern of differences between the administrators and the commanders obtains in respect to both the LBDQ-Real and the LBDQ-Ideal.

The finding support the basic hypothesis that educational,

administrators differ from aircraft commanders in both leadership ideology and leadership style. The administrators tend to show greater Consideration and less Initiating of Structure than the commanders. These differences are presumably associated with differences between the institutional settings within which the two groups of leaders operate.

Since the concept if institutional setting possesses a certain heuristic value, further comparative studies of leaders drawn from different institutional settings should increase our understanding of leadership behaviour. These studies need not be confined to the American culture, for cross-cultural studies of leadership afford an equally important area for investigation. For example, are the present findings about the leader behaviour of educational administrators peculiar to American educators; or is the same leadership style characteristic of school administrators in Germany or in England? But in spite of its heuristic value, the concept of institutional setting is limited by its lack of specificity. To know that different institutional settings foster different leadership styles is important, but we also need to know what specific factors in each setting are associated with these differences. Therefore, it would be preferable to study various specific conditions of group operation that are imposed upon both the leader and his group. Some conditions are clearly a function of the institutional setting; others are defined by the mission of the group; and others are determined by local mores and regulations, and by temporal exigencies. It should be possible, however, to isolate particular conditions of group operation and determine their relationship to different leadership styles. For example, what is the relationship between the specificity with which a group goal has been defined and the way the leader behaves? What effect does the visibility of group products have on the leader's behaviour? The speed with which the leader and the group receive feedback information on these products? In education – where goals ordinarily are broadly defined, where the responsibility for their accomplishment is diffused, where the products of group effort are not readily visible, and where considerable time often elapses before the leader and the group receive feedback on the success of the group's effort – do these conditions prompt the administrator to stress Consideration more than the Initiation of Structure? The limitations in the design of this study permit only speculation about these questions. They deserve, however, further careful investigation.

It has been noted that the leader's belief in how he should behave is not strongly associated with how his group members describe his behaviour. In examining the pattern of the four correlations in the two top rows of Table, we note, however, that the Real versus Ideal correlations are significant for the commanders on Consideration, and for the administrators on Initiating Structure. Although these correlations are low, they suggest an interesting speculation. In public education where a high value is placed upon Consideration, and Initiating Structure is not a dominant theme of the institutional mores, we find a significant relationship between the Real and the Ideal Scores on Initiating Structure. Conversely in the Air Force where a high value is placed upon Initiating Structure behaviour, and Consideration is not a major theme of the institution, we find a significant relationship between the Real and Ideal scores on Consideration. In both institutional settings the relationship between the Real and the Ideal scores tends to be greater for that aspect of leadership behaviour which is least supported by the institutional mores. This suggests that the leader's belief is how he should behave is reflected in his behaviour—as perceived by his own group members—most clearly in respect to that aspect of leadership behaviour which is least endorsed by the institutional norms. Whether this is due to a closer parallel between the leader's ideology and his actual behaviour on this score, or whether it is due instead to a closer relationship between his ideology and the discrimination with which the group members perceive his leader behaviour, is a question for further research. In either event, the implications for leadership training programs are provocative, for it this finding is corroborated by other cross-institutional studies of leader behaviour, then we should expect to find that changes in an individual's leadership ideology will be reflected in his leader behaviour principally in those aspects of behaviour that are least endorsed by the norms of the specific institution within which he functions.

Per cent of Educational Administrators and of Aircraft Commanders who Score above the Combined means of both Groups on Initiating Structure and Consideration Real and Ideal

		Per cent of Cases Educational Adminis-tration	Aircraft Com-manders	x^2	p*
Initiating	Real	40.6	71.2	1703	<.001
Structure	Ideal	23.4	727	42.45	< .001
Consideration	Real	797	50.0	15.80	< .001
Ideal		76.6	432	19.37	< .001

With 1 df. require 10,83 at p=001.

Source: From Andrew W. Halpin, "The Leader Behaviour and Leadership Ideology of Educational Administrators and Aircraft Commanders," Harvard Educational Review, 25, Winter 1955, p. 27.

10
Fiscal Matters

The subject matter of educational finance is not restricted to dollars and complicated formulas, but also involves concepts of economics, taxation, politics, and education. The curriculum and instructional programme desired must be translated into the financial resources needed through budgeting. Money must be found to fund the program. After the money has been found, it must be allocated to realize the programme desired and achieve equality of educational opportunity. In addition to these very complicated tasks, students of educational finance must conduct research on variations in fiscal capacity and effort, educational needs and costs, bases for achieving equality of opportunity, relationships between financing patterns and educational quality, and numerous other aspects of the economics and finance of education

As interest in providing equality of education for all children has increased, the study of school finance has become very important. For many years the existing differences in financial resources for education among school districts were not an issue. The rise in egalitarianism associated with the civil rights movement changed this attitude of accepting differences based upon place of residence.

The financing of education, which was once left to a small number of specialists and the will of people in local school districts, has become a state and national issue. Consequently, the field is characterized by much intellectual ferment and the development of new conceptual knowledge.

The conceptual problems in educational finance involve: (i) how to raise money needed to finance education, (2) how to allocate this money to optimize equal educational opportunity for pupils regardless of place of residence, (3) how to expend resources to optimize the attainment of organizational goals, and (4) the impact of educational expenditures on socio-economic conditions.

Economic Structure

Through the budgeting process, the desired educational programme is translated into fiscal terms. Within recent years educational literature has included much about PPBS (planning, programming, budgeting system) as a management technique for program development and budgeting. Johns and Morphet included the following important processes in budgeting:

1. Determining the purposes of the educational program.
2. Developing educational plans to achieve the purposes agreed upon.
3. Preparing a budget document to forecast the expenditures and revenue necessary to implement the educational plan during a stated period of time.
4. Presenting, considering, and adopting the budget.
5. Administering the budget.
6. Appraising the budget.

Previously, emphasis was placed upon the importance of educators knowing what they want and need as a basis of improving educational opportunities for pupils. This involves well established goals, which become the personal mission of the administrators and teachers in the system. From this point, preparing the budget document itself is largely a means problem. Seeking support for and official adoption of the budget is, however, a very important leadership responsibility involving value choices.

The Finances

Education becomes big business when one considers the financial resources spent on a state and national basis. Additional money is not easy to obtain for many reasons, not the least of which is the resistance of tax-payers and competition for scarce dollars among the agencies of government. Educational administrators must be prepared for the politics of financing schools. This involves the development of expertise in such areas as taxation, preparing budget documents, and politics.

Educational leaders must have up-to-date information to the present use of taxes to raise funds. This involves a well-developed data bank showing the present use of taxes and delineating alternatives for raising additional money. Also involved is understanding of the criteria used to judge taxes, and how the property tax, sales tax, personal income tax, corporate income tax and other taxes fit for these criteria.

The budget document should be well prepared and fully supported by supplementary documents. In preparing these documents educational leaders should use simulation to anticipate any and all possible situations and responses. There is no substitute for knowing what one wants and thoroughly documenting the position.

As is true of all major decision making in education, the decision one desires must be supported in the politics of bargaining (if practiced), politics of the board, politics of the legislature, and politics of the Congress. The educational administrator in charge of these politics must have a strategy that will win for schools the resources needed.

Money Matters

The tradition of local control and financing of education has presented a difficult problem in providing equal educational opportunity for every child regardless of place of residence. The basic problem involves variation in local fiscal ability and effort among school districts and among states. The rich states and local school districts can, with much less effort, raise many times more dollars per pupil for education than can poor states or local districts making a high effort. The range in wealth per pupil within states may be 50 to 1. As a consequence, in states having low levels of state equalization funding, the differences in programme opportunities for children, among districts are drastic.

Another significant problem in allocating funds for education is to account for factors that influence educational costs. The costs of the special education, vocational education, compensatory education, adult education, and other programmes vary from the costs of other programmes of equal quality.

As is discussed in other parts of this text, the battle for equal educational opportunity has raged in the legislatures, the Congress, and the courts. This has stimulated much activity to develop state and federal support programs to equalize financial support for schools. Authorities involved in the National Educational Finance Project developed means through which the consequences of alternative models of state financing could be analyzed and evaluated for a prototype state. Most authorities feel that complete equalization within a state requires a complete state support program. Equalization among the states would, of course, require federal funding. Either of these alternatives violates traditions of local control.

Managing Business

As mentioned previously, the operation of schools is big business. In this section the focus is upon those support services for school systems traditionally considered as school finance and business management. Both of these fields have grown so large and complex that they should be separated. School administrators are confronted with providing massive support services just to keep the schools in operation and to maintain physical facilities. Effective management must be provided to coordinate and provide these cervices

Those involved in administering business management support services also manage the expenditure of money. Because most of these support services are not direct educational services to pupils, business management activities tend to follow the norms and practices of private business. This may provide for the business official a mystique that does not extend to other professional administrators in the central office.

Candoli and associates reviewed the concept of the business functions as emerging into a planning role in addition to traditional roles assumed in educational organizations. They suggested that too much emphasis has been placed upon day-to-day operations.

Numerous concepts have been developed within recent years. The planning, programming, budgeting system (PPBS) swept the country during the 1960's. Leaders in the association of School Business officials developed the Educational Resources Management System (ERMS) as an application of management systems to educational organizations. The Program Evaluation and Review Technique (PERT), is another management technique. The planning function is further discussed in this chapter. Let us now consider some of the important tasks of providing effective business management services in school systems.

There must be appropriate accounting for the funds received and expended by the school system. Controls over expenditures must be established to assure that the funds are spent in accordance with authorized budgetary statements. Some of the functions normally performed by the business office are management of salary payments, purchasing, internal auditing of expenditures, preparation of financial reports, financial accounting, supervision of internal accounting of schools, provision for school insurance, and accounting for school property. Performance of these jobs is a major responsibility and involves many persons. Thus the volume of transactions completed and accounted for is very great each school year. The accounting procedure should serve a much broader function than the control of expenditures. Jordan stated this point well.

School accounting programmes are more than a set of abstract records which contain historical information about past activities in the local district. They provide the basic information used in making current administrative decisions and planning future activities. Since virtually every educational decision will require an allocation of financial or material resources, in its implementation, the reliability of the accounting system is one of the vital elements in the effective administration of local school district.

The Infrastructure

To keep the school plant facilities in operation in a large school system involves massive investments in personnel. The schools must be heateds. They must be kept clean and free of health hazards to staff and pupils. School grounds require constant care. The facilities must be maintained. Citizens have placed in trust millions of dollars of assets for educational purposes. It is the responsibility of the school business administrator to accept responsibility for this trust and see that this property is maintained so there will be no interruption in the educational program and maximum life and usefulness will be obtained.

The thousands of persons who inhabit a large high school each school day make the provision of custodial services necessary. These custodians must be selected, trained, and supervised.

Many school systems transport thousands of pupils daily to and from schools. This was a massive operation even before the use of buses for desegregation, but it has grown demonstrably as a result of cross busing between school centres to achieve racial balance in classrooms. For many school systems this has required the purchase and operation of many more buses than in previous years. Of course, in many city school systems the school district does not assume responsibility for transporting pupils. For the presponderance of school systems that do provide these services, however, much is involved. In most of these school systems transportation services are publicly owned rather than contracted.

In most school systems the food service programmes have also grown into a major operation. Responsibility must be assumed for administering the purchase of lunchroom supplies and equipment, planning the menus, and coordinating the services for the schools offering them. Overall coordination at the school system level must also be achieved.

Instructional and other supplies must be received, stored, and efficiently distributed as needed. This involves records of goods received and distributed. To assure economy of purchase and efficiency in having the supplies available when they are needed, warehouse facilities for storage mast be provided for all but very small school systems. Even in the smallest systems there will be need for storage of supplies and equipment, but large-scale warehousing may not be feasible.

Facilities, equipment, and personnel are needed to distribute the supplies as they are requisitioned by school principals. Efficient management of distribution services is especially important to assure that classroom supplies and equipment are available when needed. Efficient record keeping is required; an inventory is kept of what is available for distribution.

Although the services discussed are the most massive supports provided, many others must be provided. For example, school administrators in many school districts are faced with the responsibility of operating a security force for protection of persons and property. Large systems operate a mail service. Many persons are required for secretarial, clerical, printing, and other office services. Provisions must be made for administering personnel services for non-instructional employees.

Institutional Management

Much of what has been written about organizational effectiveness involves personnel. For example, in the scientific management era, a basic theme was how personnel could be led toward optimum productivity. As a task area, however, personnel administration involves numerous management functions as well as the application of complex theories to achieve optimum attainment of organizational goals.

Before we discuss some of the tasks in personnel administration, it should be pointed out that this is an area of great ferment and change. First, there is the redefinition of roles, norms, and administrative leadership associated with the growth of collective bargaining. Federal laws relative to affirmative action and assurance of equal opportunity employment practices have been initiated. These affirmative action programs have had an impact upon procedures for recruitment, selection, and promotion of personnel. As a result of the ferment in personnel administration created by teacher militancy, adoption of the industrial model for collective bargaining, federal and state laws, and other movements, school administrators and teachers and have been faced with radical redefinitions of roles.

Instead of seeing collective bargaining as a purely negative force, school administrators may. as they seek role redefinition for themselves, look upon the process as providing further access for teachers and other school personnel to participation in decision making. This renewed energy of teachers can be beneficial to education. Many of us recall a time when teachers were too docile to be of assistance politically. We believe that when there have been satisfactory redefinitions of roles, all persons will respond to good leadership. In industrial situations where collective bargaining has become a part of the accepted process and role redefinitions have been satisfactorily accomplished, opinion polls have demonstrated that most of those in labour, do not hold negative feelings toward management.

During the great growth in enrolment following World War II, school systems faced critical shortages of teachers. Most staff planning in terms of organizational missions was lost in the massive problems of recruiting, certifying, and placing teachers and other personnel just to keep schools open. With the downturn in enrolment and availability of highly qualified personnel in many areas, school administrators have the opportunity to regroup for short and long-range personnel development goals.

As Castetter suggested, the success of the organization is related to sound personnel policies.

It is generally conceded that the success of any human endeavour is closely related to the quality of personnel who perform the tasks necessary to the achievement of purpose, as well as to the conditions which affect their physical and mental well-being. This assumption is as applicable to school systems as it is to any organization of human effort.

Personnel planning involves such areas as predicting future personnel needs, recruitment, selection of personnel, placement, evaluation of effectiveness, personnel development, compensation, working conditions, and tenure.

Individual Problems

Prediction of personnel needs must be based on the objectives of the organization and the number of pupils to be educated. The goals guide the process of program development and consequently, influence estimates of future personnel needs. The planning function must also include predictions of social trends and economic developments, which will have an impact upon the number of pupils who are to be educated.

In addition to these basic considerations are the planning of strategies for recruitment, selection, placement, and other areas mentioned previously. From the determination of future personnel needs will emerge implications for the development of strategies in other areas of personnel administration.

Personnel planning should facilitate the development and adoption of policies in such areas as internal promotion and external recruitment, welfare provisions (e.g., sick leave, leaves of absence, retirement, salary), tenure, evaluation of performance, and so on. Many of these policies, of course, are subject to negotiation through either collective bargaining or other processes.

The Selection

Recruitment involves identifying and describing positions to be filled, communicating these needs, encouraging persons to apply for the positions, and collecting information on applicants. As mentioned previously, school systems must comply with federal laws on affirmative action in recruitment, employment, and other aspects of personnel activities. The aim of all recruitment programs, however, is to locate the best-qualified persons and interest them in applying.

The importance of recruitment must not be underestimated. Obtaining highly qualified personnel is dependent upon the planning and aggressiveness of those conducting the recruitment activities, Screening and Selection.

Processes must be established to screen the applicants for the variety of positions to be filled. What information should be collected about the applicants? How will screening be accomplished and who will be involved? How will eligibility lists be prepared and maintained? Through what formal processes will those eligible be selected and appointed? What policies should exist for promotion from within the organization?

Systematic procedures should be established to appoint personnel and process their assignments and orientation to positions. Nothing can compensate for warm, hospitable attention to persons taking positions in the school organization for the first time. Moreover, personal conferences should be arranged to define expectations and provide information to optimize personal orientation.

The Assessment

Procedures should be established to evaluate job performance for all instructional, non-instructional, administrative, and supervisory personnel in the organization. This is a difficult area because being evaluated is seldom, if ever, appreciated. Yet to move to where we ought to be, we must understand where we are in relation to goals.

Evaluation involves the establishment of criteria, which has a way of becoming a treacherous administrative activity. A discussed previously, personal needs and the demand dimensions of organizations frequently conflict. What persons feel that they should be evaluated on is not always consistent with what the organizational mission demands.

The process of rating performance in accordance with criteria is also sometimes emotionally demanding. Tenure, promotion, merit pay (if applicable), and other factors (including one's ego) are greatly influenced by the way one is evaluated in regard to the applicable criteria. Therefore the process must be as fair as possible and one should include provisions for appealing decisions.

11
Ideal Setup

Models are often used in the name of theory. Sometimes an advanced theory in one area may act as a model for a less advanced area, but theories and models are not equivalent, while a theory is a logically related set of confirmed generalizations, a model is constituted of propositions confirmed for one set of problems but applied to another class of problems. The major difference is that empirical theories are first empirical laws from which more abstract relationships can be derived, while scientific models first consist of abstractions which are later interpreted into empirically testable hypotheses.

In general, one subject is a model for something else when the concepts of both subjects are isomorphic. This means that there is a one-to-one correspondence between the concepts and assumptions of the model and the observed world, and the relationships take the same form. Isomorphism suggests hypotheses. For example, if a school system is like the human body, then the main office of the system may function like a brain, and decision processes may be likened to a nerve centre. Since a disturbance in one part of the body affects all other parts, the same may be expected of the school system. How ever, some of the disadvantages of models school also be apparent in the same illustration, because models are seldom perfect analogies, they can be seriously misleading. Yet sometimes they are used to the point of seeming real, they may become so sacred that the investigator is more interested in pre-serving the model than in interpreting reality. Because of such disadvantages, a model may actually obscure the actual relationships. This is especially true when models are chosen on the basis of their prestige or their success in other fields rather than any isomorphism or inherent similarities to the subject matter being studied. The prestige of physical science models may be a consideration that underlies their prevalence in the social sciences. For social science he relied heavily on physical, geological, and ecological models, and none of them are particularly relevant to social conduct. Models derived from cultural activities, such as the dramaturgical or even the musical model, have been ignored despite their possible relevance to everyday life.

Various Models

Models in which conflict is the basic process are implicit throughout this book, but, since the biological models stressing structure have been among the most popular sociological models, the conflict models will be contrasted with them. Rational-biological models of organization in particular have widespread popularity among the most eminent contemporary theorists of organization, including C.I. Barnard and Talcott Parsons.

Gouldner describes the rational model as that model in which organization is conceived as a means for the realization of announced group goals. Stress is placed on rationally directed, long-range development of the organization, or a system, toward explicitly stated goals. The model, as Gouldner points out, has called attention to the most distinguished characteristic of modern organization, its rationality. Its premises are that decisions are based on a rational survey of the situation and implemented through a codified legal apparatus, and that significant changes result mainly from planned efforts to increase efficiency. Because nearly complete rational administrative control is assumed, any recognized departures from rationality are attributed to random mistakes, ignorance, miscalculation, or other impediments to rationality. Gouldner suggests that from this "mechanical" (systemic) prospective on organization, the structure appears to be purely manipulatable, designed solely for they purposes of efficiency and the idea that "things can always be made better."

There are a number of considerations which the model ignores and, in fact, obscures. First, attempts to rationalize the organization may obscure the less formal and less rational elements of organization that also contribute to its effectiveness. The rational attitude that "nothing is sacred" in organization also ignores the fact that people become emotionally involved in the established ways of doing things, problems of organization arise precisely because the organization becomes a sacred end in itself. Nor do executives, in fact, have complete control over the organization because it is dependent upon outside forces which divert the organization persistently from its long-range goals.

The rational model is grounded in a biological model of society that underlies the structural-functional view of society. The model rests on the complacent belief that "good" organizations are essentially harmonious and static, an unmistakably selective perception of the way organizations operate. It is assumed that societies exist in a state of harmonious equilibrium maintained by the consensus of their members, and that conflict, irregularity, change, and dissent are, accordingly a "sickness" which disrupts the harmony. This view of conflict as a disease having primarily "dissociating and dysfunctional consequences" is sharply criticized as Utopian by Dharendorf in an essay with a provocative title, "Out of Utopia." His observations merit extensive reflection by persons interested in building an administrative theory. He observes that all Utopias, from Plato's Republic to Orwell's brave new world of 1984, have several elements in common. First, they are all societies from which basic change is absent, with the exception of orderly change, or a "moving equilibrium," which occurs so uniformly throughout the society that it is never upsetting to anyone. Also, Utopias are uniformly consistent and based on a universal consensus in regard to prevailing values and institutional arrangements. In these perfectly agreeable societies there is a caste like relation between the leaders and the oppressed, who would never revolt against their superiors. Recalling that Socrates finally decided that justice really means that everyone does what is incumbent upon him. Dharendorf notes, with some disgust, that modern theorists have also discovered that justice means that everybody "plays his role." Although some writers add a clever touch of realism by inventing an individual non-conformist who is considered to be a pathological case, according to Dharendorf his only role is to highlight the inherent good of conforming. Finally, it is uniformly true that Utopias are isolated from all other communities. Since citizens of Utopias are seldom confronted with demands from the outside world, the society maintains complete control over its environment and complete autonomy to establish and fulfil its goals. Dharendorf asks "if the immobility of Utopia, its isolation in time and space, the absence of conflict and disruptive processes, is a product of poetic imagination divorced from the common places of reality—how is it that so much of recent (sociological) theory has been based on exactly these assumptions, and has, in fact, consistently operated with a Utopian model of society." The same question has implications for administration.

A way of looking at society is also a way of not looking at it. The conception of school "systems" and stress on the "socialization" functions of schools already suggests selective perception about their fundamental nature. Dharendorf writes: "One of the more unfortunate connotations of the word 'system' is its closure ...there is no getting away from the fact that a system is essentially something that is...self-sufficient, internally consistent and closed to the outside." He concludes that "...it is only a step from thinking about societies in terms of equilibrated systems to asserting that every disturber of the equilibrium, every deviant, is an 'spy'...The system theory of society comes dangerously close to the conspiracy theory of history..."As a consequence "...it introduces many kinds of assumptions, concepts, and models for the sole purpose of describing a social system that has never existed and is not likely to ever come into being."

Dharendorf observes that advocates of "empirical research" and defenders of abstract theory are stubbornly similar in one respect. They have both dispensed with the prime impulse of all science, the puzzlement over concrete intellectual problems, the simple curiosity to solve "the riddles of experience." Problems, as opposed to topics or fields of inquiry, exist because they are puzzling to the investigator. Their solution demonstrates, above all, critical examination of facts, observation, and testing which generates new problems. Dharendorf believes that this loss of problem consciousness explains the Utopian state of modern theory.

One of the carious riddles of society concerns the problem of "social glue," or in other words: what holds organizations together. Why do people join organizations and "play" roles. If the bonds of organization are personal harmony and group consensus, why do they persist despite the facts of organized resistance, internal friction, intrinsic competition, and sometimes radical cleavages that characterize organizations. It is unreasonable to dismiss so common a phenomenon as conflict as "accidental" and "exceptional" to the normal process. On the contrary, perhaps it is not the presence, but the absence of conflict that constitutes the surprising and the abnormal. At the very least, what seems to be called for is a model of organization in which power and power conflict have a central place. It is proposed that power has a vital place in the maintenance of social order as consensus, and that conflict itself, as a natural adjunct of power relationships, provides a form of cohesiveness. Some premises of a conflict theory of organization follow:

1. *The Group Nature of Conflict:* Contrary to a popular view, conflict is not purely personal, or the subjective expression of individual psyches. Conflict is a group phenomenon and extends beyond the subjective attitudes of persons as group members. Barnard points out, for example, that just as a thousand loves between soldiers and enemy women is not equal to peace, so a dozen disputes between American tourists and French cab drivers is not equivalent to a French-American conflict; parties in conflict may even display affection toward one another, as in the cases of conflict between the sexes or age groups and the numerous wars fought by "peace-loving" people. Since conflict can exist independently of personal hostility, personal attitudes reveal little about group relations. Moreover, Barnard maintains that improving interpersonal relations by "getting people together" (as in the comprehensive school) does not necessarily reduce conflicts which are based on institutional differences (for example,

race), and in cases where enemies definitely have something to fight about, getting them together may simply expose their basic differences and drive them to their extremes.

2. ***Cultural Relativism:*** Historically the "good" people have usually fought the "good." Nations participating on each side in the religious crusades claimed religious justification. Modern nations each establish elaborate moral justifications for their inhumane acts of violence. The neighbours who dispute their property are likely to be "good" citizens, just as "progressive" educators and "essentialists" and authoritarians" are equally "good" people. That is, the "good" man is generally the supporters of his own groups' values, while the "bad" man is usually on the opposing side. Thus, the problem is not which side is "good," but what the fight is all about.

3. *An Organization is a Balance of Power:* What is defined as "good" may have had a long history of struggle for acceptance, as, for example, did Christianity, which was at one time the religion of a downcast minority. In this sense, the world, a society, or an organization, as each exists, is the outcome of historical power struggles and is the remnant of resulting animosities. All organizations are subject to some incipient cleavages on the basis of their previous history. Since the defeat of an idea or of a group seldom requires complete annihilation, scars remain which provide the basis for cleavage in new conflicts. For example, the relationship between North and South in the United States cannot be understood apart from the Civil War and the events that preceded and followed it. Similarly, playground fights are not entirely due to personality problems; those fighting may represent different community groups and families in conflict—social classes, racial, religious and ethnic groups. Like school-boys' fights, the more sophisticated battles between their parents, teachers, administrators and other school personnel, often reflect deep-seated animosities nourished by past events. Relationships between the school and its community are likewise molded by past struggles which may recur.

4. ***Conflicts Create Co-operation:*** Co-operation and conflict are not polar opposites, but are in fact closely related group processes; conflict between groups promotes co-operation within

groups. Because groups must cooperate intensively in order to wage conflict, the cohesiveness and discipline of a group may be indicative of impending disputes with another group. Also, as new conflicts occur, new forms of co-operation emerge. For example, competing groups within a school system will nevertheless work together when their mutual interest is jeopardized by outside groups. Superintendents intentionally employ this principle when they cast the blame for certain internal problems onto the school board. This alternating conflict and co-operation between groups, which can take place among the same individual, provides an element of unpredictability and flux in the organizational structure.

5. *Groups Must be Visible to Conflict:* Conflicts cannot occur between groups that are not indentifiable; each side in a conflict must have some physical or symbolic indentity. This requirement of visibility helps to explain why certain minority groups which are in opposition to the established order; such as the Mennonites and, more recently, the Beatniks and "hoods," deliberately maintain a uniquely characteristic appearance. Members of such groups who do not maintain the symbols (such as Mennonites who wear lipstick, or Beatniks without beards) are outcast by the group, not so much because their acts are mortal sins, but to prevent farther erosion of the group's identity. The members of one branch of Mennonites are not permitted to have telephones in their homes, but they may freely use public telephone booths because the public telephone is not identified with them. Identity is so important that as groups in conflict lose their symbolic character, the conflicts between them decline. Same distinctive groups, such as Negroes who cannot modify their appearance, must endure conflict longer than ethnic groups, such as the Italians who quickly become acculturated and accepted. Quite often conflicts disappear in this way without being resolved as the identity between those in conflict disappears.

6. *Conflict is Sustained by Ideology:* Symbolic identities have their highest expression in the statements of ideologies justifying the group's position in conflict. For example, each side of the 'town-and-gown" fights between colleges and their communities around the country has its rationale or its justification. Professors

are viewed as potentially dangerous liberals of an impractical bent by a nation that is grossly anti-intellectual, while many professors delight in thinking of laymen as crass, unsophisticated, conservative materialists. The ideology of local democratic control over the schools bolsters resistance to consolidation or to any interference in local affairs from state departments of education, while state departments justify their interference on the basis of elaborate ideologies about raising the standards of education, benevolence, and professional expertise.

Perhaps there is no more elaborate rationale for the different positions that educators take in conflict than those provided by philosophies of education. Two dominant philosophies, as described by Conant and Nock, will be briefly compared to illustrate the function of philosophy in maintaining and justifying conflicts. The two philosophers differ on the meanings of the doctrine of equality, realistic and instrumental conceptions of education, and programs of education.

(a) The Doctrine of Equality: Conant's basic value premise is equality of opportunity, not equality of reward. Consequently, he emphasizes that there should be a minimum of social class distinction to facilitate social mobility. Yet, while he is interested in maintaining an open class structure, he does not advocate homogeneity of social groups either, and he encourages diversity.

Nock also implicitly accepts the doctrine of equality, but he is less interested in explicating what it implies than in what it does not imply about education. Denying that all men are "educatable," he asserts that the doctrine is applicable only to those who are able to learn. Therefore, equality of treatment must be tempered by ability. While he grants that democracy and political equality are acceptable political values, he maintains that there is no implication from this political philosophy that the economic and educational areas of life need also be egalitarian. Therefore, while Conant concentrates on initial social opportunity, Nock emphasizes the desirable and logical outcome of the resulting competition, the survival of an intellectual elite based on ability.

(b) Conceptualizations of Education: Conant perceives education in its pragmatic, utilitarian aspects. First, it is a way to implement a fluid social structure, providing a means of social mobility. Second, education for Conant is more than a way to train an elite; it is a way to train citizens to live in a democracy. He sees education, then, as a way to make democratic society work. This is most clearly seen in his exaltation of the "comprehensive" high school which he believes will develop mutual respect among persons of diverse backgrounds who attend. He asserts that the American nation could not have developed its current coherence without the unifying influence of the public schools.

For Nock, on the other hand, there is a fundamental distinction between education and training. Education is for him a way of finding "truth" not of achieving the practical goals, even those so noble as developing an appreciation of democracy. Nock assumes that achievement of this truth requires more than direct contact with the world; it requires a "mental" grasping, which only a sophisticated intellect can achieve. And here is the fallacy that Nock sees in science, for with it, he charges, anyone can claim knowledge merely with sense experience; however, he argues that achievement of knowledge is not a democratic process, but a specialized one.

(c) Programs of Education: Conant believes that education must train persons for a variety of disciplines. He would like to have a variety of programs, designed to benefit all types of students and all types of intellectual abilities. He believes that specialized education should be at a relatively late age so that persons are not prematurely "forced" into a career pattern before their interests and abilities are known.

Contrary to Conant, Nock favours early specialization for promising students. He believes that intellectual ability can be identified early, and this allows for greater cultivation of the intellectual elite which he feels will develop anyway. Furthermore, since the object of education is to find the truth, a "bargain counter" education is uncalled for; this is merely a way of admitting that we are not sure of what the truth is. Furthermore, since "truth is truth," it can be found in Greek and Latin literature as well or better than in science. He prescribes a non-elective curriculum weighted heavily with classical studies and mathematics.

(d) Interpretation: This brief-summary of the two positions should be sufficient to suggest for the reader two basic philosophical positions under controversy today in public education. From the standpoint of conflict theory. Nock and Conant are representatives of two identifiable groups in competition over a limited social value; their philosophies are used by groups in conflict as justifications. The middle class is being justified by Conant and the upper class has been justified by Nock. From this view, one function of education is to transmit a group's values to its young; it is a training program for "new young warriors" to staff groups in conflict. Nock's distinction between education and training is illuminating. He defines training in terms of those subjects (science) which help to promote the social mobility of the middle class, and equal opportunity for all classes. Yet, it is equally obvious that "education" in Nock's terms also amounts to a training program – the training of a cultural elite. Latin, Greek, and math are symbols of identification with the upper social class, the landed leisure class that once controlled the society and still struggle for survival against the newer commercial and industrial middle class.

7. *Conflict Influences Goals:* Due to conflicts which normally exist within and between organizations, some personnel have aims which are not expressed in the official statement of purposes. This situation nourishes a diversity of organizational goals and unplanned cleavages between departments which further compromise the original goals. The operating goals, consequently, are partly forged out of the conflict process. As a note of caution, perhaps the conflict model is too pre-occupied with these spontaneous and unplanned developments of goals, but it is a pre-occupation which at least counteracts its systematic neglect in the rational model of organization.

The Effects

The important question at this point is not which model is more "real to life," but which raises the more significant questions. In the conflict model, "organization" is problematic. It calls for an investigation of organization as an initially "unnatural" state of affairs and forces the question to be asked; What causes organization? Answers to this question will provide answers to the question about the role of the school administrator.

Specific Structure

School administration is viewed in this book from a general perspective on organizations. General principles of organization and conflict are borrowed from literature on other type of organizations. This does not imply, however, that problems of administration are unrelated to the type or organizational goals, the organization's complexity, and its degree of centralization and standardization. There are certain characteristics of education suggested by Campbell which make it a somewhat special case. Yet, it will be clear as they are briefly discussed in the following paragraphs that far from denying the relevance of sociological perspective and conflict model, each special feature seems to support the critical relevance of the conflict model.

First education is a service that deals directly and intimately with people; perhaps this hardly makes education a belligerent enterprise. However, the school does things to people as well as for them; parents will be especially suspicious of some types of changes which may occur in their children. The conflict centres partly on which services the school is to render to a community with diverse interests and high hopes, and partly on the authority of the school to make that decision and to control the means of implementing it. Parents have exercised a long and, in some sense, legitimate control over administrative decisions which, however, is also legally delegated to the school boards and which is often usurped by professional doctrines of authority. The possibility that schoolmen may oppose the interest of parents lays the

Second, the development of a critical attitude is a central part of most educational philosophies, and some objectivity is generally expected of the public school system. This analytical attitude, supported by ideologies of academic freedom, is sometimes directed toward highly valued aspects of society. Consequently, there always exists a remote possibility that schools will lead pupils to revolt against certain aspects of the established order which some members of the community uphold. Public sensitivity to this possibility increases interest in the school from outsiders who can exert sometimes overwhelming pressures. Teachers, children, parents, and administrators may differ on the utility of critical thinking in practice if not in philosophy. This and the first condition suggest the inherently unstable, triadic relationship that characterizes the school's relationship to pupils and parents. There is usually some competition between home and school for the allegiance of children.

Third, there are explosive impediments to accurate evaluation of the success of schools. Policy statements tend to be so abstract that they are useless in establishing criteria of success. What is "good citizenship ?" Does it include critical attitudes toward the American government or not ? What are the criteria of good teaching ? What is a "successful" student? Often many years are required before attitude changes effected by high schools are revealed in behavior. This ambiguity in evaluating teaching success is less apparent in some phases of business, particularly in sales, where effectiveness can be measured in terms of sales volume and effectiveness of promotion campaigns. The actual criteria of success used by teachers and administrators have been left directionless by the ambiguity of goals and standards of success, and these criteria must be hammered out in practice from the different available expectations.

Fourth, education differs from other organizations in the structure of the forces that control it. School boards represent various special interests of the community and have almost complete legal control over school policies; school administrators have almost no legal status, and their job is subject to the school board's pleasure, which greatly impairs the administrator's control over his organization. He is forced to compete for the support of various special interest groups which attempt to influence school practices and he must often act as a mediator between them. Because these groups are inexperienced and untrained in education, the administrator may wish to resist some of their demands; but because they control his job, he may be in a poor position to do so.

Fifth, the school staff is professionally trained; many teachers have as much education as the chief administrator. Professionalization requires autonomy over work, a requirement which is often at variance with actual control by the administration. Their level and type of training, together with legal tenure provisions and the support of several professional organizations, gives the teaching faculty more legal autonomy than, for example, unskilled factory labourers. At the same time, teachers do not have as much authority over their spheres of work as do those in many of the more established professions in fact, perhaps no other professional group, except perhaps nursing, is so completely subordinate to its administration as are teachers. The traditional authority of laymen over the schools, the ensuing professionalization of teachers and the delegated power of administrators and school boards over teachers are basic characteristics of teaching that breed conflict between laymen, the administration, and their subordinates.

Finally, the school's physical structure and organization merit special attention. Unlike many organizations, such as the hospital, the school cannot be understood as a separate unit, for it is part of a system of units physically dispersed throughout the community and state. The fact that the superintendent's office is physically remote from the principal's office may be of some consequence for the development of unauthorized autonomy in some schools, problems of communication, and the kind of criteria used to evaluate teachers.

School administration is obviously, then, not identical to other forms of administration in all respects. The differences, however, should not be permitted to obscure the similarities; and in fact they may merely serve to highlight many of the same characteristics found in other modern organizations to which conflict models have demonstrated relevance. In any case the concepts that have proved faithful to us in studying complex organizations are those that have common rather than specific application.

Theoritical Aspects

The concepts which underlie models are tools of analysis. They set the perspective and point to the questions that are to be raised. Concepts have a fundamental role, therefore, in directing the investigation of organizations. Some of the major concepts that will appears in subsequent chapters will be previewed below. Their applications will be developed in more detail in the chapters which follow.

The Governance

Organization is primarily supported by two types of force, power and authority. Power is sometimes conceived as the non-legitimate or illegitimate threat of force to achieve an end, while authority is the right to use force, which is granted either by the consensus of those over whom it is wielded, or by delegation from other authorities. Power, then, will refer to the potential of force, and authority will refer to the right to exercise that force. Power is calibrated from minor influence at one extreme, to complete control at the other. While both power and authority involve the threat of force, force need not be actually applied in order to exert either power or authority.

Excessive display of authority may in fact dissipate power as repeated applications use up the available alternatives. Un-exercised power may also lose some of its threat, of course, but the more significant fact is that power is directly proportional to the number of alternatives available and is diminished when they are used. It is, for example, evident that persons who are willing to use illegal and unethical alternatives have more power than those who feel constrained by legal and ethical principles. Similarly, within the legal and ethical limits, each application of power consumes an alternative and simultaneously commits the organization to a line of action which further restricts its alternatives in the future. For example, in March, before the annual contracts have been signed, principals have a source of power over teachers that is not available in April after they have been signed. Similarly, a principal has more power over an incompetent teacher before the disposition of her case is decided than after she has been demoted.

A person may have authority without actually having the power to implement it. In fact, because power is a function of the alternatives available, authority and power may be inversely related. That is, the very legitimacy of authority constrains the kinds of alternatives that an authority may use in order to exercise its power. Authority is constrained by popular expectations, values, and traditions, which necessarily bind the use of power. The restraints on power that accompany authorization are apparent in the fact that fraud and bribery are very effective kinds of power which are precluded to persons in authority. The power of the principal to fire incompetents is similarly constrained by the existing community sentiments toward the incompetent, opinions of his colleagues, and humanitarian concern about how it will affect his personal life. The number of persons who can be demoted or negatively treated by the chief executive in any one year is limited, at some point resistance will develop. Therefore, the availability of each negative alternative is diminished every time it is used. Moreover the way that the principal handles a particular incompetent will set a precedent that in turn restricts the alternatives which are proper for dealing with incompetents in the future.

To summarize, power is based on the ability to control rewards - an action which may be seen as a threat, to be effective, it must be used occasionally. However, just as power increases as the range of alternatives increases, it diminishes as alternatives are actually consumed, for each application sets a precedent which precludes other alternatives. Authorized power is regulated by public opinion or organizational consensus. In the long run, though, there seems to be a tendency for those who exercise sheer power to gain public respect and legitimacy over a period of time. Because the greatest power is held at least temporarily, by persons who are not constrained within the limits of legitimization in its exercise, there is a tendency for power to become separated from authority.

Different Types

To a considerable extent, recent controversies over the appropriate models of social organization are repetitions, in another tongue, of an age old controversies about the foundations of society. To the question "What makes organizations risk ?" Some have answered, in company with Hobbes that it is sheer power – the threat of loss of job, the indirect forces of gossip and chicanery, or a compelling non of the rewards which conformity to the existing power will bring. Others prefer a more civil answer, the one Locke advocated, that it is the mutual consent of the governed which provides the authority to rule organizations.

The anthropologist Bronislaw Malinowski, has implied that rules as they relate to purposes, make organizations tick. Malinowski maintains that all human behavior begins with organization and that the particular nature of any organization is understandable in terms of the relationships between its goals and its functions on the one hand, and the relationships between its rules and its activities on the other. The goals prescribe ideal expectations and the functions represent reality; in the same fashion, the rules define ideal behaviours and the activities represent real behaviours. Organizations, change, therefore, to the extent that they are able to tolerate the degree to which reality deviates from ideality. He would hold that organizations are necessarily representative.

These various viewpoints also seem to underlie the major dichotomies of modern organizational theory. Depending on the emphasis given to each viewpoint, organizations are primarily authoritarian, or primarily representative, in terms of the power of subordinates to influence decisions. In the authoritarian (or "punishment-centered") organization, power to make decisions is concentrated at the top of the formal hierarchy, while in the representative type of bureaucracy, the entire membership has opportunity to express its consent and dissent and to influence the final decisions.

Uses of authority of power form several distinct structures

within organizations. A structure includes both a set of positions which prescribe broad functions and specific duties incumbents, and a system of norms which regulate the relationship between incumbents of different positions. Official positions in organizations will be referred to as offices. Each office constitutes a system of jobs, or roles, which prescribe the responsibilities (rights and obligations) of that office with respect to other offices in the system. Accordingly, the superintendent's office cannot be understood apart from the responsibilities of other offices in the system, including the roles of classroom teachers.

Although the term structure implies a stable pattern of relationships, it may be viewed as a variable; organizations can be more or less structured in several respects. The most structured system is the official authority system. The official obligation of superintendents is to provide facilities for teachers and to influence their direction; the principal is responsible for staffing and coordinating classrooms; the teacher is supposed to instill knowledge and values in pupils without showing favoritism, and so on. There are, however, contradictions even within the official system. Authority may have several bases. It may stem from traditional rights to make decisions, it may be delegated by political powers vested with legal and institutional authority, it may be assumed by mutual agreement among personnel, or it may be assumed by some individual because of a special competence. These forms of authority may be inconsistent, and rifts and power conflicts may develop among personnel within the organization who are committed to different authority systems.

Moreover, there are competing systems in the school, besides the official one, which create even further variability in the extent to which the overall system can be said to be 'structured' or coordinated. These competing systems give rise to several different informal authority structures in addition to the legal and official ones. Informal leaders develop among teachers on the basis of the esteem of their colleagues. Since the authority arising from these unofficial sources is independent of the legal-official structure, it in effect constitutes a separate system of authority—the informal authority structure. The informal authority structure is intermediate between the official structure and the informal power structure. In the sense that such uses of power are not officially authorized, they technically constitute a power structure, yet, in the sense that they are authorized by group opinions, they are authority structures.

Systems of completely unauthorized power, or power structures, complicate the picture still further. Informal power structures exits simultaneously with, yet independently of the informal authority structures, being unauthorized even by mutual consent of colleagues.

To summarize, there is a structural connection between authority and power, respectively, the official and the informal organizations which they underlie. It is a crude relationship since some facets of the informal structure are authorized informally, and because competing bases of legitimization exist which are decided by power conflicts. Because authority relationships are infinitely more predictable than power relations, which by definition may exist outside the normal structure of expectancy and group control, authority is an understandably popular approach to organizational theory and planning. However, because structure is a variable and because there are a variety of structures (some based on unstable power relations), change and instability must be recognized as inherent to organizations. The notion of process must be incorporated into attempts to predict and plan organizational behaviour.

The problem of predicting events based on unstable, semi-structured power relations seems to be overwhelming at this point. The problem, however, of dealing with such dynamics as a class of events does not appear as forbidding. It may be necessary and useful to incorporate a set margin of error into predictions—that is, a specific measure of error to be expected from unforeseen disturbances, shifts of power, and environmental changes. In any event, attention needs to be given to the conceptualization prediction, and explanation of power relations as distinct from authority relations.

High Position

It is by now a truism that the official and informal structures of an organization are drastically influenced by the society in which they exist. The statement, nevertheless, is a reminder that administration cannot be viewed apart from the general status system of the society and the manner in which the status is translated into organizational practices. The concept of status refers to a position in the general society; it parallels the term office, which designates positions within a particular organization. The distinctiveness of organizational and societal positions, or office and status, is illustrated by Lazarsfeld and Thielens in a study of academic freedom. College social science professors believed that they were ranked low in esteem by businessmen, congressmen, and college trustees. That is, they sensed that they held a low social status in the society. But the professors who had higher official and professional ranks within the educational system felt they had lower social status than the lower ranking professors. In other words, the professors felt that their official achievement was not accorded sufficient recognition by members of the broader society.

There are sometimes contradictions between what treatment a person may expect because of his status, and what the actual duties of his office are. A superintendent, for example, assumes the status of "educator," but his official duties may be more akin to those of a businessman and, in some smaller communities, of a records clerk. Conversely, different social statuses may be bestowed on offices with the same rank in different associations. In one study, for example, it was found that school superintendents of wealthier school systems were accorded more prestige than superintendents of the same rank in less wealthy schools. It is the variations in status between offices of the same official rank which, of course, motivates mobility patterns within the school system.

Contradictions between status and office are also sources of dilemmas. For example, age has a different meaning within the status system of the broader society and the official system of the school. For, while it may be officially proclaimed that ability is the only important consideration for promotion, within the school age is important. Because responsibility is supposed to be relegated to older persons, a young principal or superintendent in command of older persons can create a problem. Female high school principals who command a predominantly male staff may create a similar dilemma. Women officers occupy positions of incipient conflict because of inconsistent expectations of the subordinate place of women in our society.

The Bodies

Statuses and offices comprise different "social orders." Offices constitute the fundamental element of an organization, while statuses are the basis of social institutions. Together, the offices constitute the responsibilities of the school system, its jobs, or its "roles," which outline rights and duties with respect to other offices. They comprise, in other words, the organizational structure providing the organization's regularity and stability; conflicts between offices provide its dynamic quality as well.

Organization behaviour is to be understood in terms of offices rather than exclusively in terms of members' personality characteristics. Modern man lives in a "contract" society in which people react to each other without knowledge of their personalities. Administrators do business with teachers, contractors, students, and parents, sometimes with almost no knowledge of their personal characteristics, yet with relative ease and success because people are expected to behave according to their status. Little insecurity is felt by school officials when they entrust the schools' monies to bank tellers who may be virtual strangers, because even though the teller may nave dishonest tendencies, he will nevertheless tend to conform to the obligations of his office rather than give in to his personal inclinations. Similarly, teachers may be personally prejudiced against Negroes, but strive to be equalitarian with Negro students in schools where discrimination is condemned, and, conversely, personally unprejudiced teachers may be forced to racially discriminate in some systems.

While the official system is not determined primarily by the personalities of those who are in it, it is primarily affected by the institutional system that underlies it. The institutional "order" consist primarily of the statuses that compose each institution. Institutions are rules that link cultural values to specific situations. They have no official name and location as organizations do, and institutions are more abstract than organizations, comprised of values and rules that transcend a location and specify the general organizational forms. Thus, while teachers are employed by the New York City Schools, for example, and presumably have some allegiance to these organizations, they also are subject to the institutional values of teachers and citizens in other parts of the country, including the political, religious, economic, professional, and educational values that dominate the society. Each of these institutions is distinct in the sense that it is comprised of a network of interrelated statuses which are less related to other institutional areas. For example, politics is comprised fundamentally of relations between politicians, governors, cabinet members, the voting citizens, and so on. Education is comprised basically of relations among school board members, the citizens of the community, the state boards of education, superintendents, teachers, and pupils.

Since there is, in each institution, an element of the ideal, these statuses and expectations can be more or less compatible within a single institution. Thus, the job of "educator" is straightforward; he is to develop in children knowledge and character. But what is distinct about the institutional order is that there may be inconsistent expectations among institutions. A "good family man," for example, is expected to spend his evenings at home with his family, but the good community citizen is expected to spend his time working on community projects, and the good businessman is expected to use his evenings to work overtime and "get ahead." The point then is this: a single institution, such as education, is implemented in a number of different organizations besides the schools, such as the church and businesses and the military, all of which have educational programs; and a single organization, such as a particular school, is comprised of a variety of often inconsistent institutional statuses. The job of a teacher at school X is hardly described simply by her status as an educator; that job is comprised of a variety of institutions, among them business, politics, religion, and so on. In addition to teaching the children, she is to keep attendance records, chaperone parties, sell war bonds, encourage patriotic and religious devotion, and provide spiritual and vocational guidance. In these activities, educational values must be compromised with recreational, business, patriotic, religious, and other institutions in the work place. The "official" job then, comprised of a variety of institutions, is an arena of institutional conflict where compromises among political, religious, business, educational, and other value systems are carved out of the daily work routine. In the process, educational ideals are sometimes implemented, sometimes usurped, by other institutional means. This implies that the character of the public schools cannot be understood solely in terms of educational principles and philosophies, but must be understood within the context of the broader institutional order, including politics, business, religion, and other basic value systems. It also means that the official system is inherently one of conflict, the same conflict that persists in the more abstract institutional order. But the inconsistencies and conflict are more notable and severe as the teacher experiences them on the job because it is on the job where they must be reconciled and translated into action.

Again, lest it be misinterpreted, it should be noted that such conflict is not always debilitating; on the contrary, it can be and frequently is highly productive. The school like any other organization is a dynamic system. It is by virtue of the dynamic interaction of its various components that the organisation maintains what Parsons and others have called its equilibrium, or "steady states." When conflicts are severe enough to create imbalance in the system, they are responsible for readjustments, which in turn may result in or intensify other tensions.

Locals and Cosmopolitans

The simultaneous existence of the institutional and organizational orders poses conflicts of loyalty for employees. Loyalty to the employer, to the school—its customs and regulations, or its administration—is often a-precondition of success; but on the other hand, teachers may be more or less attached to various institutional principles that transcend the particular school. For example, if the school's policy forbids the teaching of religion, some teachers will feel guilty about ignoring it, or will teach their own brand of religion anyway. School systems differ greatly in their attitude toward the part which different institutions play in their operation. Some teachers may stress the educational aspect (that is, the transmission of knowledge) more than others, while other teachers may stress efficiency, or the use of business techniques, or the "politics of the game" more than others.

Institutional loyalty creates a particularly acute problem in a mobile society where the local place of employment, and particular family boundaries, no longer constrain a person's career nor exclusively define his standards of achievement. In a time when one part of the country may serve as a model for another part, it is no longer apparent that compliance with the job requisites is any assurance that the major institutional values are being fulfilled. It is possible for a teacher to be "successful" without actually contributing anything toward development of the nation's educational goals.

Members whose primary commitment is to the school's local community will seek to win the community's support for their school programme and their place in it. This makes it more likely that the community will influence the basic character of the school. However, those members whose primary loyalty is cosmopolitan in nature (that is, committed to the broader national values) will be more influenced by national and international pressures on education which, as a matter of fact, can adversely affect the interests of a particular community or region. Thus, any attempt to curtail a vocational agricultural programme in a predominantly rural community would probably meet resistance despite the well-known decline of agricultural opportunities, just as zealous attempts to integrate Southern schools in the national interest will be unwelcome.

Official Side

The dilemmas of employed professional constitute a peculiar form of the local-cosmopolitan dilemma. The bureaucratic employee is expected to reserve his primary loyalty for the school where he is locally employed, particularly to its administration. The professionally oriented teacher, on the other hand, will probably be more influenced by the stands taken on issues by professional society, by professors at influential training centres, and by colleagues across the country. Conflicts in the professional and employee orientations can become particularly acute when the issue involves racial integration, school consolidation, or relative importance of seniority and merit.

The Concerns

Although exercised by individuals, power and authority describe characteristics of the organization. Commitment and involvement, however, provide a parallel set of concepts which describe the power system from the standpoint of the individuals in it. While commitment and involvement tend to be correlated processes, they can be distinguished analytically. Considering the extremes, a person is completely "involved" when he does something solely because of personal desire without any formal obligation to do it. While there is an element of compulsion implicit in a commitment, it arises largely from the ethical and social pressures from precedented acts rather than from threat of direct force.

These concepts are useful in analyzing the strategies by which individuals and organizational leaders handle their problems. In complex organization, persons often must do what they dislike in order to obtain their preferences. As a result a person may commit himself to something and be involved with an entirely different matter. In other words, people exchange obligations for rights. Their life becomes a dynamic balance of commitment and involvement. Such systems of exchange are regulated by norms of reciprocity, which means that when a person gives up something, he can expect something in return.

The concept of commitment is also useful for the analysis of power, which, as indicated, is a function of the number of available alternatives. Every major commitment consumes one or more alternatives by binding the organisation to an irrevocable line of action. Moreover, every decision creates still other commitments, ones that are often unforeseen. Informal commitments usually accompany the formal ones. For example, when a school attempts to recruit a teaching staff that is entirely middleclass, white and Protestant, it is also committing itself to distinct practices, curriculum, and operating goals which, in turn, limit the school's alternatives for dealing, for example, with lower class Negroes.

These unforeseen and compulsory types of commitments create considerable institutional drift from long-range goals. Selznick cites two sources of these strains between actual and operating goals. First, the daily minor decisions can lead the organisation in directions it did not set out to travel. Old techniques of administration and teaching have a way of becoming sacred; thus, the goal of efficiency may actually be subverted by a seemingly minor decision to hire a tradition-directed accountant when planning to mechanize the records-keeping system. Second, drift is partly a consequence of a limited administrative perspective that naturally occurs because administrators tend to stress rationality and formal organisational goals. In stressing the rational formal goals, unintended outcomes of decisions on informal goals tend to be overlooked, or are considered to be irrelevant because they are logically irrelevant. The task of simultaneously "keeping an administrative eye on the ball" (as Selznick puts it), and systematically observing conditions seemingly irrelevant to the goals that arise independently of international acts, introduces a complexity into administration which is difficult to manage. However, both the relevant and non-relevant conditions obviously do shape the character of organisations.

The concept of commitment, then, implies a strategy of organisation as well as individuals. The act of commitment is potentially an act of change which may eventually affect the organisation's structure and goals. There is a need for organisational theorists to study this class of strategies, for the notion of commitment as a strategy calls attention to the simultaneous structure and change that constitutes the science of administration. The view stresses the flexibility of organisational structure and helps to offset some of the traditional emphasis on structure and goals as "given" qualities. It suggests the feasibility of viewing organisation as a development over time by analysing its strategic acts. The decision-making process is a particularly important crux of such analyses.

The analysis of organisational process had been so neglected, and the need for new departures so urgent, that there is some justification for taking the opposite viewpoints that process, strategy, and sheer "accident" are the "normal" states of organisation, and structure is the "abnormal" state. Pursuit of such a view would require special conceptual tools. A few of the most promising of these tools include interplay, co-operation, and reciprocity. Interplay stresses the strategic character of organisational decision-making. It is a tactical relationship wherein the action of one person depends on the unknown outcome of a previous act; an administrator's decision to fire or retain a teacher, for example, depends in part on anticipated community reaction. Reciprocity refers to the norm of exchanging favours. Persons may often engage in conduct that is not personally approved by them, but which promises the fulfilment of obligation or the return of a favour. Co-optation refers to type of compromise in which an opponent is incorporated into the leadership structure of a group in order to control him better; some control over organisational affairs is sacrificed in exchange for greater control over the opponent. These concepts describe some of the types of commitments by which organisations are guided and compromised. The important function they play within organisational processes also suggests another basis of the organisation's cohesiveness besides power and consensus—that is, constraint.

Our purpose is to communicate with each other to try to develop useful theory in educational administration. A seminar in which professors of educational administration and social scientists work together is salutary; it illustrates the progress made in the past decade—progress characterised by a marked change of emphasis in the training of administrators. Traditionally, our training programmes have stressed the "practical" and have concerned themselves more with techniques than with understanding. During the post-war period, however, administrators have become increasingly aware of the role of theory and have come to recognise the contributions that social scientists can make to our understanding of educational administration. The superintendent's job and the jobs of principals and supervisors have been viewed afresh in the light of recent human-relations research. Those of us responsible for training, administrators have welcomed research findings on leadership and group behaviour, and we have found ourselves drawing heavily upon insights into administration derived from other disciplines. But at the same time we are appalled by the poverty of theory within our own field and dismayed by the extent to which our own research has been anchored to "naked empiricism." Out of this realisation has grown our present-attempt to develop theory in educational administration.

New Trends

Several influences during the post-war period have contributed to this realisation. Three in particular deserve mention. The first was the establishment of the National Conference for Professors of Educational Administration (NCPEA) in 1947. This group, through its annual meetings and other activities, has facilitated communication among those who train administrators and has fostered higher and higher standards of training.

The second influence—one is tempted to say "revolution" — came about through the Kellogg Foundation's support of the Cooperative Programme in Educational Administration (CPEA). This programme, begun in 1950, provided much-needed support for research and development. Among other things, it opened new avenues of communication between educational administrators and the members of other disciplines. Professors of educational administration and social scientists began to talk to each other. This did not come easily, for each group was wary of the other. As members of these two groups discovered that they were not speaking the same language and found that their orientations were strangely different, their initial wariness gave way to varying shades of frustration, rejection, and hostility. It took time to overcome these negative attitudes, to develop way of communicating with each other, and to develop the mutual respect necessary for efficient cooperation. Some of the original eight CPEA centers have made substantial progress in this regard.

The third influence is that of the University Council for Educational Administration (UCEA), established in 1956. Even during its first year, the UCEA, along with the Educational Testing Service and Teachers College, sponsored a large research project designed to develop measures of the performance of school administrators. The financial support for this project comes primarily from the United States Office of Education, but also there will be contributions from Educational Testing Service, Teachers College, and others. The UCEA is also cooperating with the University or Chicago in sponsoring this seminar. Several other UCEA projects are contemplated.

As in any form of social change, progress has been slow and along an uneven front. Three recent books reflect the present state of affairs. First is the signal book by Coladarci and Getzels, The Use of Theory in Educational Administration, published in 1955 and stimulated—at least, in part—by the authors' participation as consultants at the 1954 NCPEA meeting in Denver. Coladarci and Getzels call attention to the dearth of theory in educational administration, emphasize the integrity of theory and practice, and propose one approach to a theory of educational administration. This important monograph has not yet had much time to "take"; it will require a few years for its full impact to be appreciated. The second book, sponsored by the American Association of School Administrators, is Moore's Studies in School Administration: A Report on the CPEA. Moore in reviewing the publications that have appeared thus far from the eight CPEA centres, observes that few of the investigations are theory-oriented. The bulk of the studies reviewed are exhortations, how-to-do-it prescriptions, catalogues of opinion, or normative "status" investigations which do not permit us to generalize beyond the immediate data. The third book, sponsored by the NCPEA and edited by Campbell and Gregg, is Administrative Behaviour in Education. Here again, the contributing authors found a lack of theory-oriented research. However, Griffiths in his chapter has taken steps in working toward a theory of educational administration. The current gloomy side of the theory picture that these three books reflect is of less importance than what they herald for future, more constructive efforts to develop better theory. Note that all three books appeared within the space of two years. The significant point is that they appeared at all; they examine issues that would not have come within the purview of educational administration prior to the end of World War II.

This brief historical perspective has bearing upon our task in this seminar because our progress may be impeded by the same issues that have cropped up from time to time in the NCPEA, CPEA, and UCEA. Several of these issues were epitomized in the communication problem that be set the authors who produced the NCPEA book. A few of the contributors sought to employ the social scientists' point of view and stressed the importance of theory; other contributors held to a more "practical" orientation. The writers found that they often were talking past each other. A demonstration of good will among the participants and superb tact on the part of the editors helped to achieve constructive communication between the adherents of these two groups. The development of better communication and understanding among the members of that writers' group is a story in itself and one that would be worth examining as a guide for other groups engaged in cooperative enterprises of this kind.

We are faced with a similar problem. Our seminar group is composed of people from two major backgrounds: educational administration and social science. What can we learn from the experience of the NCPEA writers' groups that will help us accomplish our present task? Perhaps by identifying the issues that have baffled others we can place ourselves in a position to approach these problems with greater rationality.

Our problems appear to arise from three major sources which we may classify roughly as substantive, communicative and motivational. These sources of difficulty are not distinct; they overlap in subtle and intricate ways, and in a sense all revolve around problems of communication. However, let us pretend that there are no interaction effects among them.

12

Various Aspects

1. Ottaway, The culture of society means the total way of life of a society.
2. Mettfww Arnold said, The best that has been thought and know is culture."
3. Ellwood, "Culture includes on the one hand the whole of man's material civilisation, tools, weapons, systems of industry, and on the other, all the non-material or spiritual civilisation such as language literature, art, morality, law and Government."
4. In the words of E.B Taytor, "Culture is that complex whole which includes knowledge, belief art, moral law, custom and any other capabilities and habits acquired by man as a member of society."

Merits

1. One comes to know about all the things then one can transmit or preserve them better.
2 One can improve one's culture update it in the light of other cultures.
3. A person culturally more sound is one who excels in one aspect, gains confidence and that helps to becoming better or other aspects of personality.

4. It adds grace to human. We, make it worth living as there is a keen desire to prosper, to flourish and to live-better and better.

5. It glorifies the nation, enriches its already rich cultural heritage.

6. One is able to understand society properly and can add to enrich it and can also root out ills from it. One can also eliminate the bad elements from the culture.

7. It trains and cultivates human powers. John Dewey said that an individual is enabled to join freely and fully in shared or common activities.

Demerits

1. Too much emphasis on cultural aim will lead to neglect or other aspects of personality.

2. It will be in line with the surrounding and the prevailing social climate.

3. It hinders the natural development of the child. In the words of T.P. Nunn, "the aim of cultural-development-hinders a child from developing according to his own interests and potentialities." He further says, "National institutions and traditions have a performance which made individual life a trivial thing."

4. A few bad things cannot be allowed to continue but in cultural aim that has to be continued. Long and fellow gap stated "Let the past bury its dead"

5. It leads to neglect of professional aspect of education which is very important to earn one's livelihood.

6. There are many cultures in the world which one is ideal and the best—it is difficult to decide, if we go on within our own culture, our vision may be narrow and may be too low.

Cultural aim of education is important but it cannot be given priority in the aims of education. It can surely assist the other aims with some broader thinking on it. In the words of Rafifidm Pwad, "India has to choose for herself a culture that derives inspiration from what is noble in our ancient culture and at the same time does not ignore demands of the present age."

The Spirituality

Education makes a person spiritually sound. A person who is spiritually sound behaves better. He/she is able to do well while being trained for social efficiency, sound moraly and physical betterment. In the absence of spiritual aha of eduction, one's life is incomplete. Spiritual aim is the pillar on which rests the edifice of total personality. Surely it is deeply linked wtth the character building aim. Spiritual aim gives strength to human soul and mind. The great spiritualists like Guru Nanak, Buddha, Mahavir, Swami Dayanand, Vivekanand, Shankaracharya, Aurobindo, Gandhi, Tagore accepted the spiritual aim of education. Views of some of them on this aspect of life are given below and they are worth mentioning down:

Aurobindo said, "Every man has in himself something divine, something his own, a chance of perfection and strength. In however small a sphere which God offers him to take or refuse. The task is to find it, develop it and use it. The chief aim of education should be to help the growing soul to draw out that in self which is best and make it perfect for a noble cause.

Finfey said, "Material progress is good thing; social and political reforms are mere valuable both to the race and the individual; their final worth lies in the aid they afford to spiritual life."

Radhakrishnan said, "The aim of education is neither national efficiency, nor world solidarity, but making the individual feel that he has within himself something deeper than intellect, call it spirit. If you like."

Merits

1. Spiritual aim of education makes a person gentle and pious.

2. It makes the students religious minded. They are able to have some values of life—and all this has its good effect on their behaviours.
3. It makes the personality of the individual strong. He/she becomes a man of character, honesty and integrity.
4. It-reduces the problems of indiscipline, conflicts, quarrels to some extent corruption, greed, aggression etc., destruction, hatred are on the increase. All these also stand checked to a considerable extent.

Demerits

1. One may think of leaving the worldly life. That is not so good for every one.
2. Spiritual aim may be achieved but one may not be so practical.

Spiritual aim of education, no doubt, is important but it cannot be given top-most priority in the aim of education. Other aims of education the vocational aim, knowledge aim, etc will to be cared for fully. Then and then and then only it will remain practical and useful to lead a good life in the society.

Harmonious development of personality is considered to be the main aim of education. In harmonious development, various facets of personality i.e. academic, social, cultural, economic, spiritual, aesthetic etc. are fully cared for and they are given equal importance. Emphasis on all aspect of personality helps to have a balanced type of personality. In the process of education, different types of education are important in their own ways. Each one has great significance. None of them should be ignored considering it insignificant. One of them or two out of them should not be considered more important than others. Due recognition to each aim and that also on proportionate basis must be given. Then only there will be harmony in the various aspects of an individual's personality. A harmoniously developed individual is an asset not only to the social group or community but also to the society or the nation he belongs to. He is good, incarnate and he is bound to emit fragrance and imbibe in others goodness wherever he is and wherever he goes. Therefore, harmonious development aim of education is important and it must be properly attended to by one and all.

The great men say so about harmonious development aims Rousseau regards education as, "The process of development into an enjoyable, rational, harmoniously-balanced, useful and hence natural life."

In the words of Ross, "Harmonious development needs the intellectual, religious, moral and aesthetic development of the child."

Pestalozzi says, "Education is natural, harmonious and progressive development of man's innate powers." By harmonious development, he means the education of head, heart and hand.

In this context Gandhiji said, "By education I mean an all round drawing out of the best in child and man—body, mind and spirit," He further says, "Man is neither mere intellect, nor the gross animal, nor the heart and soul alone. A proper and harmonious combination of all the three is required for the making of the whole man and constitutes the true economics of education."

Merits

1. An individual comes out all round good. He is successful in whatever type of situation he is placed.
2. He is academically good, physically and mentally sound, normally and culturally all right, has social efficiency and is economically a fit person for some vocation.
3. It is complete living. It makes an individual useful and self-reliant person.

Demertis

1. Development of all aspects is not possible fully in one way or the other, one may lag behind.
2. It is not possible to measure accurately whether the desired ends are reached or not.
3. Individual differences are always there.

4. Harmonius development aim is goodwithin this age of competitions where only academic aspect is the main criteria, the person may not get a chance of selection.
5. In some institutions, all facilities for harmonious development of personality are not available. Moreover, it is very difficult to decide a suitable curriculum for it.
6 The problems of population explosion, unemployment hinder the harmonious development of the individual.

The Education

Knowledge is very important these days. A person with good and uptodate knowledge is able to impress others. Such a person gets applaud wharever he is and wherever he goes. Education equips a person with adequate knowledge. It updates his knowldge aim of education. Is it the most important aim of education? The answer to this has to be thought of carefully. Knowledge is not the only thing important in life. An individual stands adorned with knowledge. Apart from academic aspect, other aspects of personality i.e. physical aspect, social, cultural, moral, educational are in no way of lesser importance. One thing is definite that knowledge about social, cultural, moral aspects is possible only if one has acquired the knowledge. That way knowledge aim may be called a foundational one. Socrates said, "One who had tre knowledge should not be other than virtuous."

Merits

The following are the merits of knowledge aim of education:

1. It is a very good instrument of education.
2. It helps the individual in making adjustment in life.
3. It helps the individual as well as the society in the proper growth and development.
4. It strengthens morality.
5. It makes an individual thoughtful.
6. It serves as a means to achieve some end.

Demerits

1. Knowledge for the sake of knowledge is not good.
2. More knowledge is good but it is add out the cost of starving the soul.

Aims of education must be related to the needs and requirements of the people. In this fast changing age when values of life are changing, life is becoming complex and to live well is a challenge for everyone. Education should equip a person to face life boldly and courageously, eradicate its shortcomings and make it worthy of living. Education must enable an individual to come out all successful in every walk of life whatever may be the situation— political, social, cultural and whatever may be the circumstances of the individual. Then and then only education will be called education worth the name—an instrument of utility and usefulness for humanity.

The Commission made a bold statement in respect of aims of education for democratic India. It stated that education must develop in its citizens habits, attitudes, and qualities of character and equip them to bear the burden of life in the changing economic structure. The Commission suggested the following aims of education :

Development of Democratic Citizenship. It is the major responsibility of education to carefully train every citizen for democratic citizenship. Such a training comprises of:

Clear Thinking. Education should equip the individual with the capacity of clear thinking. The individual should be a good democratic citizen who is clear of head and clear at heart. This makes him have clear thinking about everything.

Receptive to New Ideas. The individual becomes open minded. He welcomes new ideas at every stage. He is not a narrow thinking individual tied to the old customs and traditions. He is always willing to accept the change.

Clearness in Speech and Writing. The individual has clarity in speech and in writing. While exchanging ideas with others orally, he remains peaceful. While writing maintains clarity and is able to present ideas with full clarity.

True Patriotism. The individual is a true patriot through and through. He leaves narrow ideology of selfishness in the interest of broaded national feelings. He is well-wisher of a nation and whatever he does or says, he remains in tune with the nation.

Art of Living with the Community. The individual learns to live with others. He believes in co-operation and co-existence. He is a social being ever-ready to learn the art of living with community.

Development of Internationalism. Education imbibes the qualities of world citizenship. He believes in universal brotherhood. Today just patriotism is not sufficient. There is need of true and pure nationalism which believes in internationalism.

Improvement of Vocational Efficiency. Education must aimed at increasing the productive or vocational efficiency of young students. It includes :

(a) Realisation of the national prosperity is possible only through work.

(b) A new attitude toward work and dignity of labour.

The emphasis should be on crafts and productive work and diversification of courses. The ideas is that a large number of students may take up vocational courses.

Development of Personality. Education should develop Htence, artistic and cultural interests of the students. These are necessary for self-expression and for the full development of human personality. For this purpose subjects like art, craft, music, dancing etc should be included in the scheme of studies.

Education for Leadership. In order o make democracy function successfuHy, it is essential' To' incutctr - the qualities of leadership in youth. Education should train the youth to provide leadership in the social, poflfical, industrial and Itural fields.

Indian Education Commission (1964-66) has made very valuable recommendational regarding the aims of education. It has, in fact, turned to refer to the whote system of education through its recommendations, the Commission has stated, "No reform is more urgent than to transform education, endeavour tb relate it to the life, neiptfs and-aspirations of the people' and thereby make it a powerful instalment of social, economic and cultural transformation, necessary for the realization of our-national goals."

The Commission is suggested the following aims of education for the purpose of reforming it :

1. Increasing Productivity
2. Promoting Social and National integration.
3. Accelerating the process of Modernisation.
4. Cultivating social, moral and spiritual values.

The details of these aims are given below :

Increasing Productivity. It is very essential to increase the productivity of a country in order to ensure its progress. This objective can be achieved by education. The commission has suggested to act upon the following programmes in order to achieve this goal:

Imparting Science Education. Imparting Science Education is very essential in modern age in oroer to increase productivity. Hence science should be made a compulsory subject from the school Stage upto the University stage. Science Education must "become an integral part of school education and uttimatety some study of science should become a part of all courses in the humanities and social sciences at the university stage."

Work Experience. It is very essential to include work experience in school curriculum in order to produce interest in work. Every student should have experience of doing some work from the early school stage. Hence practical experience should be given to the students at school, home, workshop, factory etc. so that skilled workers are available in the field of work and there is a definite increase in productivity of the country. The Commission also suggested that a student should be given a certificate only when he fulfils the condition of work experience.

Application of Science to Production Process. There is a great need of connecting the knowledge of science with the activities of productivity. Modern age is the age of machines. Productivity can be increased to a great extent by the use of machines and machines can be used efficiently only with the application of technical knowledge and the knowledge of science. Hence it is essential to include these elements of science in curriculum which can accelerate the action of productivity.

Vocationalization of Education. It is very essential to impart vocational education in order to fulfil the aim of increasing productivity. Hence there should be arrangement of vocationalization of education from the secondary school stage. The students should be given the required information and guidance for the proper selection of vocation so that they are able to choose the right vocation which is according to their interests and aptitudes and which can fulfil the needs of the country.

Indian Education Commission described the promotion of social and national integration as the main objective of education because the unity of the nation is the only solid basis of the strength of a country. The Commission recommended the following steps to be taken for this purpose :

Common Schools. There should be common schools for all students, belonging to any category or community.

There is a great need of continuous progress in the country so that we should be able to walk side by side with other countries of the world. Hence there is an urgent need of accelerating the process of modernization in our country so that we may be able to stand in line with the developed countries of the world. For this purpose, there is a great need for the use of science based on technical education. There is also a need for preserving and re-evaluating the cultural heritage of our country so that we may be able to move forward in every field of life.

The commission has given the following suggestions for this purpose :

(i) Education should create the feeling of curiosity and investigation through the development of proper interests, sentiments and attitudes. There is also a need for developing the power of dear thinking and decision-making in the students.

(ii) Education should create perfect intelligentsia which should be associated with the different categories of people and which should have deep roots in the soil of the country.

Indian Education Commission had laid great emphasis on cultivating social, moral and spiritual values In order to associate education with Indian Culture Religious or moral education has always enjoyed a great importance in India. Everyone in this country wants that education should cultivate good qualities, moral values and spiritual understanding among the students so that they may cultivate these good qualities in other persons. The Commission has given the following suggestions in this connection.

(i) There should be an arrangement in the school time table for teaching fundamental principles of all religions.

(ii) The knowledge of becoming a good citizen should be made a part of education.

(iii) Social, moral, religious and spiritual qualities should be developed in students through practical working in the school.

The Culture

We should try to make a critical evaluation of the present system of education in the light of the aims of education suggested by the Indian Education Commission. The critical evaluation reveals to us the following things :

1. The present system of education has proved itself to be quite unsuccessful in creating good citizens. The standard of citizenship is falling day by day in our country because of the spread of corruption and indiscipline. And in general, there is fall in moral values.

2. Vocational education is not being given in the planned way in our country. No doubt, vocational education has been started in some schools, but the students are not

given proper guidance in the selection of suitable vocations. They are not given any information of the opportunities of employment in various vocations.

3. Unsuccessful in Creating all Round Development. The present system of education in our country is quite unsuccessful in creating all round development in students. Our education lays great stress on intellectual development only. It ignores physical, economic, social and cultural development of the students.

4. Our education has also been unsuccessful in cultivating moral values in the students. As a result of it, moral standard of people is falling day by day Many persons in the country have become selfish and greedy.

5. No religious education is given to the students in our schools. As a result of it love for all religions has disappeared in our country and fanaticism has become the order of the day.

6. Our education has proved itself to be unsuccessful in developing national unity. Our teachers and education have not been able to convey the concept of national unity to the students. Nothing has been done to establish common schools in India as suggested by Indian Education Commission. The students belonging to various religions are not given opportunities to work together freely. Hence our students have not understood and developed the concept of national unity.

Following are the ideal aims of education at the present time :

1. All round or perfect development of the personality of all the students.
2. Creating good citizens out of all the students.
3. Imbibing the spirit of patriotism in the students.
4. Preparing students for the service of humanity.
5. Enabling the students to preserve their cultural heritage.

6. Cultivating the spirit of social and national unity in the minds of students.
7. Imparting vocational education for enabling the students to earn their livelihood.
8. Making proper use of Human Resources.
9. Giving moral, religious and spiritual education to students in order to raise their moral, and ethical standards.
10. Creating awareness in the minds of the students for modernization.

National Educational Policy

National Policy of Education aims at National System of Education which implies that upto a given level, all students, irrespective of caste, creed, location or sex, have access to education of a comparable quality. (1) Common Educational Structure i.e. 10+2+3 (ii) National Computer frame work with a common core and other flexible components. All educational program are to be carried on in strict conformity with secular values.

Life Long Education. Education is a like long process. Naturally it is to continue once it has been started. Education will be provided to one and all. Universal literacy will be spread. Every person, whatever may be his profession and whatever occupation he may be engaged in, will be provided with the type of education he/she is interested in. Open school, open university, distance education centre, pace learning etc. will be provided.

Development of Manpower. The country needs manpower at different levels and in different areas of working. Education will develop suitable type of manpower of all type. Thus, it will help the country to grow and develop fully. Efforts will be to have national self-reliance.

Peaceful Co-existence. Education should help everyone believe in peaceful ways of life. It will, therefore, propagate national unity and international brothehood. All types of emotional integration will be aimed at. Mutual give and take policy, respect and regards for each other etc. will be inculcated in the people. India has always worked for peace and understanding between nations, treating the whole world as one family. True to this tradition, education has to strengthen this world view and motivate the younger generations for international cooperation and peaceful co-existence

Development of Socialism, Secularism and Democracy. Goals of socialism, secularism and democracy enshrined in our Constitution will be developed. Education will make everybody have scientific temperament, free and independent mind and.thinking Education has the accelerating role. This aim of development includes materialistic'as well as spiritualdevelopment. Education while helping in social development of all persons, leads them to, socialism, broadmindedness and democracy. It also includes economic development and political development. It aims at raising the standard of living of all persons.

Moral and ethical Values. Then being erosion of values in the social set-up of life, everything has to be geared up through the process of education. Value crisis has to be thwarted with the help of a suitable type of education. There is need of inculcating in the youth moral and ethical values from the beginning. 3asic values of life have to be incorporated in the school curriculum.

All Round Development. Education should help in bringing about all round development in the personality of the child. There should be physical, moral, social, cultural, academic development and thus an individual should be made a fit person for the Indian society who is not liable to go astray in anyway. All round development will include material and spiritual development.

Removal of Disparities. National Policy on Education lays special emphasis on the removal of disparities and equalising educational opportunities by attending to the specific needs of those who have been denied equality so far. It removes the following disparities in the field of education:

Education for Women's Equality. Eduction will be used as an agent of basic change in the status of women. In order to neutralise the accumulated inequalities, there will be well-conceived edge in favour of women. The National Education System will play a positive rote in the education of women. It would foster the development of new values through redesigned curricula, text-books, the training and orientation of women teachers and the active-involvement of education, institutions. Woman's education will be promoted as a part of various course and education stituations encouraged to take up active programme to further the cause of women's development through education.

Education of Scheduled Castes. The central focus in educational development of Scheduled Castes is their equalisation with the non-scheduled caste population at all stages of education. Following measures are contemplated for this purpose :

(a) Scholarship Schemes for Children of Scheduled Caste. Scholarship schemes will be adopted for children of Scheduled Castes from Class-1 upto Metric in order to improve their prospects of receiving essential education.

(b) Provision of facilities for Scheduled Caste students in students' hostels at district headquarters.

(c) Recruitment of teachers from Scheduled Castes.

(d) Location of school building, Balwadis and Adult Education Centres in such a way so as to facilitate full participation of the children of scheduled castes.

Minorities. Some minority groups are educationally deprived or backward. Greater attention will be paid to the education of these groups in the interest of equality and social justice. This will naturally include the constitutional guarantees given to them to establish and administer their own educational institutions and protection to their language and culture.

Education for Handicapped. The objectives is to integrate physically and mentally handicapped with the general community as equal partners in order to prepare them for normal growth and to enable them to face life with courage and confidence. The following measures will be taken in this regard:

(a) Whenever it is feasible, the education of children with minor handicaps will be common with that of others.

(b) Special schools with hostets will be provided at district headquarters for the severely handicapped children.

(c) Adequate arrangements will be made to give vocational training to the disabled.

(d) Teacher's training programmes will be renovated to deal with the special difficulties of the handicapped children.

(e) Voluntary efforts for the education of the disabled will be encouraged in every possible way.

Adult Education. The whole nation must pledge itself to the eradication of illiteracy, particularly in the 15-35 age group. The Central and State Governments, political parties and their organisations, the mass media and educational institutions must commit themselves to mass literacy programmes of diverse nature. It will also have to involve, on a large scale, teachers, students, youths, voluntary agencies, employees etc. The mass literacy programme will also include functional knowledge and skill and also awareness among learners to improve their socio-economic condition.

Different commissions and committees have put forth suggestions regarding the aims of education suitable for contemporary Indian society. The different aims must be assessed in the light of needs and requirements of the individuals as well as that of the society. Fast changing trends of life should also be viewed and reviewed so as to reach the right type of conclusions. The emerging era being an age of science and technology and the futurity of the emerging society should not be overlooked. In their true perspectives, suitable and very apt aims of education only should be well tested and that way research based conclusions be arrived at and put to use for maximum benefit to the whole humanity.

13

Further Studies

To plead for the greater dissemination of research findings in education is to enjoy cozy harborage beneath the wings of angels because everybody applauds such a plea even as everybody cheers for God, Country, and Mother. The slogan—"the dissemination of research findings in education" is unbeatable. We in America may not always be sure what education should be some of us, indeed, may conspire to degrade the college degree into little more than a passport to suburbia. Yet we are "all for education." And pity the parent, the legislator, or the admiral who dares to question ou budgets, our competence, or our motives.

No Brahma cow is more slavishly hallowed than is our "idea of research. Yet, as Woodruff has noted, the role of research i education is still only foggily conceived:

> Educational research is a phrase that currently stands fo everything from the use of reference books by elementa school pupils to the most rigorous and systemat experimentation by trained personnel. A great deal c what passes as educational research is of extremel doubtful validity. Although a subjective version of researcl literally runs wild among administrative and teaching personnel, the role of good research in education is still undefined.

Of course, many weird activities get designated by the name of "research," for in contemporary América we delight in "upgrading" everything. Every cramped, jerry-built ranch-house in the brash, new suburban development of Futility Acres is described as an "estate." The regular-sized box of detergent on the supermarket shelf is described as the "SUPER" size, while the slightly larger size is identified as the "EXTRA GIANT SIZE." You will have noticed that the detergent is purchased not in a market, but in a "super" market. Similarly, an art teacher's anecdotal report—biased and scarcely literate—of how he has enriched his students' experience by teaching them cartooning is upgraded and "dignified" by the name of research.

In education we have become proficient in justifying the debasement of research. We console ourselves with the notion that "not all research has to be statistical; some of it can be simply 'descriptive." And we always have recourse to that seductive formula, "action research." As I observe what occurs in our colleges of education in the name of research, I am repeatedly amazed at our capacity for self-deception.

Finally, who would be fool hardy enough to question the value of "disseminating" information? In a society that fosters "communication engineers" and that, at every turn, assaults our eyes and our ears with vulgar commercials, it is sacrilegious to suggest that communication, *per se*, is not a sacrosanct end. It is therefore not surprising that we encounter in education the naive assumption that if only we could disseminate research findings effectively enough, and could disseminate them to a wide enough audience, rapid and constructive changes would promptly take place in our schools. I fear that much of this effort proves to be a case of artificial dissemination.

If we are to progress at all in making research more viable, we must recognize slogans for what they are and we must rid ourselves of them. Often, when we seek to identify the realities which the slogans presumably represent, we find ourselves beleaguered by amorphous concepts.

At this point I cannot get too excited about the failure to disseminate research findings in education. We suffer less from a poverty of findings than from the lack of sufficient courage to act upon those findings that we do possess. For example, our state colleges and universities are plagued by a high incidence of student failure during the freshman year. This rate fluctuates little from year to year and we have at hand, even now, reasonably accurate means for predicting which students will fail. Yet, for political reasons, university administrators persistently maintain that every graduate of a state high school has the right and the privilege of attending a state university. This privilege includes, of course, the privilege of foredoomed failure at the cost not alone of heartbreak for the student, but also of the pointless expenditure of scarce tax funds.

Like wise, at the national level we currently hear vociferous laments about the teaching of English. Indeed, the United States Office of Education is currently sponsoring a broad research program in this area: Project English. Here again, I believe that the issue is less a need for more research than it is a need for courage to act upon our present knowledge. If we want to raise the students' standards of English, then there is one obvious way to do it: raise the standards and raise them immediately. But we must really mean it, and the students must know that we mean it. The blunt fact, then, is that students who fall short of the standards will be failed and, if necessary, failed repeatedly, irrespective of whether their parents can, or cannot, exert pressure on the Board.

But who shall help us enforce these standards? Here we discover a situation so embarrassing that some professors of education would prefer to deny or repress available information; it reflects too unfavourably upon the teaching profession itself. The information is stark and simple: a significant proportion of the teachers in our public schools and universities mangle the English language.

Let me give a specific example of "standards" in English, as displayed by a group of school administrators. Marcella Miller has analyzed the written compositions of a national sample of 232 elementary school principals. In each 100 written words the men made 4.8 grammatical errors; the women, 3.6. Several principals wrote 250-word compositions that contained only two or three genuine sentences; the remainder of each composition was jammed with sentence fragments. Roughly 73 per cent of the words that the principals used were among the first 1000 most frequently used words in the language. On a measure of linguistic flexibility these principals scored lower than a sample of college freshmen and lower, indeed, than a sample of schizophrenics. On an index of the use of subordination in sentence structure (the use of dependent predicates and other forms of complex sentences), the principals scored below the level reported elsewhere for a sample of students in grades four through eight.

Here is our plight. If our students are to respect standards in English and to achieve effective communication, we must train personnel—administrators, teachers, and professors—to recognize such standards. It is no accident that our colleagues in the colleges of liberal arts refer to the jargon of educators as "pedagese." Nor will I accept the counter argument of those of my colleagues in education who say, "I have read some papers in the liberal arts college and they, too, are bad." The point is that we are teachers and, as such, we have accepted responsibility for setting high standards for ourselves and for others. The time is past for seeking to justify relativistic and elastic standards. We must admit the fact that our society will continue to produce generations of high school and college students who use sloppy English just as long as we continue to graduate and hire teachers who themselves use sloppy English.

I have dealt at length with these two examples that of drop-outs among college freshmen and that of poor standards in the teaching of English in order to emphasize that what we need is not more research or even a wider dissemination of preset findings. We need only the courage to act on what we already know.

Whenever we reach such a schism between knowledge and action, it is fascinating to observe the regularity with which some professor or superintendent introduces an all too familiar ploy designed to immobilize any constructive effort for action. The ploy is thus: "But after all, we really don't have enough information yet. We need more research on the subject." This technique uses the plea for "further research" as a delaying tactic in the same way that a wily administrator assigns a sticky problem to a committee "for study and action," knowing full well that the problem will get buried in committee, and that he thus will be relieved of responsibility for acting upon it.

Furthermore, I suspect that our drive to disseminate more and more information has an anxiety-relieving function; constant pressure to disseminate help us to feel that we are doing something, and thus relieves us of the responsibility of facing up to our failure to act a failure not at all due to a lack of research evidence, but solely to our own obeisance to political expediency.

There is another reason why I cannot get excited about the failure to disseminate research findings in education; many of the so-called findings are not worth disseminating. Indeed, the general quality of research in education is so inferior that I feel we had better attack the question of research standards before we worry too much about disseminating findings that possess only dubious dependability.

This is a good juncture at which to clarify a point that might otherwise be misconstrued as a contradiction. I have declared, first, that in education we do not suffer from a dearth of research findings but lack the courage to act on those findings which we do have. I also have said that I cannot be too concerned about the failure to disseminate research findings because many of the alleged findings we seek to disseminate are not worth disseminating. Paradoxically enough, both statements are true. To explicate this paradox we must examine the difference between the training of professors of education in the 1920's and 1930's as compared with the training of present professors.

Inherited Knowledge

Our major legacy of findings in educational research comes to us from the period of the 1920's and the 1930's. Men of the caliber of Thorndike, Gates, Buswell, Symonds, and Pressey — to mention only a few names and to make no attempt at ranking them - enjoyed the advantage in their own graduate work of rigorous, "tight", and uncompromising research training. Also, they secured this training outside of colleges of education. In turn, these men introduced their own students to the same research tradition. Many students of this first generation, after they received their

Ph.D.'s, were fortunate in being able to work in settings that made it possible for them to maintain the tradition. (Lorge, a direct heir of Thorndike, was a superb example.) But more than this, they had the courage to demand high research standards of their own students, no matter how disgracefully their colleagues in other part of the college might allow standards to sag. But there were others of this same generation, especially during the depression years, who had to settle for jobs at Catatonic State Teachers' College. Here they found that few of their colleagues understood, let alone respected, a tradition of research. Because jobs were scarce, these new members of the Catatonic faculty decided that it was expedient for them to adjust to the local mores. And gradually, as they ceased to do research themselves and let poorer and poorer students slide by, they found themselves in the position where, piously as they might prattle about research, their own behaviour made it starkly clear to their students that research was to be construed as merely an exercise.

Meanwhile, enrolments in colleges of education across the country increased as more and more teachers and administrators felt that they must get an M.A., an Ed.D. or a Ph.D. But at the same time that the demand for the degrees increased, the supply of Professors who themselves had been trained in a solid research tradition decreased at an infernal rate. By now we have reached a point where the majority of our present professors of education simply are not competent in research. Whatever they do teach about research can be described best as derivative, it is not intrinsic to their own experience and knowledge. In Colloquial language, what these professors do in the name of research is not 'for real.'

Positive Side

The entire picture is not dismal, for certainly there are men today whose competence equals or exceeds that of any of their predecessors, and who can more than hold their own in any group of social scientists. For example, one thinks of men such as Cronbach, Getzels, Ryans, Thelen, Robert Thorndike, and J Torrance—to mention a few names and, again, with no intention of ranking. One must also take into account men not affiliated with colleges of education, whose research findings are of extreme importance for education: Hemphill and Calvin Taylor are cases in point. Even today we can find departments, colleges, or schools of education in which a great tradition of research is respected and lived up to in every way. Certainly anyone who spends even a few hours in Judd Hall at the University of Chicago quickly senses the central and viable role of research at that institution. The entire picture is not dismal, but neither is the prospect for the future encouraging. The pathetic point is that one finds few other colleges of education that maintain a research tradition like that found at the University of Chicago. Similarly, when one looks at university bureaus of educational research, institutions such as the University of Indiana, the University of Illinois. The Ohio State University and the University of Minnesota stand out prominently. But whether we look at the men who are producing top quality research, at the universities which support a strong research tradition, or at those bureaus of educational research that operate constructive programs, we encounter the same situation: a few highly visible names at the top of each group are prominent, but then the list diminishes rapidly. Nor do we find a smooth, continuous distribution of quality; rather, we are faced by a chasm between the great and the mediocre.

A research tradition in a university can never be made viable unless it is supported by a majority of the senior members of the faculty. A common and a serious mistake made by many deans is to appoint a professor who is charged with the responsibility for upgrading research standards in a department or a college of education. The faculty usually concurs in the man's appointment at the time because, to a man, they are, at least verbally, in favour both of research and of high standards. But when the new professor does indeed try to do what he has been charged to do, he quickly finds himself viewed merely as a gatekeeper. And then, both the graduate students and the other professors devise ingenious stratagems for getting the students past the gatekeeper. Those professors who have never done a respectable piece of research in their lives and who incur violent psychosomatic symptoms at the very thought of bringing their own knowledge of research up to date by reading a few books, suffer embarrassment in their classes at questions raised by able students who have learned, from the research professor, modern ways of conceptualizing and attacking research tasks. Nagged by their own embarrassment, these professors next seek to punish the research professor, either by isolating him or by extruding him from their midst.

Let me illustrate this deplorable situation by three examples chosen from different parts of the country. About a decade ago, the school of education of a major western university appointed a professor who was assigned to teach courses in research methods and statistics required of all graduate students. The professor is a well-trained man who has exacted high standards. Because the first letter of his name happens to be "C.," the Ed.D. alumni now categorize themselves as having taken their degrees either B.C.- that is, "Before C," or A.C.-"After C." The excruciating point to this instance is that the professors in one of the departments actually jest with the students about this "A.C." versus "B.C." joke. The jest is highly symptomatic; these professors fail to give "C." full support in that they become party to the students' game of how to devise a dissertation that will most painlessly set them Past Professor "C."

The second illustration comes from another university, on the east coast. The professor concerned, who also gives a research methods class required of all graduate students in the school of education, has stated to me in a personal letter:

You might be interested to know that I made a resolution this summer not to write any more articles critical of education. They take time and effort, and their effect is not worth the time and effort. Few people seem to pay any attention to articles that are critical of education and that are, at the same time, written within the profession.

I'm trying to avoid being any more discouraged than I have been in the past by the utter lack of understanding by educators of what might be called an intellectual revolution. Last year I even wrote an appeal to our faculty ... on the cultural or academic lag which we should do something about. It got almost nowhere. It made a slight impression, but very slight, I'm afraid. So, I'm viewed with a bit of hostile or affectionate suspicion, depending on the personal feelings of the particular colleague involved.

The third illustration is taken from a state university situated between the two coasts. A professor was appointed a few years ago to give a research methods course required of all graduate students, and to upgrade the research standards within the college of education. It did not take too long for his colleagues to denounce him for trying to exact standards that were "too high" and for failing to "adjust to the local mores" Several graduate students who dread a tight course of any kind have now for two years delayed taking the research methods course that this professor offers, hoping that he will leave. The department chairman recently solved the students' problem, this quarter the course is being taught by another man—a man who has published nothing in any research journal but who does "understand the local mores."

Incidents such as these are being repeated in all parts of the country. They are relevant in the present context for an obvious reason: it is pointless for us to try to disseminate research findings in education unless we first equip people to understand the meaning of research and to comprehend research findings. If members of the teaching profession fail to secure a solid foundation in research or fail to gain a modicum of respect for it during their graduate training. I do not know where or how we can expect them to secure such an understanding once they have left the university.

I repeat that if we are to disseminate research findings in education we first roust produce a wide audience that understands the structure of scientific thought. With rare exceptions we do not posses such an audience in education today. In their training and experience, our teachers and administrators have been shielded from solid instruction in the philosophy and the language of science. How many men are there indeed to teach them? As I listen to many professors of education, I am shocked at their ignorance of the nature of scientific thought, of what constitutes competent research. Yet men who themselves have never published a creditable study in a respectable research journal, guilelessly teach courses on research methods in education and have the audacity to direct master's theses and doctoral dissertations. This is tantamount to having a man teach art who has himself never painted a canvas, or who, indeed, cannot discriminate between "calendar" art and the work of a Matisse or a Wyeth. The result of this procedure is to sanction mediocrity and to inculcate in students the belief that research is just a necessary hurdle that one must jump to secure the degree that will put one up a further notch on the salary scale.

Many professors reinforce these negative attitudes through their own conspiracy of silence that fails to damn as shoddy much of the material that their students and colleagues perpetrate in the name of research. A great portion of that material does not deserve to be disseminated, and the students know this. For the most part, training in research in our colleges of education has become a farce. And even if an occasional student does manage, in spite of the system, to learn how to do competent research, what reward does he find in a school system? He receives scant encouragement. Indeed, if he insists that educational decisions be based upon research findings, he may even imperil his job. Why?

I suggest that there are two major factors which contribute to this impasse. The first is that the objectives of education are unclear and that its avowed purposes, even to such extent that they are clear, fail to receive unequivocal support from our society. The second reason for the impasse is that public education is a virtual monopoly in most American communities. Let us examine each of these points in turn.

Ambiguous Aims

The objectives of education are not clear because we have tried to make the school mean all things to all people. To the partent who insists upon high standards of scholarship of his children we say that we are maintaining high standards; conversely, to the parent who is concerned mainly with the social and personal adjustment of his children we say that this adjustment is our primary concern. To one parent we say that we are selective; to another, that we are, indeed, "democratic" in "meeting the needs" of every child at whatever level. We insist that we are dedicated to quality and quantity and seldom do we recognize the utter absurdity of this claim.

In America's status-obsessed society the school has become the individual's foremost social escalator for "getting ahead." Whether a person becomes "educated" or not is irrelevant. What he seeks is a seal of approval that presumably will allow him to compete more effectively in the job market. This situation has reached such a stage of travesty that some employers advertise in the newspaper for a "college-type man." This does not mean that the applicant even needs to have attended college, but he must look the part and dress conservatively for the part.

In our graduate schools of education, for example, we declaim publicly that we maintain high standards. But because a professor's effectiveness is too frequently measured by the number of people that attend his class to be exposed to his dubious wisdom, most professors lack the courage to extirpate from their midst those students who are intellectually unfit and who grace or disgrace— the campuses for reasons that have nothing whatsoever to do with the purpose of a university.

Indeed, it is instructive to compare the research situation in education with what we find in medicine or in the defense establishment.

In medicine the purpose of the physician is clear to improve the health and prolong the life of his patient. If the physician fails consistently, he soon finds himself without patients. If he is too grossly incompetent, or if he violates the ethics of his profession, his colleagues may restrain him. To stay in business he must keep abreast of new research developments in his field and be must be able to deal directly with new research evidence—without the aid to an interpreter or a middleman. The physician's purpose, of course, receives unequivocal endorsement from society

The defense establishment too has a clear purpose to protect our nation against a potential enemy. Here again, our society gives unequivocal support to this mandate. Moreover, the role of research in this effort —as in the space and missile programs, for example is abundantly evident to all Americans. The industries that support the nation's defense programs vie with each other to produce better and more efficient equipment. The competition for research "brains" is vigorous and, at times, almost piratical.

There is an obvious difference between the reliance placed on research in medicine and defense as compared to the cavalier treatment it receives in education.

This brings us to the second reason for the impasse we face: education is a virtual monopoly in most American communities. In respect to this monopoly, we need only note the difference between a school and any private industry. For example, if I should open a small factory producing a new household gadget, it behooves me to make my product, at its price, as good, if not better, than the product of my competitors. Furthermore, it is quite possible that I shall encounter competition on a national, rather than a strictly local, basis. If, as president of the company, I should fail to show sufficient profit to meet my payroll and to declare dividends, I probably would have to resign.

Neither an administrator and a staff operate a good school or an inadequate one, the school still stays in business. Win, lose, or draw, the superintendent will undoubtedly keep his job. Superintendents do get fired, but usually for political reasons that is, for failing to please the "right" powers in the community, rather than for failing to provide the children with an educational program of high quality. Moreover, whereas competition in industry is based upon a national market, such competition as we have in education is based, at best, upon a highly provincial, local market. It is only in such instances as the national drafting of men for the armed services or in the awarding of merit scholarships on a national basis that we get a glimpse of the glaring way in which schools across the country differ in their academic accomplishments. In short, we in education do have the same incentive to improve our operations as do men in industry.

Carlson has nicely described school systems as "domesticated" organisations:

School systems belong to a class of organizations that can be called "domesticated"; that is, they are not compelled to attend to all of their needs. A steady flow of clients is assured, and although they do compete for resources, support is not closely tied to quality of performance. The business firm as a competitive industry, on the other hand, can be seen as existing in a "wild" setting. It is not protected at vulnerable points as the school system.

Furthermore, I am inclined to suspect that school executives enjoy their "domesticated" status, and by devious means seek to become more and more "domesticated." For example, I surmise that in education we deliberately keep our objectives muddy so as to minimize the possibility of an open and objective comparison between one school system and another. In short, I think we go out of our way to avoid an objective appraisal of what our schools are accomplishing—or failing to accomplish. For this reason, although we may give lip service to the importance of research, we do not want to use it in a real situation because we are afraid that it will reveal, both to ourselves and to the public, many flagrant flaws in American education.

It would be intriguing to speculate on some of the dynamics of personal choice that produce this situation. One wonders to what extent our dilemma is due to the kinds of people who enter education. Our profession is composed, for the most part, of gentle people, many of whom have entered teaching in the first place because they dislike the rough and bruising competitiveness of business. And these gentle people abhor the idea of seeing their organizations become more "wild" than "domesticated." This reluctance might be justifiable were it not that the stakes in the game have now been radically changed by the present international situation.

Now, one salient characteristic of the "wild" environment is that its denizens, either through personal predilection or through coercion from the environment itself, place greater emphasis upon what McClelland and his associates have identified as Need-Achievement, in contrast to Need Affiliation. The scientist or research man is marked by a high degree of Need-Achievement. Conversely, teachers and school administrators are marked by a high degree of Need-Affiliation. Indeed, one recent unpublished study of the biographical characteristic of a sample of 232 elementary school principals shows that the principals fit neatly into the pattern of what has been described clinically as the "good child": they are more preoccupied with conformity to group mores and with being liked than with a strong drive to achieve. To achieve, one must excel over others and must risk not being liked by those over whom one excels; the person with high Need-Affiliation is loath to take this risk.

This brings us to what I consider the crux of the entire educational research issue, of which the dissemination question is merely a facet. The problem is the collision between two "cultural systems." View, for a moment, American education from pre-school classes through the graduate school as one cultural system. Likewise, view the world of the scientist as another cultural system. Historically, the cultural system of education has developed in one way, that of science, in another. Each has attracted to its fold different kinds of members, and each has crystallized for its members different customs, rules of the game, and myths. There are some educators who would like to pretend that there is no real difference between the two cultures. I cannot subscribe to this belief. Furthermore, I contend that, if an accommodation is to be achieved between the members of both cultures, we must first quit denying that differences exist and must next boldly delineate both the focuses of these differences and their inexorable implications.

Because education operates within a political milieu, much of what we do in our schools reflects the consumer-orientation of American society. Guided by the slogan that "the customer is always right," we have tended to tailor our action to the "needs" or rather, the wants" of the customer. The result is an effort to make everything as palatable as possible to the customer. The classics are watered down to the comic strip level to make for "easier" reading, and we indulge in even such atrocious simplifications as the caption used to introduce a recent movie version of Hamlet: This is a story about a man who couldn't make up his mind. To appease the customer, our courses throughout the school system are marketed in terms of their painlessness. Bradbury has made a pertinent and perspicacious observation about the British schools, and it is one equally applicable to our own.

Consider, for instance, the change in the meaning of the word educational. Once it meant "enriching, elevating, enlarging", it now means "of little or no entertainment value; fuddy-duddy; square," One of our current problems is to divorce our school and university system from the smear of being educational; our Minister of Education has pointed out that some forms of education are congenitally dreary, and if they can't project a new image, they had better go.

Not content with Instant Coffee and Instant Soup, we are determined that we now must have Instant Learning-drip-dry, crease-resistant, and effortless. Also synthetic!

In the aspiration for painless Instant Learning, many educators believe that were we only to find the "right" formula we could then translate all educational research knowledge into the language of everyday life. Both the search for this formula and those who pursue it are doomed to failure for a simple but fundamental reason the language of science is different from the language of everyday life. This difference is not merely a difference of vocabulary the very structure of scientific thought a radically different from the structure of thought that governs our daily life. The language of everyday thought can be described in one respect as the language of metaphor, in another, as the language of politics. The language of science, however, is concerned with the precise description of events and experience. It is based upon a "probability" view of the universe, and it seeks to purge itself of value-commitments and exhortations to action, the evidence must speak for itself. Conversely, the language of politics, a George Orwell has nicely demonstrated, trades upon ambiguity, double-talk, and escape clauses. It is patterned upon an Aristotelian rather than a Galilean view of the universe, and it is designed to persuade, to exhort, and to incite listeners to action—an action often so partisan that it violates very scientific rule of evidence. A chasm exists between those of us who think primarily in the language of science and those who think principally in the language of politics. Of course, to some extent we all use both languages, but, since phylogenetically the language of politics is the older of the two, it is the more common and the more entrenched.

The similarities and the differences between these two languages, then, cannot be treated as analogous to the similarities and differences between, for example, English and French. One cannot indiscriminately translate the language of science into the language of politics because the structure and purpose of each language is totally different from that of the other. If one is to understand the words of science he must also understand the structure of scientific thought, there is no short cut.

The scientific method is a way of thinking. The meaning of every concept in science can be understood only in terms of the complete set of operations which constitute its definition. Thus such concepts as "common variance," "degrees of freedom," and "level of statistical significance" each represent shorthand expression for a long and complex set of operations. Not one of these concepts is comprehensible without a precise understanding of a basic course in statistics. Similarly, the meaning of the "authoritarian personality" cannot be understood apart from the long and complex set of operations reported by Adorno, Frenkel-Brunswik, and others on the development of the "F Scale."

As an example of the scientific method in the field of educational administration, consider a recent study by Hemphill, Griffiths, and Fredericksen of the administrative performance of a national sample of elementary school principals. This cogent study, which has dramatic implications for the selection and training of administrators, employs an elaborate factor-analytic procedure. One cannot reduce a report of such findings to the level of "You, Tarzan – me, Jane." Indeed, the administrator who would capitalize upon the findings of this study must be sufficiently knowledgeable to understand the concept of factorial dimensions.

The attitude taken toward such a study by different groups of administrators starkly illustrates the core of the dissemination issue in education. The majority of administrators is loath to expend the effort necessary to read and fully appreciate this study. These executives will complain that the study is too "technical" and too "deep" and that it contains a "lot of statistics." They will insist that in order to reach a broader public the same findings should be rewritten in "easier" language. The abiding faith nurtured by the proponents of this strategy is that it must be possible to translate the concepts of every research investigation into a form that approximates primer talk. Had this same strategy been applied to the field of physics, Albert Einstein would have undoubtedly remained an unknown and the application of his findings to nuclear power would have been stillborn. He never knew enough to "meet the needs" of the lay reader. He did once propose, however, that his theory of relativity could be "explained" to laymen in the form of the innocent question, "When does Zurich stop at this train?"

There is a minor group of educators, composed mainly of those who actually engage in research, who respond quite differently to the dissemination issue. They recognize that a slogan approach may be effective for stimulating impulse buying in a supermarket. They also recognize that, since the dissemination of research findings entails more than memorizing a new brand name, this advertising gimmick is inappropriate to our purpose. The real dissemination task is to increase the "literacy" of the consumer. But in education we seem to have preferred to dilute information in an attempt to "meet the needs" of the consumer rather than to raise his skills, so that he may "meet the requirements" of the situation. I am reminded of the exquisite remark made by Edith Wharton while she was working with the American Red Cross in Paris during World War I: "America is the only country in the world where, when two people meet and the first uses a word which the second doesn't understand, it is the first person who is embarrassed."

The difference between meeting the requirements of the situation and meeting the needs of people illuminates the differences between the culture of the scientist and the culture of the educator. The scientist, confronted by the host of complex phenomena presented by the universe, seeks to wrest from Nature her secrets. The phenomena he seeks to understand often are intractable, for Nature is sometimes unwilling to surrender her secrets to the first cavalier who flirts with her: the suitor must measure upto her requirements. The scientist must carve meaning from the phenomena with which he deals even as a Rodin or a Calder must carve from marble or metal whatever figure he gives to the world as his creation. Nature "meets the needs" of neither the scientist nor the artist; instead, she defies them both to meet her demands. Alberto Giacometti gives us beautiful insight into the creative drive.

"Why does one paint or sculpt?" he said. "It's the need to dominate things, and one can only dominate by understanding. I make a head to understand what I see, not to make a work of art."

Nor is the creative artist's motivation dissimilar to that of the scientist. For this reason, only those men and women who possess a strong achievement motivation are attracted to careers in science and the creative arts, and only those whose achievement motivation is strong enough and persistent enough survive beyond the point of dilettantism.

There was a time in American education when the requirements for graduation from either the elementary school or the high school were stringent and unequivocal; a time when a doctoral degree from a university attested to its bearer's scholarship and research competence. In this era each child was given the opportunity to receive as much education as his demonstrated achievement warranted. But beginning roughly with the post-World War I period, as rapid industrialization and urbanization took place in America, and as instalment buying increased and the Advertising Age flourished, we witnessed new and tumultuous pressures for greater social mobility. Even as the traditional anchorages of society gave way under pressures, so did the schools succumb to the demands of a consumer-oriented society. The teachings of Freud and the doctrines of those anthropologists who stressed cultural relativism provided convenient rationalizations for a shift in the American character from inner-directedness to other-directedness. During this process what originally was conceived as an opportunity to receive an education became converted into the right to receive an education.

During those days when Teachers College was the Mecca for American teachers, the Jeffersonian idea of American democracy was prostituted into a cheap and sentimental equation between "democracy" and equality." Yet this was after all, only one of the specious political slogans nurtured by the national temper during the years of the great depression. Egregious misinterpretations of

John Dewey's doctrines, cocktail party versions of Freud, and a desperate and obsessive urge to meet the needs of all students combined to produce new generations of teachers who were only too willing to reflect in their classrooms the most meretricious features of a consumer-oriented society. Candidates attracted to the education profession increasingly became characterized by a high motivation for affiliation in contrast to a high motivation for achievement. Further impetus was given to this change by the group dynamics movement which was ardently embraced by many colleges of education; professors happily pitched the tone of their classroom to a new note of "togetherness" and "group-think." In short, the culture of the school system came to emphasize among its personnel human qualities and motivations that are antithetical to the motivations of the scientist and the research man.

Influencing Factors

A recent incident that occurred at a meeting of educational administration professors pungently illustrates the difference between the dominant values of educators and scientists. I had met for the first time a highly competent psychologist who had been conducting important research in education. While he and I were chatting informally, along with a coterie of his graduate students, he asked my opinion about a colleague whose publications he had read but whom he had never met. I hesitated a moment and then replied. "He's a very nice person." The graduate student smiled knowingly. The psychologist's eyes twinkled with amusement, and he commented laconically, "That's what I thought," (And the next tumbrel lumbered upto the guillotine.)

If one teacher was to make this identical remark about another- "He's a very nice person"-it would be interpreted as high praise; for a scientist, such a judgment is the embrace of death Why? Because for a scientist the salient criteria are a man's knowledgeability, competence and productivity. His products must stand on their own merit, and their worth is not to be judged either by their own popularity or by the personal popularity of the investigator. Contrarywise, in teaching, the major criteria are a man's social skills. How well does he get along with other people? Is he pleasant and affable? Does he "adjust" to the local mores?

Yet, at the same time that our society and our schools were promoting togetherness, other-directedness, and ethical relativism, other forces were stimulating a tremendous growth in technology, with the result that the research man suddenly found himself invested with a new and Messianic aura. For the schools to fail to jump on the bandwagon of scientific research was unthinkable; research was made into a shibboleth, even though the concept of research was hideously diluted in the process. And this is where we stand today. In education we are seeking to merge the culture of education and the culture of science. We want to combine the flabbiness of a consumer-orientation with the intellectual rigor demanded by scientific research. One is reminded of a current TV commercial for an American, compact car. The announcer greasy with affability, discourses at length upon the "compactness" and economy of the ear. Then, without pausing for fresh breath and with the smile of a complacent camel, he adds, But it is a big car, too, and extols its bigness. In a society that accepts, with no ravage to its sensibilities, the claim that a car is both a small car and a big car too, is there any wonder that we also accept the claim that our schools provide for both quality and quantity?

It is not surprising that educators naively expect teachers, selected and trained in the consumer-orientation of education, also to perform effectively as productive members within the achievement oriented culture of science. But here I surmise that we are asking for the impossible. And the sooner we recognize the irreconcilables within our demands, the better off will we all be. The crux of the issue is that in a consumer society most of us are reluctant to admit that we must inevitably lose something in every choice we make.

As Griffith has noted, our society fosters the superficial and discourages the original and the thorough:

Considering the nature of their work, most people feel rushed. Creativity itself in such a climate must account for its time, and often cannot wait on inspiration but must adapt what is close to hand. We thus tend to take a decorator's interest in other cultures—ransacking museums or far-off places for combinations of colours or design motifs we can borrow from them and no wonder that we "use up" these other cultures so fast and move on to something new. Fashion can never stay long enough to discover what a culture was really about, but moves on restlessly like one of those crop-picking machines that whooshes across an entire field, gathering in its claws all that it can profitably pick up and leaving behind what would have been uneconomic to pause over. This year a Polynesian theme, next year the Etruscans. The present temper of the arts, to satisfy people's longing for something more than the bleak and efficient functionalism of our uncrafted homes and offices, runs toward diluted borrowings (simplified Victorian, etc.). The designer's task, in adapting a past elegance, is to see that what is intricate be made simple, or capable of easy reproduction, for we no longer have time to be original or thorough: we adapt, we imitate and we multiply, and are becoming a society of tomb robbers.

And in a footnote to this passage, Griffith adds:

And since our pace is what it is, we then have soda fountains which are another form of profitable approximation: we must have speed and therefore accept clutter if we demand economy and must tolerate crowding and rapidity of turnover. Drugstore counters are a hurried substitute for restaurants, and the American, understanding their function, puts up with their annoyances. While a counterman slops an egg into a pan and whips up some ready-made tuna mash, an adman at a low unit cost has been at work on the menus, spreading his crispy crunchy promises that have no relation to what will be delivered, for it is the American custom never to acknowledge a lowering of standards in service or product, but to deny stoutly that anything has been lost along with what has been gained.

Americans persist in suppressing from our consciousness the discrepancy between the glowing advertisement and the product itself, between the promise and the fulfilment. Even as the readymade tuna mash served at the drugstore fountain belies its savory image on the menu card, so do our devout statements about what we are doing in education give the lie to our accomplishments. Thus within the citadel we devise mouth watering descriptions for our educational menucard – "The Pursuit of Excellence." "Education for Creativity." "Special Programs for the Gifted," "Guidance," "Teaching Geared to Individual Differences," "Education for the Space Age." But any correlation between the slogans and the mash served to the students is purely coincidental. And even as the decorators pursue a Polynesian theme one year, and an Etruscan one the next, so do our preschool faculty conferences establish a new, enticing theme – with slogans to match – for each new school year. At the start of the school year the administrative staff whips up a new froth of enthusiasm, appetizing enough to make the teachers forget – at least, for the moment – that last year's froth provided no nutrition.

But in a society where words have been ripped loose from their semantic moorings, it is easy to become anesthetized to the fraud of our empty, verbal litanies. Indeed, it is an anesthesia of this very kind that makes us fail to see how inevitable the collision must be between the culture of education and the culture of research.

Nor are we going to solve the dissemination problem by trying to force the culture of research into meeting the needs of the culture of education. If an accommodation is to be achieved between these two cultures, I submit that the change will have to be made the other way around, the culture of education will have to be modified to meet the requirements of the culture of research. And I am not sure that we in education are at present prepared, or even willing to accomplish this.

These remarks about the dissemination of research findings in education would not be complete without comment about a popular suggestion that has been offered as a solution to our dilemma. We develop "middlemen" who will function between the scientist and the practitioner and who will "translate" the findings of the scientist into a form more comprehensible to the practitioner. This is, indeed, a tempting idea. There is only one thing wrong with it, it will not work.

The advocates of this idea gloss over the fact that nothing remotely similar exists in other professions. The physician, in his training, must learn to read and understand medical research, he is trained to draw upon primary sources. Popular opinion notwithstanding, I must denounce as a canard the suggestion that the Readers Digest functions as the middleman for the medical profession. The lawyer, too, must deal with the precedents of prior cases and must be equipped to function without an interlocutory middleman. Likewise, the engineer must have sufficient knowledge of physics and structural mechanics to apply new research findings to the practical tasks with which he deals from day to day. Indeed, in proposing that educational middlemen be trained to function between the scientist and the practitioner we admit to a failing that—at least in this respect disqualifies education as a profession. The core of this failing is not bard to find, we need only look at our undergraduate programs (and, sadly, even at our graduate programs) for teachers to see how seldom our students are required to deal with primary sources. This is in marked contrast to what takes place in such disciplines as psychology and biology. To spare our students from effort and boredom, the material in education textbooks is presented to them in the form of predigested pap. Indeed, some of the textbooks seem to be so removed from primary sources that one surmises that they have been "written" by applying scissors, Scotch tape, and a table of random numbers to the ten most popular books previously published on the same subject.

The notion of the educational middleman is based upon another fallacy. The ideas of the research man can, or even need to be translated into another language. To some extent, the scientist himself is at fault in failing to communicate effectively, and I do not intend to exculpate him for this. When his jargon blocks communication he must be condemned. But here I believe that we must take into account the often-disregarded point that there are two kinds of jargon—sacred and profane. Let me deal with these in reverse order.

Profane jargon is composed of cliches, half-formulated concepts, slogans, loaded words, and parades of abstract terms for which there are no clear referents. Jargon of this kind usually results from the infrangible fact that the author's ideas are not clear. Because his ideas are not clear he covers his bed of imprecise ideas with a blanket to match—a patchwork quilt of fuzzy language. This jargon is marked by a dearth of concrete images, by an array of inert, passive verbs, and by nouns that have been converted into new, grotesque verbs. In these instances, the scientist is inclined to invent new words simply because the poverty of his own language and his cursory acquaintance with literature prevent him from recognizing that most of his ideas could be expressed in sample, and often vigorous, English. This type of vocabulary must be condemned because it fails to communicate even what few clear ideas it may contain. But even more, profane jargon must be denounced on aesthetic grounds, it is ugly.

Jargon may also mean the technical language of a science. Because science must be conceived, in large part, as a special language, and because the syntax of science is as important as its content, we cannot eliminate the use of special language and special concepts in scientific writing. This jargon results not from fuzzily conceived ideas but from ideas that have been defined operationally and usually with devastating clarity. This is sacred jargon, and it is not to be defiled for the blandishments of the popularizers.

Here is where we run into a refractory problem. The scientist's critic feels uncomfortable in the presence of new concepts and concludes that the author's technical terms are just new words for old ideas; he then summarily condemns as jargon not only the words but the concepts themselves. This allegation misses the point. The scientist has created, in fact, not just new words, but new ideas. In creating new ideas the scientist classifies phenomena into fresh categories-boxes that do not always coincide with the categories presented by naive experience. These new categories cannot always be described in orthodox, everyday language. Faced with this contradiction, the critic speaking to the scientist, resorts to the gambit, "Can't you use ordinary words to say what you mean? Don't you really mean...?" In short, the critic tries to force the scientist's concepts into the structure of his own verbal categories. The only answer the honest scientist can give is, "No, I don't really mean that at all. I mean precisely what I have said." The critic bristles, for he considers his own categories inviolate. To understand what the scientist is saying, the critic must now relinquish his preconceived categories. In order to understand any single concept in the scientist's language, the critic must first understand the total theoretical context within which each concept is imbedded. This requires greater effort than the critic is willing to expend; it is easier for him to ridicule the scientist's legitimate use of jargon than for him to exert the energy necessary to understand it. The scientist's own abusive use of profane jargon allows the critic to justify his own unfounded attack upon the scientist's use of sacred jargon. Unfortunately, many scientists make themselves easy victims for such attacks.

Misunderstanding on both sides arises out of inertia or sheer laziness. Profane jargon impedes communication, and the blame must be placed on the scientist's slothful attitude toward clear writing. This critic's resistance to sacred jargon equally hinders communication, and the blame rests with the critic's failure to differentiate between the language of science and the language of everyday life.

The Difficulties

These obstacles to the success of the middleman proposal are formidable enough, but typical attempts to follow through on this proposal are quickly grounded by another starkly practical problem: where do we find competent middlemen? Certainly, the fatuous and condescending attitude of both the scientist and the educational practitioner toward prospective middlemen is less than decent. Even the advocates of the middleman plan imply that the middleman should serve as a type of editorial assistant, at a status level only slightly above that of the average secretary and certainly below that of the research technician. The men who hold to this view become chagrined when they discover that they cannot locate a suitable candidate for the job. I have known only two or three people who could qualify. Although these people were interested in this work and had been interviewed for such jobs, in each instance they could only reject with contempt the niggardly salary offered. Nor were they willing to be treated as sub-professional lackeys. I think that we must recognize an uncomfortable truth. A competent middleman must possess skills of a different, and possibly higher order, than those of either the scientist or the practitioner. The middleman jobs are top-level positions that should command salaries commensurate with the skills demanded. But I know of no college of education, and certainly of no school system, that has budgeted enough funds for a skilled middleman. Further, I do not believe that the ego of either the scientist or the practitioner will permit him to be gracious in granting a middleman the status he deserves. I repeat, this is not a job for a young manuscript editor or a part-time employee from the English department and it is not a job for an indigent but well-intentioned doctorate student in education. If the middleman proposal is to work at all— and I am not sure that it will—then we would have to create a new occupation. We would have to budget ample funds for the men and women to fill this role and would have to devise a rich program for training a new professional breed. If this were done, and were done with sufficient support, perhaps the effort would pay off. But we should realize at the outset how enormous a task this would be.

Yet, even if we should be able to persuade legions of top-quality middlemen to devote themselves to the dissemination task in educational research, their work would be futile unless we can simultaneously accomplish four objectives:

1. Raise the standards of research so as to produce a professional crops which can understand, respect, and act upon research findings.
2. Recruit for the profession, and retain in it, young men and women who possess strong achievement-motivations, conjoined with the intellectual and creative capacities required for research careers.
3. Strengthen teachers' motivation to do research by rewarding such efforts and by developing within our schools an organizational climate that encourages creative inquiry.

4. Incite competition among the schools and ruthlessly publicize not alone those schools that are doing exemplary work, but also those that are not.

These views can be construed as being gloomy, but we could not be so scathing in my indictment of the present situation in educational research did I not trust in the ultimate victory of rationality and possess deep faith in the future of American education. To save the patient, a surgeon sometimes must cut deep. Yet a responsible physician will not even bother to operate unless he believes that there are greater than chance possibilities that the patient will survive, and unless he knows, too, that the risk of the operation is a lesser evil than are the imminent and certain ravages of the disease itself. Analogously, in the surgical role that I have taken toward the "culture" of education, I, too, take risks. But I take these risks not because I despise the patient, but because I love and respect him and because I am gravely worried about his welfare.

14
The Researchers

Today, science has gained tremendous prestige— but for the wrong reason. What we in America seem to have responded to most avidly have been the technological, and even the gimmicky, aspects of "science." Our zeal has been accompanied by only a remote understanding of the essential ideas that undergird all critical and creative inquiry. In the same way that we in America have bureaucratized corporate, governmental, and university life, we have also sought to bureaucratize research. The increasing federal and foundation aid to social science and educational research that has stimulated the research scene since World War II has been accompanied by several attendant evils, not the least of which is the virulent, contagious disease that now ravages many of our campuses: "projectitis." To have a research proposal approved by most fund-granting agencies, the investigator must stress design and must indicate what data will be gathered. Data are treated as so many units of production, almost as if they were automobiles on a production line. We have come to revere technique; I fear that, at times, substance has been sacrificed to method. We are guilty of what Lord Dunsany once described as the tendency to place technique above inspiration. He noted that if this notion was to spread we would have the diamond cutters valuing their tools more highly than the diamonds, with the result that, as long as they cut them in accordance with the rules of the craft, they would then cease to care whether they cut diamonds or glass, and finally would cease to know.

Basic Concepts

Far too many of us who aspire to be scientists miss the point that the foundation of creative inquiry lies in observation, in identifying what is "out there." I grant that such observation never can be random and always is more fertile when it has been guided by an explicitly stated theoretical formulation. But we must start with observation; all our techniques—including the clinical and the statistical are just that: techniques. Yet no technique, no matter how elaborate, can pull important generalizations from raw data that are, themselves, not viable. We sometimes are in such a hurry to count things that we fail to take enough time to decide whether or not what we do count is, indeed, worth counting. This defect arises out of a misguided effort in education and the behavioural sciences to mimic the more prestigious physical and biological sciences. But the prestige of these older sciences has been earned not so much by the use of quantitative methods as through insightful, patient observation. As Feibleman has noted: "A scientist is not one who can see better but one who can watch more intensely."

However rich any set of observations may be, they are useless to science and to mankind unless the investigator can communicate his findings to others. Thus J.Z. Young, professor of anatomy at the University of London, states, "Science consists in exact description of one's observations to other people."

In other than a face-to-face situation there are only three languages by which one can communicate a description of events or experience to other people: by words, by numbers, or by pictures. Irrespective of which of these three channels the scientist uses he must recognize that his language becomes an integral part of his behaviour as a scientist, that his language is not merely an appendage to his "scientific" activity. Without endorsing to the hilt the Whorfian hypothesis, we must, nonetheless, accept Whorf's major conclusion that the language in which each of us is acculturated cuts up our perception of events and experiences in specific and limiting ways. Indeed, the greatest benefit any one of us can derive from command of one or more foreign languages is the inexorable realization that language itself structures our experience, that our concept of reality is restricted in part by the very words that imprison us.

Since the structure of our language can distort our reporting of experience, and even can interfere with our apprehension of experience, I believe that the first unit in a course in research methods in education or for that matter, in any of the social sciences—should be devoted to the topic "Language and Events." In an introductory course on research methods that I teach, I start the students with readings from Wendell Johnson's People in Quandaries and Young's Doubt and Certainty in Science. I encourage the most competent students to acquaint themselves, too, with Cassirer's penetrating essay on "Science," and also to go directly to Korzybski. I repeat Korzybski's theme: "Words are to events as maps are to territories."

Let it be noted, too, that in this course we also remind the students that words are man made: because a word exists we have no guarantee that there exists "out there" a "thing" that corresponds to the word.

Some of the logical positivists—even, for that matter, Percy Bridgman himself—have, to some extent, recanted. Bridgman, for example, is no longer as unreservedly enthusiastic about the value of operational definitions as he was when he first discussed such definitions in The Logic of Modern Physics. Yet at the present stage of our knowledge in educational research, I would rather see students err in the direction of insisting upon operational definitions than have them submit to the enticement of the vague, exhortatory slogans which characterize so much pap that masquerades as "research" in education.

The Promotion

Scientific advancement consists in finding ways of conceptualizing a new our experience. This means that one endeavour of science must be to define our experience in new terms—new language, unfettered by previous concepts and stereotypes. If man can make words, he also can unmake them or to state the point differently, man can eliminate from his vocabulary those words and concepts that create greater confusion than they are worth.

Having started the research methods course with a discussion of general semantics and having illustrated the advantages of using operational definitions, we next explicate the role of theory in research. We emphasize that theory must deal with "is's" not "ought's" and note why the models that we use can never be declared as either valid or invalid. The question of validity is irrelevant: the only relevant test is an heuristic one. Models are "as if" statements that we use to generate "if ....then" statements which we can, then, test empirically.

Just before the curtain falls on Act I of the course. I deliver what usually turns out to be a telling blow: I suggest that language itself can be construed best as a theoretical model —an "as if" statement about experience and events. Furthermore, this "as if" statement must be subjected to continual revision.

The map can never be the same as the territory; the map is an abstraction designed for a specific purpose. Thus the language-map of the poet is not the same as the language-map of the scientist. This, of course, does not mean that one map is better than the other, only that each map is different from the other. To ask whether a map is "true" is silly; the relevant question is whether a given map is useful for a specific purpose at a specific time and at a given stage in our knowledge. This point of view comes as a distinct shock to many students who for a long time, have enjoyed the spurious security that faith in the word seems to have afforded them. To illustrate how word can get between us and our experience, let me quote from Harold Taylor's excellent book, Art and the Intellect:

> The trouble is that most kinds of education are devoted to teaching students how not to be themselves, but instead how to cover up, how to gain enough knowledge, for example, in a survey course in Western civilization so that no one will ever know that you haven't read any of the authors or that you haven't ever really understood the works of art you were asked to observe. The usual kind of education—that is, the kind that is divided into courses, condensed into textbooks, put out in three lectures a week, tested by examinations, and rewarded by three academic

credits a throw—is designed to give answers to questions which nobody asked and to inhibit the student in discovering his own truth and insight. The lectures and the texts do all that sort of thing for you. They provide a way in which the student can cover up his true self by finding a vocabulary acceptable to most people and a set of facts which generally known among people generally considered generally educated.

Once this skill of covering up has been acquired, the student may never be called upon to say what he really thinks or feels at any point in his education or later life. This is what makes bores, and produces college graduates who are ignorant and dull, but successful and plausible.

What I have been saying is simple: no man or woman can presume to do research unless he first becomes knowledgeable about the relation between language and events. Yet it is on this very point that most textbooks and courses in educational research have failed. Those authors start the student with techniques and "cook-book" recipes and assume—erroneously, I believe that the student already understands the pitfalls of language and the essential nature of theory in science. Furthermore, the premature introduction of the student to technique tends to cripple his skill in observation. We already have too many scientists who choose their research topics not in terms of the importance of the domain but because techniques for measurement in the particular domain they choose happen to be available

Such a situation recalls the story of the policeman who one evening discovered a drunk fumbling his way around a lamppost, evidently searching for something. The policeman asked the drunk, "Lose something?"

"Yes, my wallet."

"O.K. I'll help you find it."

After several minutes of diligent but unsuccessful searching around the lamppost, the policeman asked, "Are you sure you lost it here?"

"Who shed anything 'bout here? I lost it up the street." "Then why in hell are we looking for it here?"

The drunk assumed a weaving posture of dignity and, with haughty condescension, replied: "More light!"

The issue for us is not one of "more light," but rather of "Mere light on what?" Technique as technique is not enough; we persistently must ask whether whatever technique we use is, indeed, applicable to the research task in hand.

I do not want to disparage the value of technique; I would like to see only that it be kept in perspective. The student should not be introduced to technique prematurely: instead, he should be made to understand that observation does come first. The student should discover how to observe events and experience and learn how to report these events free from verbal stereotypes.

A'fred North Whitehead has stated the issue succinctly:

> My point is that a block in the assimilation of ideas inevitably arises when a discipline of precision is imposed before a stage of romance has run its course in the growing mind. There is no comprehension apart from romance.

To help our students freshen their observations, we had better rid ourselves of some illusions. We must quit thinking of research as research with a capital R. Instead, we should seek to encourage creative and critical inquiry without being concerned obsessively with a form of empiricism that is ridden with what Whitehead has called the error of "misplaced concreteness." Let me offer two examples of perspicacious observation. In the first example the observer is a distinguished historian; in the second, a great novelist.

Raymond Aron, professor in the Faculty of Letters at the University of Paris has published an exquisite study on "The Situation of Democracy," in which he compares the history of Western political institutions in the twentieth century. He reports not a blessed standard deviation or Pearsonian correlation, not even a mean! Yet here I find a rich mine of concepts that can be extrapolated from nations to formal organizations. Why, Aron asks, do some nations provide a stable base for the development of a democracy, whereas others do not? Why, for example, do we discover in the Latin American nations a history which shifts between populist democracies and military dictatorships? Aron gives us a host of provocative cues for new concepts in the study of administration, for new ways of conceptualizing the dimensions of organization?

He reports, in particular, new dimensions by which we can more accurately describe a democracy. With the guide of Area's reasoning, it requires no wild leap of the imagination to see why many organizations-school systems, and even universities – reveal a history of organizational policy characterized by wide and repetitive swings from one extreme to another similar to those found in Latin American countries. Aron's skill, in short, is his skill in observing, is not being blinded by the filter of words which obfuscates the vision of so many of us.

Empirical View

The second example of clear-sighted observation is that of the Irish novelist, Lawrence Durrell, whose brilliance is vividly displayed in his tetralogy, The Alexandria Quartet. His topic is love in our times – actually, love in any time.

In the first book of the tetralogy, Justine, Durrell tells the story of the infatuation of Darley, a young teacher, with Justine, the wife of a wealthy and politically influential Egyptian. At the end of the first volume. Darley gives his manuscript – that is. Justine – to one of the characters in the story, Balthazar.

In the second volume, Balthazar, Durrell has Balthazar return the manuscript to Darley, with corrections. In effect Balthazar says, "You are all wrong. It wasn't that way at all. Justine was not in love with you. You were only a 'cover' for her affair with somebody else." So the second volume deals with the same material as the first, but with the events seen through the eyes of a different character.

In the third volume, Mountolive, Durrell relates the life of Mountolive, a British diplomat. Darley, Justine, and the major characters of the first two volumes do not enter the story until about half way through the book. The same events are then viewed through a third pair of eyes. The first three volumes end at about the same point in time; only in the fourth and final volume, Clea, does the story move forward in time. Yet even at the conclusion of the tetralogy the reader is not certain which version of events is "true" — in a sense, they all are.

I urge students to read Durrell if only to shatter many of their verbal and perceptual stereotypes, to let them watch Durrell demonstrate the complete "as if" quality of every man's perception of his own experience.

At this point, a few colleagues must be wondering, "But what about objectivity?" To them I reply, "Let us quit deceiving ourselves." No scientist is nearly as objective as he pretends to be or would like to believe that he is. Note, for example, recent studies by Rosenthal and his colleagues at the University of North Dakota. These investigators have shown how, even in simple laboratory experiments, experimenters are able to obtain from their human or their animal subjects precisely the data the experimenter wants, needs, or expects to get. Indeed, I respect objectivity, but I resent the blind, compulsive pursuit of it, especially if, in this pursuit, we deceive ourselves. It is past time for us to ask why some of our colleagues persist in doing meticulous, "objective" research on arid topics.

Consider the instance of a professor who enjoys a national reputation in the field of educational research — a man who does excellent research on learning. Yet, when one his ablest graduate students proposed to him a Master's thesis in which she sought to study certain attributes of a national sample of elementary school principals, he courageously said, "If you find what you think you will, do you really think it is a good idea for you to do a thesis that may reflect against the teaching profession?" The student demurred and naively declared that she thought science was dedicated to a disinterested search for truth. He replied: "You do plan to take your Ph.D. in this department, don't you?"

I propose that we bring fresh observation to the entire issue of objectivity. I endorse objectivity, but I deplore the fraud of insisting upon objectivity in dealing with trivia while we slyly smuggle into the system errant subjectivity in respect to the central issue of what topics we do study. The subjectivity that enters into our choice of what topics we study is the most dangerous form of subjectivity, for it involves not a piçayune question-for example, that of inter-rater reliability but a question of far greater import: the morality of the investigator. Does he have the courage to study what is really worth studying? This aspect of subjectivity—the morality of the investigator—is one that should worry us all.

But when we move to the question of subjectivity in respect to technique, the scene changes. I grant that dependable (that is, reliable) measures are desirable, yet I refuse to get frightened by the introduction of subjective elements in research. I fear that much of the effort made to reduce subjectivity is futile. On this score, I believe that more of us need to follow the sweep of the exciting argument presented by Michael Poiyani, originally a physical chemist and now a social scientist and philosopher. In his monumental book Personal Knowledge, Poiyani rejects completely the ideal of scientific detachment. He declares that knowing as an act of comprehension involves a change in the person carrying out the comprehension. Accordingly, comprehension must remain non-critical in that there exists no permanently fixed framework within which a critical testing of that comprehension can take place.

In science as well as in other areas of living, there are times when we must have the courage to take a gambler's risk. At certain junctures I would be willing to risk slightly less objectivity, were I to see a chance to gain richer human insight and fresher observation. Of course I would not have us resort solely to feelings, and certainly not at the expense of intellectual rigor. A scientist cannot afford to adopt the stand of Iphigenia in Goethe's play: "Ich untersuche nicht, ich fuhle nur."

No, I would not have us become Iphigenias. But I will wager that it is a touch of Iphigenia-a controlled touch,, perhaps, yet a touch of Iphigenia-that gives Ross Mooney his creative insight into the nature of research. Anyone who has been privileged to read the opening chapter of the book Ross Mooney is now writ ting will sense immediately that here is a warm, sensitive human being, attuned to man's aesthetic impulse. Nor do I consider it accidental that a research scholar as distinguished as Jacob W. Getzels should have done his early graduate work in comparative literature and should posses a discriminating taste in art. Yet I suppose I should remember, too, that Iphigenia was sacrificed to Artemis, the goddess of wildlife and bunting, and that even today the Iphigenias are placed at the mercy of hunters faculty committees.

Conversely, I look at the work of other research investigators—men who are industrious and exacting but whose inquiries are mundane and whose findings are passionless. Let me return to the learning-experiment professor I referred to earlier. One day he drew himself up to his full height of high dudgeon to declare to me: "I have never read a novel." Men who take such pride in their cultural illiteracy have turned the art of science into a business. I pity them.

Over and over again I find that the scientists whose work I admire most are men who are at home not alone in the sciences, but in the arts and the humanities as well. Why? Because the essential human quality that enables a man to engage in creative inquiry is sensibility. Accordingly, I quote the conclusion of Harold Taylor:

> It is for this reason that the arts, since they have most directly to do with the development of sensibility, are an essential component of all learning, including scientific learning.

The temper of the scientist must become more and more akin to that of the artist, not to that of the businessman and the production engineer. No longer can we, as civilized human beings, afford what C P. Snow, the physicist and novelist, has referred to as the tragedy of The Two Cultures.

How long, I wonder, will it take us to learn that the model of the physical and biological sciences may be the wrong one for us in education to ape? Since the events with which educators must deal are human events, they have closest affinity to the spheres of the philosopher, the poet, and the novelist. Too many orthodox psychologists are rigid: they are quick to treat with disdain any knowledge other than that which is empirical. But consider the relevance of the insightful analysis of the logic and language of teaching that recently has been reported by Bob Gowin at the University of Chicago. Also, study Language and Concepts of Education, edited by Smith and Ennis, and read especially the chapter by Smith entitled, "A Concept of Teaching." In these instances we discover compelling evidence of the unique contribution that logical and philosophical inquiry can make to educational research.

Yet we cannot rely upon the final stability of logical analysis any more than we can trust a naked empiricism. The mathematician Godel, in his startling theorem, has demonstrated wholly unsuspected and staggering imperfections in any system of deductive logic. He has shown that it is theoretically impossible to prove the consistency of any set of postulates which is, so to speak, rich enough in content to be interesting. The question, "Is there an inner flaw in this system?" simply unanswerable.

Let us reiterate now in a slightly contrapuntal way, the themes that I have been seeking to develop. In short, let me suggest four specific, yet broad ways by which we can improve the quality of educational research.

First, we must enlarge the pool from which we draw trainees; I would secure young men and women who have a broad, liberal arts training and who, therefore, are likely to be more sensitive to the nuances of the human condition. Part of our difficulty is that the present system is rigged so that we discourage from research careers in education some of our ablest undergraduates. There is nothing to be gained by belaboring the point that most of us already know: many of our brightest undergraduates get discouraged by the banality of courses in education; they flee from our ranks. To attract to our profession bright young men and women who will make creative contributions to educational research, we must improve our undergraduate program. Not the least task in this respect is to rid our colleges of education of their surplus of "old maid" professors—both sexes.

The second job is to improve the morality of those professors responsible for the training of research workers. Young people seek to emulate men whom they can respect. But I fear that the image of morality created by many professors is not one we would like our students to copy. For example, the amusement with which a professor refers to graduate students as a supply of cheap "slave labour" does not change the intrinsic, exploitative attitude that prompts him to make such a remark. On my first research job, the senior investigator blandly told me, "I'm exploiting you, Halpin. Of course. I know it. But that's all right; later on you'll get your chance. You'll have some graduate students of your own, and you'll get your chance to exploit them." This attitude sets up a shabby example of morality. We had better realize that a professor's responsibility is to liberate the creative capacity of the young research people who work with him. And we had better police our ranks to eliminate those men who use their positions not to liberate the young, but to exploit them.

Third, we need to examine the institutional arrangements within which research is conducted. Research in our universities has become Big Business. The universities are eager to have professors secure "outside" money. Nor is it without significance that when a contract has been negotiated the universitiy's comptroller immediately deducts from the allotment the university's own "cut" for the project. In the case of "co-operative" contracts where the institution is supposed to make a matching contribution, it certainly is no secret that much of the "matching" money is, in effect, only "money on paper," and that the amount does not represent actual funds set aside in a separate account for this purpose. The investigator and the contracting agency are forced to engage in a conspiracy of silence about these shenanigans. Here again we encounter a procedure of dubious morality. How do we overcome it? I suggest that in some way the universities, themselves, need to be coerced into assuming greater responsibility for providing research funds on their own. Perhaps one criterion for deciding whether funds should be granted to a university by an outside agency would be an index of the amount of research funds that the university provides, entirely on its own, for its own research personnel. For example, personnel on research projects, particularly those people who do not hold faculty rank, frequently are viewed by the university as peripheral, if not indeed, expendable employees. What happens, for example, when a gap in time occurs between two research projects? Does the university itself pay the personnel so that competent people can be kept on the campus until a new contract is negotiated? I expect we know what usually happens.

. The young people who work within institutional arrangements such as we now have quickly learn that research is a "dog eat-dog" affair. Because the university itself is loath to assume full social responsibility to these young people as human beings, they, in turn, tend to become cynical and at times, I regret, even predatory. I doubt that this is a healthy atmosphere for developing creative scientists.

Fourth and last, we need to examine the sponsorship for educational research. The Co-operative Research Program of the United States Office of Education has been a boon to all of us. Yet, I am disturbed that we in educational research are forced to rely—for the most part—upon a single, major source of research support. The "portfolio" is not diversified enough.

Furthermore, we should examine another central danger in the entire project-proposal activity. Hans Selye, perhaps the most eminent endocrinologist alive today, remarked at a recent conference, "The research studies that you can put into proposal form for a government contract are probably the ones that are not worth doing in the first place." Perhaps Selye exaggerates, but, nonetheless, there is a vital point in his riposte: too much of our research endeavour encourages activity at the cost of creativity. It seems that we are afraid to support a man simply to give him a chance to think. I would like to see a few government agencies and foundations show enough courage to underwrite researchers without restricting them by any form of contractual commitment. An outstanding exception to the indictment I have made is the Centre for Advanced Study in the Behavioural Sciences. Another research agency that shows a sophisticated respect for the "care and feeding of researches" is the Office of Naval Research.

The man with a business outlook usually is aghast at the suggestion of giving anyone such a blank, signed check. His first rejoinder is, "How can we be sure that the man will work? If we pay him this way, maybe he'll simply take a vacation or retire." To this I can respond best with a comment made by Andrew Wyeth, one of our most gifted, contemporary American artists: "If I can't paint, I die." Likewise, creative research investigators are, indeed, "driven"; they can no more refrain from doing research than can a nightingale refuse to sing.

To those who think that my suggestion is impractical I would say that probably the price of a single B-70, placed instead into an endowment fund, could pay the salaries of a solid core of capable research workers for the rest of their lives. But here again the decision of how we, as Americans, spend our resources is a moral one. Do we want to spend the bulk of our resources with the tacit assumption that war is inevitable? Or are we willing to devote a moiety of these funds to a few human beings who embrace a more hopeful view for mankind?

In making these proposals for the training of research workers, I know that I invite criticism for emphasizing so strongly the importance of feeling, as well as that of intellect. I do not intend to disparage intellect. A competent research worker requires skill in conceptual thinking. Indeed, I do not care to accept as an advanced graduate student an applicant who scores below a reasonably high critical level on the Miller Analogies Test. But intellect is not enough, especially if it is rooted in an arid personality. We have inducted into our graduate training programs too many young men and women who are so dedicated to intellectualism and objectivity that they deny their own emotional impulses and also shut off from themselves a whole range of aesthetic experience. Literally, such people are deformed. We prefer to encourage into scientific careers men and women who are at least whole human beings.

15
Social Factors

The leadership is not merely a personality characteristic, neither can it be understood exclusively in terms of the leadership tasks just alluded to. Drucker says of an institution, that it is "like a tune; it is not constituted by individual sounds but by the relations between them." The same can be said of leadership; it is a function of the social relations expected of certain social positions. These expectations both support leadership actions and restrain them.

The content of the leader's orders is normally as important as he who gives them. For no matter who the leader is, his orders cannot be arbitrary, that is, outside the realm of normal expectation. For example, it has been found that small group leaders cannot maintain their leadership positions unless their orders are in agreement with the traditions of the group.

The view of leadership as a social relation directs attention away from the personal qualities of the leader and toward the fundamental nature of leadership, the demands made by one party on another. Leadership occurs when subordinates comply with an order. A leader's acts cannot be understood out of context of his relationship with his subordinates. The nature of that relationship is reviewed below.

The leader has a unique role with respect to his subordinates. It is a role which is indispensable to their jobs and to the organization. It is characteristically a role on which others depend.

This characteristic is a matter of degree and is present in many roles. Thus, a member of a group is a leader to the extent that others in the group must depend on him to fulfil his tasks. Leadership, in other words, is not an all-or-none category, but is a variable. People are not simply either leaders or followers. There are as many leaders of an organization as there are shared dependency roles; the same person may lead and be led as he changes roles.

The criterion of a leader, then, is the fact that all other members must depend on the leader more than he depends on any one of them. Thus, while every member of the assembly line performs a minor task, the foreman is less dependent on a particular assembly worker than each is on him—for parts, for wages, vacations, and so on. As specialization increases, there is opportunity for more individuals to become indispensable at various times during their careers; but conversely, it becomes increasingly difficult for a single individuals to be completely indispensable and dominate the leadership structure.

This element of shared dependency differentiates "small group" leaders from large organization leaders. In the former case, group functions are limited and so there are only one or two leaders because all members can be served by a single person. But in complex organizations with diverse functions, it is difficult for any one or two persons to serve the entire membership. They have neither the skill nor the social capacity to do so. This difference makes it hazardous to generalize in both small and large group leadership studies.

Social Relationship

Two component of the leader's relationships to his subordinates are of special importance. On the one hand, the leader is expected by superiors to initiate ideas, maintain group norms, and act as final arbitrator of decisions. At the same time his relationships to subordinates concern "taking care of others," maintaining a humanitarian or, at least, an objective attitude, and in general not acting "like a big shot." When emphasis is placed on the consideration role, the leadership is sometimes loosely characterized as "democratic," while emphasis on initiating activities is often attributed to authoritarianism. Several studies have shown that skills in fulfilling these "initiation" and "consideration" roles are associated with good leadership ratings. One investigator concluded from a study of chairmen of liberal arts college departments that chairmen with good reputations as administrators are those who rate high on both the consideration and initiation dimensions. A similar conclusion was reached from a study of eighty-nine aircraft commanders. Good ratings of the commander by his superiors were associated with high initiation structure scores (originating new ideas or practices, maintaining standard operating procedures with his crew, giving regular and clear assignments to subordinates). Good ratings by his subordinates, however, were associated with high consideration scores (doing personal favours for crew members, being friendly, treating the subordinates as a social equal, looking out for crew welfare).

There are times when these two relationships require the leader to behave inconsistently. Telling others what to do and maintaining official standards may create resentment among subordinates, while establishing equal relationships with subordinates may prevent the leader's taking official action against them, and may jeopardize his relationship with his own superiors. A division of leadership labour is one solution to the dilemma. Some leaders seem to depend more on their initiation role, letting other members of the group take care of the needs and feelings of subordinates. This division creates at least two distinct types of leaders, those responsible for pursuing the group tasks and supporting its official structure, and those who are responsible for maintaining group sentiments, or its cohesiveness.

There is also reason to believe that the relative emphasis which an official leader gives to each of the elements is conditioned by his rank and his advancement opportunities. In one study of military leaders, it is reported that army officers, more than non-commissioned officers, competed openly with their peers and with their superiors, while they competed less with their own subordinates. On the other hand, although non-commissioned officers were more aggressive with their subordinates, they maintained less "social distance" from them than officers did. The lower ranking officials seemed to rely on the consideration leadership behaviour more than higher ranking officers did. The consideration function is perhaps left to informal mechanisms to a greater extent at high levels of command than lower ones. Similarly, initiation seems to be more informal at lower echelons.

Like so many other characteristics of the organization, their initiation and consideration behaviours often necessitate compromise in practice. Styles of leadership are undoubtedly associated with the nature of these compromises. Halpin has developed a typology of leadership styles in terms of four combinations of initiation and consideration structure. School superintendents who were high on both dimensions were assumed to be the most effective; only eleven of fifty superintendents were placed in that category by both their staffs and the school board.

Class Distinction

The initiation and consideration roles are no different that subordinates and superiors, leaders and followers, are characteristically separated by formal and informal barriers. Of this, one school superintendent has said, "You can become too—maybe too putting yourself on too much of an equal—to be too friendly. Now there has been some little thought that has come to my mind that maybe I have been a little too friendly. Some of the superintendents in a Massachusetts study followed a policy of having no intimate friends in the community in which they worked, and they were reluctant to develop friendships with their staff member. The social distance that characterizes leader and subordinate relationships is most apparent in the military where there are official restrictions against fraternization, and separate social, eating, and sleeping places (they even wear their status on sleeves and shoulders).

In maintaining social distance from subordinates, the leader is handicapped in understanding them and their wishes, which generally prevents the most effective fulfilment of the consideration role. This is a structural source of ignorance which may leave the needs of subordinates unanswered. This social distance is one reason that informal leaders arise within the subordinate ranks to take care of the consideration roles neglected by distant superiors.

If it handicaps the consideration role, then why is social distance so characteristic of leadership positions? From an examination of this question, one investigator concludes that it is not because subordinates' feelings of familiarity with their leader hinder their own effectiveness; nor is it because the knowledge which subordinates have of their leader's defects reduces their confidence in him. Rather, social distance is designed to protect the leaders' performance of initiating behaviours. Barriers protect the leader from any involvement with subordinates which might influence his ability to reach decisions that contribute to the goals. As one school superintendent put it, I mean they would feel, 'He's an old buddy of mine.' If you had to crack the whip a little bit, or set down some rules, then they'd be offended quicker. Social distance seems to produce an atmosphere favourable to rationality by preventing unnecessary personal commitments from interfering with the leadership role.

This is not to say that social distance is without benefit to subordinates, for it does benefit them. At the same time that he is aloof to his subordinates, the leader is associating with other, perhaps more influential people—that is, school and community leaders. This puts him in a position to make contacts with those who can achieve salary increases and otherwise protect the interests of his subordinates, advantages which they could not have achieved themselves.

One researcher suggests that social distance is partly explained by virtue of the fact that the satisfactions realized through peer relationships might be jeopardized by too close relationships with superiors.

It is relatively more difficult for leaders in some positions than those in others to maintain social distance. Lower ranking officials are often in closer physical proximity the subordinates than higher officials are to theirs. This may help to account for relatively greater emphasis (noted earlier) that lower officers give to consideration. Teachers, for example, having no office of their own, cannot completely withdraw from students as principals can withdraw from teachers. They are under pressures to be popular and a "good Joe," with no intermediary to bear the brunt of resentment; and not having particularly high social status, as well as being subject to the ridicule of their students and parents, teachers are especially likely to rely on their consideration role, which makes them vulnerable to the charge of "favouritism." There is always a threat that the teacher will succumb to humanistic conceptions of students rather than to official ones, that they will like some of their pupils and dislike others, because of their close special relationship.

Nature of "Subordinates." The concept of leadership is meaningless except as it implies a set of relationships. It cannot be understood without understanding the other positions with which leaders must deal. Of particular importance is the nature of the subordinate position. The practice of speaking about subordinates categorically obscures their characteristic diversity. Subordinates do not represent a unified front, but rather a mixture of subgroups which support or resist different leaders in various degrees. In a study of sociometric choices in a training school for girls, for example, it was reported that there was very little overlap among individuals who supported different group leaders. Large organizations, particularly, are characterized by heterogeneity and dissent among subgroups who are divided among themselves on the basis of their allegiance to different leaders.

This heterogeneous character of subordinates influences the structure of leadership. An array of leaders develop who are supported by various factions of subordinates. A portion of the power of the leader is dependent on the relative power of his supporting (action compared with the elements that oppose him.

Societal Means

Bennis has characterized leadership in operational terms as comprising the following fundamental elements: (a) an agent; (b) a process of inducement; (c) subordinates; (d) the induced behaviour; and (e) a particular objective or goal. He explains that the process of inducement may be defined as power- that is, the ability to control rewards and punishments and thereby control the means for the satisfaction of subordinates' needs. The behaviour that is induce is denned by Bennis as influence. Putting these elements together, leadership may then be denned as ".....the process by which an agent induces a subordinate to behave in a desired manner."

Interaction and Informal Leadership. Like the ancient alchemists who sought a man-made substitute for gold, administrators understandably seek a set of rules, or "principles of administration" which apply unconditionally to most situations. There are at present no such rules. However, also like alchemists, the belief in them causes some persons to glibly accept the prescriptions of "more experienced" persons on faith. One writer cautions that it would be dangerous if there were such rules because, although they might work for a time, they would become inappropriate under new conditions. This in fact is the epitome of "trained incapacity," this is, the substitution of rules for aims. Yet this is precisely what the administrator who wishes to learn only from experience seems to be seeking.

Rather than look for a set of administrative rules, the administrator is better advised to look for underlying principles of human interaction in large scale organizations which will provide a method for understanding situations in which the aims must be achieved. Although the search for rules of administration assumes that situations are consistent, the quest for principles of interaction starts with the variability of situations.

Homans chooses to investigate small processes in terms of four concepts: activity, interaction, norms, and sentiment. Activity refers to the tasks of the work group. Interaction occurs whenever one person's activity is stimulated by the activity of another; it includes verbal and non-verbal communication. A norm is a standard held by work group members that prescribes what ought to be done; orders are norms which anticipate changes in established ways of doing things. Sentiment refers to the subjective qualities of members, their likes and dislikes, drives, emotions, motives, and attitudes. The underlying assumption of the conceptual system is that a change in one element modifies the others. Thus, for example, by increasing the group's activities, interaction will increase among the members, and in increasing interaction they are more likely to get to know one another on a personal basis, either as friends or personal enemies." "The more frequently persons interact with one another, when no one of them originates interaction with much greater frequency than the other, the greater is their liking for one another and their feeling of case in one another's presence." On the other hand, ".....the more frequently one of the two originates interaction for the other, the stronger will be the latter's sentiment of respect (or personal hostility) to ward him....." That is to say, hostility or respect, rather than friendship, is a more likely outcome when superiors interact with subordinates.

The concept originating interaction provide a clue to the detection of informal status relationships. Action is originated for another when he obeys requests, volunteers to satisfy the wishes of other, seeks information, and so on. Often persons who are not in official leadership positions originate interaction for others. The assignment of persons to high-ranking offices does not guarantee that they will necessarily exercise leadership initiative, for there are many factors in the official structure that may prohibit the exercise of initiative. Key subordinates may be in a better position to exercise unofficial leadership because of their close affiliation with the public, with pressure groups, or with influential community leaders. Leadership depends partially an access to crucial information about what is going on the group and within the community; this may involve access to files. For example, the school psychologist is in a position of leadership because he controls secret information about students.

Since intelligent leadership requires that outside influence be considered and used in making decisions, the leadership position will be one that provides a wide variety of outside contacts. This is, the higher the formal or informal social rank, the more interaction there is between that position and the outside groups. For similar reasons, informal leaders will have contact with more of the organization's personnel than those who are not leaders, and consequently they are in a position to develop intimate knowledge of the group norms. That is to say, the leader's knowledge of group norms is no accident. It is gained through a complex network of communication with all members of the group. In other words, "the higher the person's social rank, the wider will be his range of initiation" within the group as well as outside it. This suggests that informed leaders arise from those group positions which afford a range of internal and external contacts and that provide readymade channels of communication. Because communication generally flows toward and away from the leader in greater volume than to other members, it seems reasonable that informal leadership develops at communication centres. Thus, the higher an individual's informal rank, the larger the number of persons for whom he will initiate interaction, in official rank. This high rate of interaction of informal peer group leaders with other group members facilitates the development of mutual sentiments; informal leaders, therefore, can be expected to rely more on consideration and friendship and less on deference, respect, and initiation than official leaders. The view that leadership is a social relations process calls for special consideration of sociological explanations.

The influence of the situation on leadership is unmistakable. Roosevelt and Hitler were products of their time who would not have risen to fame and infamy apart from the situation. The nature of the situation greatly influences the type of leader that will be selected. The shy boy may become an aggressive leader when an issue close to his heart arises or when his special skills are demanded; as one writer points out, the lowly army private may assume command under severe battle condition, when his lieutenant's skills are no longer sufficient, and the most flagrant criminal who has knowledge to survive under times of stress may be entrusted with leadership during a community disaster. It must be concluded that leadership is a combination of a situation, demand for special skills, and a sense of common destiny, as well as personal ambition.

Social Movement

The fact that the situation is important does not make personal background irrelevant, however, Personal career patterns (as opposed to personality traits), for example, constitute one aspect of the "situation." Most administrators of the largest and most influential school systems achieve their positions after a long succession of upward moves. The exact degree of mobility among chief school administrators is variable. Carlisle reports an eight per cent average turnover of local administrators. Turnover is inversely related to size of units; administrators tended to move because of desire for higher salary. In New Jersey, districts look for a new superintendent at least once every six years, while turnover in twelve mid-western states was found to be nearly twenty per cent annually; the highest turnover there was reported in the smallest districts, and the greatest stability was reported in medium-sized districts of 40 to 200 teacher?

Local and Cosmopolitan Leadership Patterns. Carlson notes several principal ways in which the patterns of leadership differ among local (place-bound) and cosmopolitan (career-bound) public school superintendents. Place-bound superintendents are "insiders" promoted from within the system; they constituted thirty-five per cent of a nationwide samp'e of 59 superintendents, while sixty-five per cent were "outsiders." Three types of outsiders were identified: hoppers, specialists and statesmen. Hoppers move frequently without benefiting their status and without leaving a lasting impression on the schools they serve. Specialists are hired to do a special job-financing or building and do leave a lasting impression, but go away when their job is finished. The statesman leaves only when he feels he can do no more for the system. Largely because of what the statesman has been able to do for the system, the school board is usually satisfied with the system as he leaves it, and hires an insider as his successor. Insiders are often represented in larger systems. Outsiders are looked to for creativity, while insiders are hired to maintain stability. No insider reported that his board was dissatisfied with his predecessor. It would be difficult for the insider to effect change even if he wanted to. He would not be as likely to have the school board's support and he risks being identified, on the basis of his past and by virtue of his promotion, by the teachers as the "school board's man." If there is any creativity in such a system, it must come from the teaching profession rather than from the administration. Carlson concludes: "The insider adapts or modifies himself to fit the office; his performance adds nothing new to the role. It is not creative.The place-bound superintendent seems to derive satisfaction from the office; he does not bring status to it. Coming from the outside, cosmopolitans are in a better position to bargain that are insiders, and accordingly they receive between 51,000 and 85,000 more a year than beginning insiders, and the insider never catches up. This demonstrates the crucial relationship that connections with the outside market have on the salary level. Persons not willing to enter the market or leave their present employment cannot command the present market salaries.

Both types of superintendents studied by Carlson engaged in rule-making upon taking office. Rule-making creates the impression that the successor is engaged in important activities, that he is going to "do" something, forcefully bringing to everyone's attention the fact that he is on the scene, in the process of making rules, the successor also learns who will support him on larger issues and who will resist. Insiders and outsiders, however, were concerned with different types of rules. Insiders made rules which essentially sustained the *status quo,* while eighty-five per cent of the outsiders' rules altered internal commitments or external ties of the system. Insiders' rules typically pertained to the technical-managerial facets of the school; for example, "All individuals are responsible for making classroom observations and follow-up conferences." But outsider's rules affected the institutional level of the organization and changed its character; for example, the outsider might establish a kindergarten or employ social workers to serve the school.

When the successor was an outsider, the informal organization also showed signs of change and realignment of conflict relations. One noticeable effect of the outsider was a temporary solidification of informal relationships within each level of the hierarchy; that is, interaction increased among elementary principals and among secondary principals, but decreased between them. Such solidification was less likely where the successor was an insider, and when it occurred it took place across hierarchical levels. This means that, unlike the insider, the outsider inherits strong. The insider knows who his friends are and who his enemies are, and he has had years in which to build up a personal following. Consequently, outsiders more frequently increased their staffs than did insiders. Even new outside superintendents added more positions than old outside superintendents, while the reverse was true for new and old insider superintendents, which indicates that additions by the outsiders are viewed as strategic replacements necessary in the early years. Thus, school systems changed more quickly when outsiders were brought in.

Insiders "lasted" in office longer than outsiders. The mean time in office for insiders was ten years, while outsiders lasted a mean average of eight years. There was some evidence that insiders were able to persist longer because of more thorough political adaptation to outside interests. One insider who served twenty-seven years in one system never permitted himself to take a position in conflict with his school board, but he was willing to sacrifice principle for expediency; he also spent his time in community projects making personal contacts.

Although there are periods when insiders are needed. Carlson concludes that "two insiders in a row may be one too many." Two consecutive insiders would mean that the system has endured an average of twenty years of leadership without any major adaptations to the environment, less than ten per cent of the instances of succession were concurrent insiders. However, about half of the cases were consecutive outsiders, fifty-three per cent of 209 instances were outside to inside, and thirty-nine were inside to outside successions. Carlson conjectures that by comparison with business organizations, which exist in a "wild" environment where adaptation is necessary, public schools are "domesticated" in the sense that they are assured of clients and income. They can exist longer without adapting.

Thus, it is apparent that turnover is a crucial aspect of the school's character, and that the type of person a board hires—outsider or insider—may be a more significant determinant of his leadership than personality traits.

This process of promotion, mobility, and aspiration to positions of greater authority affects the leadership style. In a study by Seeman of fifty school administrators, results of a leader behaviour description questionnaire developed by Halpin disclosed that while measures of career mobility showed little relationship to administrative behaviour, it was significantly related to a mobility aspiration scale designed to test the administrator's ambition to succeed. By combining mobility history with mobility aspiration, a four-way typology of administrators was developed as mobile nonstrivers, mobile status seekers, stable nonstrivers, and unsuccessful status-seekers. Both the mobile strivceptive, the mobile nonstrivers displayed relatively uniform controls over the organization and low responsiveness to needs of the group. The finding demonstrate that the career pattern and aspirations influence the style of leadership.

Social Objectives

Another facet of the mobility pattern which conceivably influences leadership style concerns what leaders strive for. Some ambitious persons seem to be seeking to "become something," and are awed by the style of life or the prestige of the leadership position itself. On the other hand, some ambitious persons seem to aspire to leadership in order to *"do something"*—they want to effect a program, or change one currently in effect. Conceivably, these two types of leaders display different leadership styles upon taking office. For example, the "**strong**" leaders, who resist pressures that deflect from their goals, are perhaps more likely to be found among the latter type. "Weak" leaders, who succumb to power of outside interests or who allow subordinates to ultimately assume command, are conceivably of the former type; for having no program, they seek out clues from others about how the role is to be played. In this case, it is the interplay between ambition and social pressures that constitutes the "situation."

Often, the personal goals that lead individuals into an occupation are not the ones that hold them there. One investigator classified nurses on the basis of shifts in their goals during their career: the "dedicated" had initially strong allegiance to nursing, which was retained throughout the career; the "convert" entered nursing with a low estimation of it, but radically altered her opinion of her career; the "disillusioned" entered the occupation with a high estimation of it, which later deteriorated. The "uncommitted" had neither entered the occupation with a high estimation of it nor developed one during the career. In short, it is conceivable that the leadership styles change with fluctuations in degrees of emotional involvement and formal commitment during the career.

The mobility pattern and expectations regarding it have far-reaching significance for the style of leadership. The question can be analyzed further by directly examining aspects of the succession process separately.

A person's style of leadership can be affected by his anticipation of promotion to another office. This anticipation, in-turn, can modify the behaviour of the promotable's own subordinates who are "next-in line" and develop new expectations because of it. The leader's behaviour seems to change with a cycle of promotion which includes the opportunity to be promoted, the promotion itself, and re-entrenchment afterward. Levenson has observed for example that while striving to gain favourable ones he knows that he will be promoted, he again relaxes control, having less time or incentive to police subordinates as he learns his new job. At this same time, the leader also scrutinizes his subordinates for a replacement which, in turn, undoubtedly constrains some of them. Moreover, in training someone to fill his position, the leader exposes much information about the work that was formerly secret. Then, for a time following his promotion, the promotable is obliged to "prove" himself to the superiors. He may retighten control at this time, but once he has demonstrated himself, the leader may adopt still another style of leadership until there are prospects for another immediate promotion. Thus, cycles of authoritarian and democratic control, and other leadership characteristics which are often attributed to personality traits, are actually variables produced by the pressures of the situation itself.

The unpromotable supervisor probably has as significance effect on his subordinates' behaviour as the promotable. For when the supervisor is unpromotable, his subordinates' opportunities are restricts as well. Levenson outlines four possible reactions to unpromotable. First, the unpromotable one may withdraw, that is, leave either the organization or the profession. However, whether this alternative is feasible depends on still other situational factors, such as age commitments and financial and social commitments. Or, he may region himself completely to the situation by abandoning ambition and other rewards, such as esteem and seniority. He may also adopt uncreative tactics designed to make supervisors notice him; he may "overcomes," or try to please indirect superiors, or become assertive at meeting. Finally, the unpromotable may rebel, and seek to displace his immediate superior, he may stage a show-down, seek to embarrass his supervisors every himself more cleverly, and so on.

The presence or absence of opportunity, then clearly administrates the influence that the situation has on behaviour. Aggressiveness withdrawal, and ritualism can be accounted for by the dead-end character of some jobs rather than personality traits. To the extent that the "dead-end" career is characteristic of the teaching profession, the about thesis is a promising point of departure which may have far-reaching significance for an understanding of the behaviour of teachers and their supervisors.

In periods of organizational crisis, leaders tend to assume note authority, to centralize power, and to demand greater conformity even subordinates. Conceivably, as organizational stress relaxes, decentralization may increase (though not necessarily as quickly as centralization develops from crisis), randa, and delays at promotion and contract time are well designed to imbue the organization with an element of minor crisis.

A great deal can be learned about patterns of leadership by observing organizational tempos, the rise and decline of pressures generated by deadlines and by close supervision. For example, the school principal will sense that he has more authority, greater responsibility for the school, and more obedience from subordinates when the school is being "inspected" by the superintendent or visited by State Department of Education representatives or by a parent group. Similarly, teachers seem to be more "official" with students on the first day of school, and more informal on the last day. They also probably assert more officiousness at test time. When an important bond issue or consolidation vote is deciding the fate of the school, the administrator tends to become more directive. In general, during crises the consideration role declines in favour of the initiating functions, and subordinates' wishes become less relevant to the concerns of the leadership. Halpin's typology of leaders based on their relative stress on initiation and structure needs modification to include the cyclical changes in these styles over a period of time as pressures ebb and flow. Theories of action provide the best means for confronting those organizational variables which are complicated by changes through time. We refer to natural system models such as that of Talcott Parsons. More will be said about this toward the end of this chapter.

Precisely because he is granted more authority in times of crises, the leader's position in most vulnerable then. To fail at a time of major crisis usually means the loss of the leadership position, for ineffective leadership is at no time more apparent nor more fateful. Consequently, the defeat of an important bond issue may result in a change of administration.

However, even the administrator who has won his cause—a bond issue, or a fight with the city council or the school board—may have jeopardized his position if he had to wield too much power or alienate too many persons in the process. The successful leader usually makes enemies in the process of a fight, or he may have become so committed to his supporters that the alternatives which remain open to him are so severely restricted by his obligations to them that his power is virtually destroyed. Often his best recourse after an all-out fight is to resign, whether he won or not.

"Busy-ness." An element of crisis, at least the appearance of it, is also used by some subordinates to strengthen their authority. "Busy-ness" is the art of appearing busy. It must be admitted as one of the effective ploys of "impression management." It conveys to observers the subordinate's assumed importance. Indeed, "busy-ness" is so effective that the casual observer cannot distinguish the busy from the productive members of the work group. However, in announcing his presumed importance the busy person is announcing his ambition to be important, which is significant in itself. It is this common element of "ambition" which links the unimportant and the important busy persons.

"Busy-ness" assumes characteristic levels of activity among various occupational groups. Most nurses, for example, complain that they are "too busy." Yet upon observing them at work in hospitals, it seems that the complaint is voiced more consistently than the actual workload would warrant. That is, even when she is not personally busy, a nurse will complain of it. Occupation-wide ideologies create exaggerated illusions of overwork. The statement that "most people in the occupation are busy" comes to mean that "I am busy." Characteristically, occupations striving for greater social status, including those in the process of professionalizatton, complain most about being busy. It is symbolic of dissatisfaction and ambition. Applied to teaching, the question is, to what extent do teachers' complaints about being overworked reflect dissatisfaction with their status. Without implying that most teachers do not work hard, it may be that complaints about hard work are indicative of a more fundamental condition of the occupation the drive for the status that comes with busyness.

The way a leader performs the leadership function depends to some extent on the risks he is both able and willing to endure. The leader's feelings about the security of this position vary independent of such personality traits as "confidence." His security is dependent on the permanency of his position and the guarantees that he will continue to occupy it. His personal commitment to the position is also important, of course. His position is important to him to the extent that there are few other acceptable jobs available to him. In short, his security is a function of the permanency of the position, his power to hold it, and the available alternatives. During periods of proposed change his position is particularly vulnerable. A principal may resist efforts of the school board to bring in an "outsider" to fill the position for which he aspires. He may also resist the establishment of a position which has authority over his, thus decreasing the authority of his position. But he will not resist such a position if he expects to be promoted to it.

Similarly, for example, whether one reacts conservatively to proposed school district reorganization plans depends not only on whether the plans threaten to displace him, but on his commitment to the job. It is precisely because volunteer groups such as the PAT are not fully committed to their position that they are in a position to take a liberal stand on proposed educational changes.

As suggested, the amount of commitment to a position depends upon the relative availability and importance of other positions.

In addition to personal commitment to his position, it was also suggested that the leader's behaviour depends on the security of the position itself. A person needs a certain amount of security to take a risk. So, it can be expected that the leaders who support educational changes hold positions in the largest school systems in the country which have the backing of the nation's most powerful economic and political leaders. This is somewhat contrary to the stereotyped notion that persons most entrenched in power are the most conservative defenders of the status quo. This may have some basis in fact, the upper class is both powerful and conservative—but historically the striving middle class has probably been more anxious and insecure about its status than the upper class.

Considering the organization, the question of who is the most conservative leader depends on the relative balance between commitment to office and the security of the office. Where commitment is lowest and the office is most secure, leaders can afford to be less conservative. Conversely, conservatism is highest among leaders who are most committed to relatively insecure, unpowerful positions.

The size of an organization is another facet of the leadership situation. From one study of 500 students who described the groups of which they had been a member, it was found that as group becomes larger, demands upon the leader's role become greater and more numerous, tolerance for leader-centered direction of group activities increases, and the group generally becomes more bureaucratic - that is, rules are enforced impartially, concern with administrative problems increases, and firmness toward subordinates increases.

These findings have several implications. First, they stress the fact that the problems of leadership become accentuated with bureaucratization. The challenge of leadership in the future will increasingly be the problems generated by bureaucracy, and as these problems become more complex there is little prospect that they will be solved by "experience" or with mediocre training. Second, with his organization increasing in size, it is difficult for the leader to give attention to the special problems of subordinates. It becomes more difficult to display the special leadership qualities of consideration; but perhaps consideration is also less demanded of the official leader as informal leaders assume this function through specialistic divisions of leadership functions. Finally, the evidence points to the dangers of projecting small group laboratory studies of leadership to complex organizational settings.

The Effects

The skills of leadership, like other skills, are developed through training and experience. However, because of the variety of situational contexts, it is by no means apparent what type of training and experience are most beneficial. However, there is reason to believe that, in face of the overwhelming variety of situations, the most effective training is at the level of principles of interaction and social analysis.

The highly specialized courses in administration, which grew like Topsy, do not seem to reflect these theoretical principles. Separate administrative courses usually offered for elementary, secondary, and other special types of school organization did not emerge as a result of evidence that there are different leadership principles for each level of school organization; they emerged instead from "experience" oriented assumptions that what is important to know are the system. But contrary to this, research evidence indicates there is more similarity between large organizations of different purposes than there is between small organizations of different purposes. Such characteristics as system size, school size, situational influences, complexity, and degree of bureaucratic administration perhaps provide a more meaningful basis of differentiating course work in administrative training programs than grade levels when it comes to examining leadership problems in education.

The situational context also challenges the fetish of experience. Not only may experience in one situation be unrepresentative of another, but it may close alternatives and become so technique—oriented that the broader principles of administration are never fully realized.

From the situational viewpoint, the training program is another "situation," and from that perspective it also influences leadership patterns. When for example, the training program is closely geared, either officially or unofficially, to a particular school system, or when the training amounts to on-the-job training, the practical benefits are often more than offset by the lack of perspective and critical imagination which could be derived from systematic consideration of theoretical principles.

The recent trend toward theory development, utilization of social science models, and the application of these to ease situations appears to be a move in the right direction. Training programs which include intensive study in discovering the world of reality through social science techniques, and the application of their knowledge to analysis of the administrative world through case studies, field studies, and simulated situational materials are recent and promising additions to preparation programs for administrators in many universities.

Social Hierarchy

Although the situational approach calls attention to the influence which the immediate setting has on leader behaviour, it still underestimates the extent to which social factors condition the leadership role. For beyond the official organizational setting is a cultural one, the outside society, which seriously influences the leader's internal functions.

Seeman broached the question of how the leader's social status influences his leadership roles in a sample of seventy-five public school superintendents in Ohio. It was found that their leadership style was affected by their conception of the place they hold in the community and in the general culture. Measure of status were designed to assess (1) the leader's community status, (2) discrepancies between economic and social status; and (3) distortions between the leader's perception of his social status and his followers' perception of it. The measures were compared to the subjects' ideologies of leadership and to subordinates' evaluations of their leadership effectiveness. Regarding status differences, when the leader gave himself high self-ratings on community status, he also claimed high responsibility and authority and tendency to delegate authority to his subordinates. Also self-rated, high-status leaders who perceived a significant difference between themselves and their followers were judged by subordinates to be receptive to change, communicated frequently with subordinates, and did not express "separateness" (social distance) attitudes toward subordinates. Moreover, those high-status leaders who perceived a relatively great status difference between themselves and their subordinates received favourable evaluations from subordinates.

Because this last finding seems to be contrary to the egalitarian concept of leadership, it bears further consideration. Given a democratic bias among subordinates and a demand for personal consideration, one might expect that subordinates would prefer school executives who are similar to themselves in community status. But the reason they do not is suggested in the same data, there is a positive correlation between "separatism" of superintendents as described by teachers, and percentage increase in teachers' salaries. That is, higher-status leaders were in a better position to enhance their subordinates' positions by virtue of their social distance, that is, the fact that they associated with community influential rather than with teachers.

Leaders who exaggerated their status in relation to teachers' placement of them, and who "underestimated" teachers' status (relative to teachers' self-placement), exhibited high separatism attitudes toward teachers and were unresponsive to change; these leaders received low ratings from their subordinates. In general, the findings suggest that a basic requisite of good leadership is the ability to accurately judge the attitudes of the total membership on relevant issues (though not necessarily on non-relevant issues).

The importance of social status appears to lie in the relative security it provides. When the leader is clearly of higher status than his subordinates, he is not threatened by them, and his response is both one of high communication and delegation of authority. Also, his community status places him in a more opportune position to support his subordinates. However, when his community status is not clear, either because of disparities between economic and prestige ratings, or because his own status aspirations create distortion, the leader is threatened by his subordinates. Under these conditions, his leadership style displays personal status enhancing and conserving tactics, which probably reduces his overall leadership effectiveness.

Besides the limited sample and its obviously exploratory nature, one major shortcoming of the study, recognized by Seeman, is that no attempt was made to differentiate the school leaders' status in the local community from his status in the general society. The findings may apply only to "locally-oriented" executives, whose reputation and status in the local community is important to them. To the extent that school executives are mobile, often marginal community members, operating in a nationwide or statewide framework, their overriding status identification may typically be to professional and national sources outside the community rather than to the local community. This reservation does not detract from the study's significance. However it is evident that training in "human relations" and "social skills" do not encompass the leadership task. Leadership training stops no shorter than consideration of the cultural context.

16

Individual Growth

An evaluation system that does not have procedures to overcome limitations for optimum performance is inhuman and irresponsible. School systems have traditionally left the development of competencies to the individual. Within recent years, however, school administrators have seen the need for comprehensive staff development functions or so-called in-service education programs, which assist personnel throughout the system to function productively in relation to organizational goals.

In the past, school boards have not been led to provide much support of staff development activities. Instead, teachers and administrators had to pay for their own development. This left the preparation in specialties to the personal interests of individuals. Consequently, many who worked for master's degrees, for instance, prepared themselves not to perform better in their present positions, but to be promoted to other fields. This situation is dysfunctional. School systems should greatly increase finding for staff development programs to meet personnel resource needs.

Moreover, there has been too much interest in retraining teachers in comparison to retraining administrators. If school principals and other administrators and supervisors do not keep in touch with current trends, they may thwart the attempts of teachers to improve classroom instruction. Harris and Bessent emphasized the primacy of personal participation of teachers and administrators in planning in-service programs. Moreover not enough resources have been provided to train non-instructional personnel.

Within recent years the use of auxiliaries to supplement teaching and school administration has gained popularity. The auxiliary has been used by hospitals and other organizations for many years.

Abbott suggested that auxiliary teacher programs (e.g., tutors, parent participants, student aides) are making important contributions today. These programs appear to be growing in significance. Leadership is needed to keep these programmes focused upon the objectives of the school.

Recruitment Process

The pupil personnel services examined in this section are certain operational services, and not the curriculum and instructional services discussed previously. Included in pupil services are such areas as school census, admission and registration, accounting, discipline, promotion, health services, and counselling.

School administrators should always perceive the organization conceptually as it relates to pupil personnel services. Carlson provided an interesting classification system of organizations based upon their relationship to their clients. He classified organizations into wild and domesticated types. Such organizations as proprietary schools, private colleges, physicians' offices, and lawyers' offices were classified as wild organizations because (1) there organizations control who they admit as clients and (2) the clients of these organizations can decide whether they care to receive the services offered by the organizations. Wild organizations must struggle for survival.

The public schools were classified as domesticated organizations because (1) they must accept the clients assigned to them and (2) the clients normally cannot select the school they attend. Many persons believe that the public school's survival is assured.

What are some of the consequences for clients inherent in the domesticated type of organization? According to Carlson, the public schools have no choice except to divide pupils according to some criteria that would result in efficient management. The pupils range tremendously in ability, motivation, and interests. Consequently, schools must segregate the pupils into various types of special education categories, programs of studies, abilities, interests, and client demands. Thus the public school cannot concentrate on one specialty as physicians or lawyers may specialize in one aspect of their professions.

Many parents who have been alienated from the public schools, for whatever reason, have advocated privately administered alternative schools. Fantini has advocated moving toward consumer choice of public schools. Persons advocating personal choice should always consider the reasons people have for wanting to choose the schools their children attend. Why do persons decide not to cooperate with other citizens in building and maintaining strong, viable school systems? Why do people desire to escape racial, ethnic, or culturally different persons and construct cells of their own liking? What are the consequences of such a policy for the culture and the continuation of the society? Americans must decide whether cultural feudalism is better or worse for the good life than cultural congruence and whether balkanization is better than national unity.

We believe that there should be no alternative to making all American public schools into the highest-quality schools known. Public school administrators, teachers, and other school personnel should be mindful to their functions in relation to pupils. This mindfulness should motivate school personnel to overcome the problems in the domesticated structure. The school systems will have to struggle for survival because if they do not set missions acceptable to clients and attain them, public education may not survive.

Guidance and Counselling

The counselling program should provide special opportunities for the school and the pupil to reach accommodation and for the pupil to realize optimum educational progress. References to counselling services are not restricted to the professional guidance personnel. Specially educated counsellors are essential for helping pupils achieve educationally productive adaptations and for the school to be responsive to pupil needs. However, counsellors cannot themselves achieve these purposes. School administrators, teachers, and other personnel interact with pupils continuously. Whether the pupil makes a satisfactory adaptation and the school is characterized by responsiveness will depend much more on the persons who see the pupils every school day.

School authorities are required by law in many states to conduct periodic censuses of pre-school children. Some authorities have recommended continuous contact and enumeration of the census. These data are important in planning for the admission of pupils to school for the first time.

In many instances the admission of children to an educational programme is the first contact parents have with the school. This is also the first step of the child away from the home. Consequently, school officials should plan and execute well the processes for the admission of pupils. Provisions should be made for the orientation of pupils during the admissions procedure.

Discipline has been a recurring problem area in pupil personnel administration. For decades polls of teacher opinions have shown that discipline was among the top concerns. The volume of disciplinary cases experienced may be related to the quality of responsiveness exhibited by school personnel.

Accounting for pupils is also a very important administrative task. This includes massive record systems to locate pupils, to account for attendance and to record changes in membership.

Most school systems provide some health services for pupils. Any activity of the school to determine the health condition of pupils, to aid in correcting health defects, or to provide first aid may be classified as health services. Most school systems have individual inventory services, including a variety of individual and group testing services. Other techniques may be observations, socio-metric analyses, rating scales, and health screening. The mounting interest in employment opportunities and in evaluating school effectiveness has brought demands for better placement and follow-up services. Individual schools must provide processes for evaluating and reporting pupil progress.

Construction of Premises

The great growth of pupil enrolments following World War II placed heavy leadership burdens upon school administrators to provide new school plant facilities. These facilities cost the tax-payers many billions of dollars. Even though the nation may reach zero population growth, providing new school plant facilities will continue for many school districts. Population shifts will cause many school districts to grow in pupil enrolment. Programme changes, changes in population, and other conditions will cause many school buildings now used to become obsolescent.

Administrative responsibility for satisfactory physical environment is not limited to providing new facilities. Existing school plant facilities must be maintained. Another management task is to oversee the operation of school buildings—to provide proper lighting, ventilation, temperature, and so on.

In the planning, construction, and renovation of school plant facilities, school administrators come face to face with the ancient philosophical problem of humanistic versus material values. Should school buildings be designed to represent the values of ancient Greece or should they be designed to provide desirable physical environments functional for school programmes? The noted architect Walter Gropius wrote that the "sickness of our present chaotic environment, its often pitiful ugliness and disorder have resulted from our failure to put basic human needs above economical and industrial requirements." Gropius further contended that our obsession with designing buildings based on values of the past and imitating existing designs were symbols of our "spiritual bankruptcy."

Numerous studies have shown that in the construction of new facilities material values have held supremacy over humanistic values. The classroom environments in a high percentage of the buildings are devastating to the learning process. In the great press to house the war babies during the 1959's and 1960's, some occurrence of poor facilities was understandable. However, the incidence of failure to maintain high standards and functional facilities is too frequent to understand. Those espousing materialistic values have won over those adhering to humanistic values when, in reality, neither should win but both should interact to support attainment of educational goals.

The main objective in planning new school buildings is to construct facilities that will be congruent with the school programme. The facilities should be planned to provide a functional, attractive, comfortable classroom climate, which facilitates the learning process. Planning flexibility to adjust to changing educational programmes is crucial in preventing rapid obsolescence. Comprehensive studies of population growth and change, school programs, and socio-economic developments in school districts are essential in the development of school building programmes.

Future school sites must be located to serve pupils in school districts experiencing rapid growth, and locations should be avoided that would make the schools unsatisfactory in the future. Numerous factors are important in selecting school sites. Among these are size, accessibility, elevation, drainage, nature of soil, cost, and general environment in which the proposed site is located. Campbell's study demonstrated that inappropriate location and other conditions of school sites were leading causes for the abandonment of schools.

Success in planning new school plant facilities depends upon how well the leaders of a school district have visualised their educational mission and developed educational programs. Although school buildings should provide a good physic environment for teachers and pupils, they should also be designated to help school personnel attain the programme objectives. Therefore the participation of many persons concerned with program development in planning new plant facilities is essential to success.

Projections of school facility needs through adequate planning can be used to estimate the financial resources needed. Expert assistance is required to translate school plant facility needs into financial needs and project a financing program. Few school districts can finance school building programs through a pay-as-you-go plan. Therefore the financing program in most instances must propose long-term bonded indebtedness. This will usually require a public referendum and will involve school officials directly in political leadership. If the referendums are not successfully passed by the electorate, the new buildings will be delayed indefinitely and the school programme curtailed.

Selection of architects, preparation of educational specifications, and development of architectural plans are very important tasks. Architects should be selected who will work closely with professional educators. Architectural plans are based on the educational specifications for a building. The preliminary draft of the architectural plan should be studied and reviewed by teachers, administrators, and other personnel. Other tasks involved in the construction of new buildings are awarding construction contracts, monitoring construction, final inspection and acceptance of the building by the board.

System at Work

The primary aim in operating school buildings is to provide for teachers and pupils an optimum environment for learning. Studies have shown the importance of maintaining a good thermal environment. The temperature should be maintained at between 70 and 75 degrees Fahrenheit. Humidity must also be controlled to provide an optimum thermal environment. Ventilation is necessary to prevent facilities from becoming stuffy, with odors. The trend has been to provide for year-round control of the thermal environment. School administrators should be wary of architectural, fads that use large amounts of energy and prevent maintenance of an optimum thermal environment. One such fad in the past has been to construct buildings with too much glass, making the control of heating, cooling, and lighting difficult.

Other areas of school plant operation include maintenance, custodial services, and health and safety precautions. Because these were discussed previously under support services, they will not be enlarged upon here.

In enumerating the problems school administrators face, those concerning community school relations are among the most frequent. Educators must communicate information about the school to citizens to promote understanding of programmes, help clarify and build commitment to goals, and promote cooperation among the institutional functions of society. Effective interaction with other institutional leaders is essential in promoting interinstitutional understanding and functional congruency.

Throughout the history of public education in the United States educators have gone through cyclical periods of interactive cooperation with citizens followed by isolationist withdrawal from the public. Associated with these cyclical trends is growth in public confidence and then damaging loss in credibility of educational leaders. Within the past decade educators have been faced with lack of credibility in many, but not all, school districts. The basic conceptual problem in this area is to promote public understanding as a basis for community – school communication and cooperation in the establishment and attainment of educational goals.

Many volumes have been written concerning the development of good public relations programmes. Realizing their obligation to report upon school conditions to the public, many school systems have a director and staff for this purpose. Studies have demonstrated the need for informing the citizens about school programmes. Many citizens have only superficial and in many instances erroneous understanding of the schools. One crucial objective, then, of the public relations programme is to help the public understand schools and how they are operated, McCloskey emphasized this approach to administering public relations.

Public relations programmes that build an image of the schools that cannot be substantiated may eventually create a credibility gap, and loss of public confidence can have serious consequences. Careful planning of long-range public relations programmes is important.

Effective effort to create and maintain public understanding requires careful, long-range planning. Since attitudes and opinions evolve slowly and modern communication is so complex, poorly planned effort will be misdirected and may even contribute to public misunderstanding.

Of primary importance in providing information to increase public understanding of schools is identification of what is worthy or communication. From the viewpoint of the schools' leaders, those things that contribute most to communicating how the schools are achieving their mission should have priority. Recurring subjects of communication with the parents include (1) marking and promotion practices, (2) homework, (3) methods of instruction, (4) materials of instruction, (5) special services available to pupils, (6) schedules, and other routine practices involving children.

Deciding how best to encode and transmit information about the school to the public is a difficult task. How can the information be put into language, pictures, and graphic materials readily communicated and understood? A lot of dry factual information in stilted language is almost useless.

Often overlooked in public relations programs, however, is the importance of personal interaction with other citizens. How are persons treated by teachers, school administrators, and other personnel of the school? How well prepared are school personnel to talk intelligently about the mission of the schools and how they are attempting to accomplish this mission? In most of their interaction with parents and other citizens, do school personnel create more friends than enemies for the public schools? Every attempt should be made to promote effective processes of personal interaction with the public to promote understanding, warmth of human relationships, and bases for future cooperative interaction.

School systems and schools have made use of citizen committees to promote cooperation in improving educational effectiveness and promoting public understanding. Other procedures used include cooperative-type surveys, social activities, and special advisory groups.

Many years ago Alexis de Tocqueville observed that Americans had a great propensity to form and join civic organizations. Membership in these organizations provides many personal interactions and opportunities for community leadership.

Therefore, educational administrators should encourage active participation of school persons in community organizations.

This accomplishes several functions. The interaction provides opportunities to inform leaders in other institutional sectors about schools. Through leadership in community affairs, the interests of educators in the society in general are promoted. Effective personal relationships for future cooperation of educators and other community leaders are fostered.

As discussed in the community school·has grown in significance as a result of the interest of the developmental programmes in Michigan. The early development of the programme was based upon the school-centered concept. Within recent years the community school movement has moved to community wide programming; the term community education is more descriptive of the thrust today. Seay and associates have recently published a comprehensive discussion of the community education movement.

Certainly the community school was concerned with humane values and humanitarian issues. Educators and other community leaders tuned to it as the educational answer to increasingly complex problems. By the sixties, however, communities had become increasingly urbanized and their members were more expectant of educational services in great variety for everybody throughout his life cycle. And larger numbers of agencies appeared with educational programmes aimed toward diverse education needs within the community.

One very important aspect of the community education programme is to encourage the participation of large numbers of citizens in the educational improvement of the community.

Fixing Responsibility

School systems, colleges, and other educational organizations have invested resources in research and development, or so-called institutional research. Within recent years large investments have been made in the evaluation of education. This increase in effort was in response to the loss of credibility and public interest in accountability. The "accountability movement" resulted in intensive examination of allocation of responsibility and evaluation of academic productivity. Planning is another important activity frequently associated with research and evaluation.

The first important task in developing the research programme is to define what kind of research is desired. There are different definitions of research. Consequently, employing persons trained for research without reference to their definitions of research may not fulfil organizational expectations. Let us consider some alternative ways in which research programs have developed and how research is defined.

Many school administrators view research as a process of collecting, organizing, and reporting factual information. School administrators constantly must report massive amounts of factual data to state and federal agencies concerning faculty, pupils, programs, physical facilities, and many other aspects of school operation. This 'research" is not concerned with the development of new conceptual knowledge. It is what might appropriately be referred to by social-book-keeping (fact-collecting) research. This type of research is prevalent in state education departments, where it is used for making statistical reports about education.

Another definition of research is what some have referred to as action re-starch or process improvement research. The aim of this type of research is to develop information for solutions to problems faced by the personnel of the school district without reference to generalizing knowledge. Thus the activity starts with troublesome problems, and the aim of the research is to develop and test knowledge useful in solving these problems. External validity of the findings is not of primary concern. In this approach, however, the researchers try to produce information useful in solving problems confronting personnel in the organization and they are concerned with the applicability of the findings in the local situation.

Another version of research is primarily concerned with the development of new knowledge that is broadly applicable. This is frequently referred to as basic research. A basic research program might involve testing of ideas by numerous cooperating school districts to provide sufficient replication to make the knowledge developed generalizable beyond the individual school districts. This knowledge would be assumed to be universally applicable.

What is the most appropriate research program for school systems? Before responding to this question, let us consider some concepts of evaluation and the relationship between research and evaluation.

Examination System

Evaluation in education emerged as measurement. During the period of behaviourist, neorealist influence, the test makers developed many standardized tests to measure pupil achievement, adjustment, personality, and the like. This was eventually expanded to include observational inventories, questionnaires, and other instruments to produce quantifiable data concerning practically every aspect of school operation. Large amounts of quantified facts could be manipulated statistically.

A different concept of evaluation is what Stufflebeam and associates referred to as the congruence definition, in which evaluation is seen as the process of determining the degree of congruence between organizational goals and performance. This concept of evaluation was developed under the leadership of Ralph Tyler in the Eight-Year Study sponsored by the Progressive Education Association. In this sense the main purpose of evaluation is to collect information and make judgments concerning how well the school system is meeting stated goals.

Thus the evaluation process moved away from the aimless process of collecting objective scores on anything and everything and focused upon organizational purpose.

Stufflebeam and associates have offered what they refer to as the judgment definition of evaluation, in which evaluation is a process that links value, information, and decision-making situations in making professional judgments. This concept of evaluation would avoid the ex-post facto effect of the congruence or measurement approaches and make evaluation influential in the decision-making process, rather than simply determining what constructive or destructive effects had already occurred. Evaluation is a key factor in making professional, enlightened decisions.

The answer to the question of which research and evaluation services should be provided depends on the purposes of the organization and the demands made on it by its clients, on the strategic location and resources available for basic research, and on decisions concerning the allocation of resources. Authorities estimate that the costs of basic research to make breakthroughs in education comparable to those made in medicine and the physical sciences will be many billions of dollars. Education is a much more complex field, and very little has been invested in basic research. The "pay-off" of basic research is very, very slow, and great patience is needed as large investments are made. Greatest progress will be made when the best scholars are organised to produce a concerted attack upon massive problems. Therefore we offer the following proposed tasks for the development of research programmes in local school systems.

First, the local school district should cooperate in and vigorously support the development of state and federally funded research centers for basic research. The research specialists in school districts should cooperate with regional research agencies by submitting problems needing testing, suggesting solutions to be considered, and assisting in the development and testing of ideas. Moreover, they should help local school administrators interpret and use the results of basic research.

The costs alone, not to speak of the demands upon school systems, dictate that basic research be a cooperative effort through a regional research and development organization, such as a well-staffed university or a research corporation. In fact, the generalizability of findings would indicate the need for a national effort. Educators might well consider the agricultural model with both federal and state support and at least one critical massing of resources for basic research in each state.

Second, research directed by local school districts and state departments of education should be for process improvement. The school district research and evaluation program should emphasize designs with local applicability to assist school officials in valuing the consequences for pupils of the alternative choices considered. The research should be of high quality and offer solutions to organizational and instructional problems. This concept of research is consistent with what the Phi Delta Kappa National Study Committee on Evaluation referred to as judgment evaluation.

Third, the research and evaluation programmes of school districts and state education agencies must continue to conduct factual measurement, social-book-keeping studies, and evaluations. Valuable as judgment evaluation is in improving professional decision making, legislatures and other agencies will continue to demand measurement data and factual information. The accountability demands are also in the direction of program auditing procedures in some states.

Perusal of professional journals in education will reveal many articles involving the term accountability. The tenor of some articles is that school administrators should be made accountable to a particular person or group. Some authors attempt to blunt the modern thrust of the movement by pointing out that accountability is thousands of years old, and not new, as many presume.

Many educators believe that accountability is one of the many fads that come and go in education, and it may well be. But the modern fixation on accountability is symptomatic of deeply ingrained problems in the administration of public schools. It is symptomatic of the lack of professional development, low level of research-based knowledge about how children learn and lack of political power among educators. It is symptomatic of the loss of creditability of educational leaders and of a gulf of misun derstanding among educators, their clients, and other citizens. The demands for accountability, however, are symptomatic of much deeper social and cultural problems than these.

Remember the God is Dead movement of the 1960's? The ministers caught the brunt of this movement. All of us recall the anguished public outcry about the Vietnam War, followed by the tragedy of Watergate. The politicians are reaping the consequences of being held accountable for these events. Physicians and lawyers also come in for their share of public criticism for lack of accountability. Underneath the reasons already given for the flood of demands for educational accountability is a deep public disappointment with the basic institutions of the society. The pent-up frustrations are vented upon any institutional sector in which glaring weaknesses are obvious.

Thus the demands for accountability are based upon the belief of many citizens that education, among other institutions, has failed them. Specifically, it is a belief that educators need to be held accountable for mal-practice. The much discussed Peter Doe case in San Francisco was, in reality, a mal-practice suit against educational officials. Let us examine two views of how educators may achieve accountability.

One view is that educators should only be accountable for the processes (or treatments) used but not the end product. In support of this view, educators point to the data, which show rather clearly that what a child learns depends on many variables within systems not controlled by the school (e g., the family, neighbourhood). Therefore holding the school accountable for producing all merit scholars would be like holding the minister accountable for not converting all souls to a religious faith or holding the physician accountable when the patient dies, even though all standard treatments were used.

Product accountability, however, focuses upon the output of the system, with less concern about the processor (the school) or the variation in inputs. Proponents of this view believe that educators should be answerable and responsible for outcomes, regardless of inputs.

These renewed demands present challenging implications for educational administrators. They are challenging because educators have not demanded a strong basic research programme to establish a basis of process accountability as is possible in the practice of medicine. These demands are challenging because educational administrators have not been careful enough in specifying what education can and can not do and thus promised too much to too many. They are challenging because educators are not as strong politically as they should be. There are other challenging aspects not discussed here. What educational leaders must do, however, is respond to these challenges.

First, there must be cooperative participation in the development and legitimization of attainable educational goals and objectives. The people, who ultimately hold the schools accountable, should be encouraged through appropriate processes to participate in the development of educational goals. The school administrators who will be held accountable, should provide leadership through the use of public relations and political techniques to legitimize cooperatively developed and officially adopted goals.

Second, professional processes and performance expectations must be developed. In response to public demands for accountability, educators must lead in developing a concept or what can reasonably be expected of the school. This should include the compilation of careful programme descriptions of specified processes for attaining the objectives. The aim should be to develop and legitimize the best processes for treating variations in learning and to specify what can be reason-ably expected from these processes. In summary, educators must become much more professionally respectable than they have been in dealing with learning problems.

Third, basic research and development programs are needed. Responding to accountability requires a scientific approach to the solution of educational problems, rather than the traditional authoritative approach. There is a desperate need for the development of processes in basic research through which educators can specify that research-based practices will assist educators in specifying what education can and cannot perform.

Fourth the criteria for accountability must be specified. Leaders should see that such criteria are consistent with the accepted goals of the organization. Acceptability places greater emphasis on specifying predetermined expectations and performance objectives than was traditionally found in education.

Fifth, responsibility must be fixed. School people must also decide who should be held accountable for what Is the principal going to be held accountable for what pupils learn? If so, for what is the principal accountable? If the principal is accountable for using the correct process control of programs need not be decentralized. If produce accountability is emphasized, the principal and faculty should be given autonomy in the selection of teaching processes.

Plan Method

Although textbooks about educational administration have exhorted the significance of planning for years, new developments have made planning an absolute requirement.

The need for planning arose with the intensified complexities of modern technological society. Problems such as population, manpower needs, ecology, decreasing natural resources and haphazard applications of scientific developments—all place demands on educational institutions for solution. If educational organizations are to meet these problems, then planning becomes a necessity and planning competence becomes mandatory.

Among the specific tasks involved in planning are assessing educational needs, establishing educational goals, identifying resources and restraints, generating and evaluating alternative choices, making and implementing decisions, and monitoring, and revising processes. Thus, contrary to what some presume, the entire process involves literally hundreds and possibly thousands of persons.

Planning may also involve the use of many theoretical formulations. The planning process includes decision making. Planning may be approached as the management of change or as a part of organizational renewal. Application of the management-by-objectives concept, PERT, and various future-forecasting techniques may be a part of the process.

Additional Reading

Bhaskara Rao, Digumarti (1994). *Scientific Aptitude,* New Delhi: Ashish Publishing House. ISBN 81-7024-658-X.

Bhaskara Rao, Digumarti (1995). *Animal Kingdom.* New Delhi: Discovery Publishing House. ISBN 81-7141-274-2.

Bhaskara Rao, Digumarti (1995). *Batracology.* New Delhi: Discovery Publishing House. ISBN 81-7141-279-3.

Bhaskara Rao, Digumarti (1997), *Scientific Attitude.* New Delhi: Discovery Publishing House. ISBN 81-7141-308-0.

Bhaskara Rao, Digumarti (1996). *Scientific Attitude vis-à-vis Scientific Aptitude.* New Delhi: Discovery Publishing House. ISBN 81-7141-308-0.

Bhaskara Rao, Digumarti, Editor (1996). *Encyclopaedia of Education for All,* 5 Volumes. New Delhi: APH Publishing Corporation. ISBN 81-7024-759-4 (set).

Vol. I *Education for All: The World Conference.* ISBN 81-7024-760-8.

Vol. II *Education for All: The EPA-9 Summit.* ISBN 81-7024-761-6.

Vol. III *Education for All: Quality Education for All.* ISBN 81-7024-762-6.

Vol. IV *Education for All: Planning and Monitoring.* ISBN 81-7024-763-4.

Vol. V *Education for All: The Indian Scenario.* ISBN 81-7024-764-0.

Bhaskara Rao, Digumarti, Editor (1996). *Global Perceptions on Peace Education,* 3 Volumes. New Delhi: Discovery Publishing House. ISBN 81-7141-319-6.

Bhaskara Rao, Digumarti, Editor (1996). *National Policy on Education*. 2 Volumes. New Delhi: Anmol Publications Pvt. Ltd. ISBN 81-7488-323-1.

Bhaskara Rao, Digumarti, Editor (1997). *Care the Child*, 2 Volumes. New Delhi: Discovery Publishing House. ISBN 81-7141-394-3.

Bhaskara Rao, Digumarti, Editor (1997). *Education for the 21st Century*. New Delhi: Discovery Publishing House. ISBN 81-7141-389-7.

Bhaskara Rao, Digumarti, Editor (1997). *Reflections on Scientific Attitude*. New Delhi: Discovery Publishing House, ISBN 81-7141-319-6.

Bhaskara Rao, Digumarti, Editor (1997). *Success Story of a Primary Education Project*. New Delhi: APH Publishing Corporation. ISBN 81-7024-850-7.

Bhaskara Rao, Digumarti, Editor (1997). *World Food Summit*. New Delhi: Discovery Publishing House. ISBN 81-7141-386-2.

Bhaskara Rao, Digumarti, Editor (1998). *Adolescence Education*. New Delhi: Discovery Publishing House. ISBN 81-7141-432-X.

Bhaskara Rao, Digumarti, Editor (1998). *Community and School Nutrition Education*. New Delhi: Discovery Publishing House. ISBN 81-7141-435-4.

Bhaskara Rao, Digumarti, Editor (1998). *District Primary Education Programme*. New Delhi: Discovery Publishing House. ISBN 81-7141-396-X.

Bhaskara Rao, Digumarti, Editor (1998). *Earth Summit*, 2 Volumes. New Delhi: Discovery Publishing House. ISBN 81-7141-435-4.

Bhaskara Rao, Digumarti, Editor (1998). *National Policy on Education: Towards an Enlightened and Humane Society*, New Delhi: Discovery Publishing House. ISBN 81-7141-426-5.

Bhaskara Rao, Digumarti, Editor (1998). *Reforming School Education*. New Delhi: Discovery Publishing House. ISBN 81-7141-403-6.

Bhaskara Rao, Digumarti, Editor (1998). *Teacher Education in India*. New Delhi: Discovery Publishing House. ISBN 81-7141-406-0.

Bhaskara Rao, Digumarti, Editor (1998). *World Summit for Social Development*. New Delhi: Discovery Publishing House. ISBN 81-7141-420-6.

Bhaskara Rao, Digumarti, Editor (2000). *Education for All: Achieving the Goal*, 3 Volumes, New Delhi: APH Publishing Corporation. ISBN 81-7648-152-1.

Vol. I *The Global Consensus*. ISBN 81-7648-155-6.

Vol. II *Mid-Decade Review Reports of Regional Seminars*. ISBN 81-7648-154-8.

Vol. III *Issues and Trends*. ISBN 81-7648-155-6.

Bhaskara Rao, Digumarti, Editor (2000), *International Encyclopaedia of AIDS*, 11 Volumes in 13 Parts. New Delhi: Discovery Publishing House. ISBN 81-7141-6 (Set).

Vol. 1 *Introduction to HIV/AIDS*. ISBN 81-7141-523-7.

Vol. 2 *HIV/AIDS—Issues and Challenges*, 2 Parts. ISBN 81-7141-524-5.

Vol. 3 *HIV/AIDS—Socio Economic Realities*. ISBN 81-7141-524-3.

Vol. 4 *HIV/AIDS—Law Ethics and Human Rights*, 2 Parts. ISBN 81-7141-526-1.

Vol. 5 *AIDS and NGOs*. ISBN 81-7141-527-X.

Vol. 6 *AIDS and Home Care*. ISBN 81-7141-528-8.

Vol. 7 *STD Case Management*. ISBN 81-7141-529-6.

Vol. 8 *HIV/AIDS Prevention and Care—Teaching Modules for Nurses and Midwives*. ISBN 81-7141-530-X.

Vol. 9 *HIV Prevention Education for Education for Educational Institutions*. ISBN 81-7141-531-8.

Vol. 10 *Instructional Modules for AIDS Education*. ISBN 81-7141-532-6.

Vol. 11 *School Health Education to Prevent AIDS and STD—A Package for Curriculum Planners*. ISBN 81-7141-5338-4.

Bhaskara Rao, Digumarti, Editor (2000). *International Encyclopaedia of Science and Technology Education*, 11 Volumes. New Delhi: Discovery Publishing House. ISBN 81-7141-548-2 (Set).

Vol. 1 *Science and Technology Education*. ISBN 81-7141-568-7.

Vol. 2 *Science Education in Developing Countries*. ISBN 81-7141-570-9.

Vol. 3 *Organisational Structure of Science*. ISBN 81-7141-570-9.

Vol. 4 *Science Education in Asia and the Pacific*. ISBN 81-7141-571-7.

Vol. 5 *Science and Technology Education for All*. ISBN 81-7141-572-5.

Vol. 6 *Values, Ethics, Talent and Girls in Science and Technology Education*. ISBN 81-7141-573-3.

Vol. 7 *Popularization of Science and Technology Education*. ISBN 81-7141-574-1.

Vol. 8 *Science, Power and Society*. ISBN 81-7141-575-X.

Vol. 9 *Information Technology*. ISBN 81-7141-576-8.

Vol. 10 *Teacher Training in Science and Technology Education*. ISBN 81-7141-577-6.

Vol. 11 *Teacher Training in Science and Technology: A Curriculum Framework*. ISBN 81-7141-578-4.

Bhaskara Rao, Digumarti, Editor (2001). *Distance Education in Different Countries*. New Delhi: APH Publishing Corporation. ISBN 81-7648-229-3.

Bhaskara Rao, Digumarti, Editor (2001). *Decentralised Management of Education (Management of Education in Panchayati Raj and Municipal Bodies)*. New Delhi: Discovery Publishing House. ISBN 81-7141-617-9.

Bhaskara Rao, Digumarti, Editor (2001). *Electrochemistry for Environmental Protection*. New Delhi: Discovery Publishing House. ISBN 81-7141-619-5.

Bhaskara Rao, Digumarti, Editor (2001). *Global Educational Studies*. New Delhi: Discovery Publishing House. ISBN 81-7141-616-0.

Bhaskara Rao, Digumarti, Editor (2001). *Global Synthesis of Educational Assessment*. New Delhi: Discovery Publishing House. ISBN 81-7141-613-6.

Bhaskara Rao, Digumarti, Editor (2000). *International Encyclopaedia of Human Rights*. 7 Volumes in 13 Parts. New Delhi: Discovery Publishing House. (Royal Size). ISBN 81-7141-567-9 (Set).

Vol. 1 *International Instruments of Human Rights*, 2 Parts. ISBN 81-7141-595-4.

Vol. 2 *Regional Instruments of Human Rights*. ISBN 81-7141-604-7.

Vol. 3 *Human Rights and the United Nations*, 2 Parts. ISBN 81-7141-605-5.

Vol. 4 *Fact Files of Human Rights*, 3 Parts. ISBN 81-7141-605-3.

Vol. 5 *Study Stories of Human Rights*, 3 Parts. ISBN 81-7141-607-3.

Vol. 6 *International Meetings on Human Rights*, 2 Parts. ISBN 81-7141-608-X.

Vol. 7 *Professional Training in Human Rights*. ISBN 81-7141-609-8.

Bhaskara Rao, Digumarti, Editor (2001). *Jomtein Decade of Education*. New Delhi: Discovery Publishing House. ISBN 81-7141-618-7.

Bhaskara Rao, Digumarti, Editor (2001). *Nuclear Materials: Issues and Concerns*, 2 Volumes. New Delhi: Discovery Publishing House. ISBN 81-7141-611-X.

Bhaskara Rao, Digumarti, Editor (2001). *World Conference on Education for All*. New Delhi: APH Publishing Corporation. ISBN 81-7141-274-9.

Bhaskara Rao, Digumarti, Editor (2001). *World Conference on Higher Education*, New Delhi: Discovery Publishing House. ISBN 81-7141-610-1.

Bhaskara Rao, Digumarti, Editor (2001). *World Conference on Science*. New Delhi: Discovery Publishing House. ISBN 81-7141-612-8.

Bhaskara Rao, Digumarti, Editor (2003). *Inspiring Experience in Teacher Education*. New Delhi: Discovery Publishing House. ISBN 81-7141-656-X.

Bhaskara Rao, Digumarti, Editor (2003). *International Studies in Education*, 3 Volumes, New Delhi: Discovery Publishing House. ISBN 81-7141-647-0.

Bhaskara Rao, Digumarti, Editor (2003). *Military Conversion: Impact on Science and Technology*, New Delhi: Discovery Publishing House. ISBN 81-7141-578-4.

Bhaskara Rao, Digumarti, Editor (2003). *United Nations Millennium Summit*. New Delhi: Discovery Publishing House. ISBN 81-7141-632-2.

Bhaskara Rao, Digumarti, Editor (2003). *World Assembly on Aging*. New Delhi: Discovery Publishing House. ISBN 81-7141-637-3.

Bhaskara Rao, Digumarti, Editor (2004). *World Conference on Human Rights*. New Delhi: Discovery Publishing House. ISBN 81-7141-661-6.

Bhaskara Rao, Digumarti, Editor (2003). *World Education Forum*. New Delhi: Discovery Publishing House. ISBN 81-7141-639-X.

Bhaskara Rao, Digumarti, Editor (2004). *Education Employment and Human Resource Development*. New Delhi: Discovery Publishing House. ISBN 81-7141-681-0.

Bhaskara Rao, Digumarti, Editor (2004). *Successfully Schooling*. New Delhi: Discovery Publishing House. ISBN 81-7141-677-2.

Bhaskara Rao, Digumarti, Editor (2004). *European Education and Teachers*. New Delhi: Discovery Publishing House. ISBN 81-7141-702-7.

Bhaskara Rao, Digumarti, Editor (2004). *Teachers in a Changing World*. New Delhi: Discovery Publishing House. ISBN 81-7141-694-2.

Bhaskara Rao, Digumarti, Editor (2004). *Learning to Live Together*, 4 Volumes. New Delhi: Discovery Publishing House.

Vol. 1 *International Conference on Learning to Live Together.*

Vol. 2 *Globalisation and Living Together.*

Vol. 3 *Curriculum for Learning to Live Together.*

Vol. 4 *Science Education for the Contemporary Society.*

Bhaskara Rao, Digumarti (2004). *International Guidelines on Open and Distance Education*, New Delhi: Discovery Publishing House.

Bhaskara Rao, Digumarti, Editor (2004). *Adult Learning in the 21st Century*. New Delhi: Discovery Publishing House.

Bhaskara Rao, Digumarti, Editor (2004). *Educational Practices: Research and Recommendations*. New Delhi: Discovery Publishing House.

Bhaskara Rao, Digumarti, Editor (2004). *Chernobyl: Never Again*. New Delhi: APH Publishing Corporation.

Bhaskara Rao, Digumarti, Editor (2004). *Virology and Immunology*. New Delhi: APH Publishing Corporation.

Bhaskara Rao, Digumarti, C.A.P. Swami and B.S.V. Dutt (1997). *Self-Evaluation in Student Teaching*. New Delhi: Discovery Publishing House. ISBN 81-7141-374-9.

Bhaskara Rao, Digumarti and B.S.V. Dutt, Editors (2003). *Education: Programmes and Policies*. New Delhi: APH Publishing Corporation. ISBN 81-7648-470-9.

Bhaskara Rao, Digumarti and D. Naresh Kumar (2004). *School Teacher Effectiveness*. New Delhi: Discovery Publishing House.

Bhaskara Rao, Digumarti and D. Sridhar (2002). *Job Satisfaction of School Teachers*. New Delhi: Discovery Publishing House. ISBN 81-7141-652-7.

Bhaskara Rao, Digumarti and Digumarti Pushpa Latha (1994). *Achievement in Biology*. New Delhi: Discovery Publishing House. ISBN 81-7141-264-5.

Bhaskara Rao, Digumarti, C. Sridevi and K. Vijaya (1995). *Achievement in Social Studies*. New Delhi: Discovery Publishing House. ISBN 81-7141-281-5.

Bhaskara Rao, Digumarti and Digumarti Pushpa Latha (1995). *Achievement in English*. New Delhi: Discovery Publishing House. ISBN 81-7141-283-1.

Bhaskara Rao, Digumarti and Digumarti Pushpa Latha (1994). *Achievement in Science*. New Delhi: Discovery Publishing House. ISBN 81-7141-280-70.

Bhaskara Rao, Digumarti and Digumarti Pushpa Latha (1995). *Achievement in Mathematics*. New Delhi: Discovery Publishing House. ISBN 81-7141-278-5.

Bhaskara Rao, Digumarti and Digumarti Pushpa Latha, Editors (1998). *International Encyclopaedia of Women*. 5 Volumes. New Delhi: Discovery Publishing House. ISBN 81-7141-410-9.

Vol. 1 *Status of World's Women*. ISBN 81-7141-494-X.

Vol. 2 *Women, Education and Empowerment*. ISBN 81-7141-498-1.

Vol. 3 *Women Challenges and Advancement*. ISBN 81-7141-497-4.

Vol. 4 *Women and Family Health*. ISBN 81-7141-497-4.

Vol. 5 *Women and International Action*. ISBN 81-7141-498-2.

Bhaskara Rao, Digumarti, Digumarti Pushpa Latha and Digumarti Harshitha, Editors (2001). *Biological Warfare*. New Delhi: Discovery Publishing House. ISBN 81-7141-597-0.

Bhaskara Rao, Digumarti, Digumarti Pushpa Latha and Digumarti Harshitha, Editors (2001). *Women as Educators*. New Delhi: Discovery Publishing House. ISBN 81-7141-602-0.

Bhaskara Rao, Digumarti and Digumarti Harshitha, Editors (2001). *Education in India*. New Delhi: APH Publishing Corporation. ISBN 81-7141-207-2.

Bhaskara Rao, Digumarti, Digumarti Pushpa Latha and Digumarti Harshitha, Editors (2001). *Assessing Learning Achievement*. New Delhi: Discovery Publishing House. ISBN 81-7141-601-2.

Bhaskara Rao, Digumarti, Digumarti Pushpa Latha and Digumarti Harshitha, Editors (2001). *Energy Security*. New Delhi: Discovery Publishing House. ISBN 81-7141-598-9.

Bhaskara Rao, Digumarti, Digumarti Harshitha and K.R.S.S. Rao, Editors (1999). *Advanced Biotechnology*. New Delhi: Discovery Publishing House. ISBN 81-7141-516-4.

Bhaskara Rao, Digumarti and K.R.S. Sambhasiva Rao, Editors (1996). *Current Trends in Indian Education*. New Delhi: Discovery Publishing House. ISBN 81-7141-311-0.

Bhaskara Rao, Digumarti and K. Vijaya (1995). *A Text Book of Evaluation*. Ambala Cantt: The Associated Publishers.

Bhaskara Rao, Digumarti and N.V.M. Mohana Rao (2002). *Problems of Mentally Handicapped Children*. New Delhi: Discovery Publishing House. ISBN 81-7141-645-4.

Bhaskara Rao, Digumarti and S. Chandra Mohan (2002). *Sports Management*. New Delhi: APH Publishing Corporation. ISBN 81-7648-467-9.

Bhaskara Rao, Digumarti and Sk. Johni Basha (2004). *Teachers' Population Education Awareness*. New Delhi: APH Publishing Corporation.

Bhaskara Rao, Digumarti, V.V. Rao, V.V. Lakshmi and V.V. Krishna, Editors (1999). *Status and Advancement of Women*. New Delhi: APH Publishing Corporation. ISBN 81-7648-169-6.

Babu, P.C., Author and Digumarti Bhaskara Rao, Editor (2004). *Flowers of Wisdom*. New Delhi: Discovery Publishing House. ISBN 81-7141-695-0.

Bhagya Lakshmi, Lingineni, Author and Digumarti Bhaskara Rao, Editor (2000). *Reading and Comprehension*. New Delhi: Discovery Publishing House. ISBN 81-7141-543-1.

Bhuvaneswara Lakshmi, Gadde, Author and Digumarti Bhaskara Rao, Editor (2000). *Attitude Towards Science*. New Delhi: Discovery Publishing House. ISBN 81-7141-541-6.

Devraj, T.A.S., Author and Digumarti Bhaskara Rao, Editor (1997). *Trace Analysis of Uranium and Thorium*. New Delhi: Discovery Publishing House. ISBN 81-7141-375-7.

Durga Rani, K., Author and Digumarti Bhaskara Rao, Editor (2000). *Educational Aspirations and Scientific Attitudes*. New Delhi: Discovery Publishing House. ISBN 81-7141-555-55.

Dutt, B.S.V. and Digumarti Bhaskara Rao (2001). *Empowering Primary Teachers*. New Delhi: Discovery Publishing House. ISBN 81-7141-615.2.

Ediger, Marlow and Digumarti Bhaskara Rao (1996). *Science Curriculum*. New Delhi: Discovery Publishing House. ISBN 81-7141-321-8.

Ediger, Marlow and Digumarti Bhaskara Rao (2000). *Teaching Mathematics Successfully*. New Delhi: Discovery Publishing House. ISBN 81-7141-552-0.

Ediger, Marlow and Digumarti Bhaskara Rao (2001). *Teaching Science Successfully*. New Delhi: Discovery Publishing House. ISBN 81-7141-600-4.

Ediger, Marlow and Digumarti Bhaskara Rao (2001). *Teaching Social Studies Successfully*. New Delhi: Discovery Publishing House. ISBN 81-7141-596-2.

Ediger, Marlow and Digumarti Bhaskara Rao (2002). *Philosophy and Curriculum*. New Delhi: Discovery Publishing House. ISBN 81-7141-631-4.

Ediger, Marlow and Digumarti Bhaskara Rao (2002). *Improving School Administration*. New Delhi: Discovery Publishing House. ISBN 81-7141-633-0.

Ediger, Marlow and Digumarti Bhaskara Rao (2002). *Elementary Curriculum*. New Delhi: Discovery Publishing House. ISBN 81-7141-658-6.

Ediger, Marlow and Digumarti Bhaskara Rao (2003). *Language Arts Curriculum*. New Delhi: Discovery Publishing House. ISBN 81-7141-657-8.

Ediger, Marlow and Digumarti Bhaskara Rao (2004). *Teaching Language Arts Successfully*. New Delhi: Discovery Publishing House. ISBN 81-7141-678-0.

Ediger, Marlow and Digumarti Bhaskara Rao (2004). *Teaching Mathematics in Elementary Schools*. New Delhi: Discovery Publishing House. ISBN 81-7141-687-X.

Ediger, Marlow and Digumarti Bhaskara Rao (2004). *Teaching Science in Elementary Schools*. New Delhi: Discovery Publishing House. ISBN 81-7141-709-4.

Ediger, Marlow and Digumarti Bhaskara Rao (2004). *School Curriculum and Administration*. New Delhi: Discovery Publishing House. ISBN 81-7141-709-4.

Ediger, Marlow and Digumarti Bhaskara Rao (2004). *Modern Elementary School*. New Delhi: Discovery Publishing House.

Ediger, Marlow and Digumarti Bhaskara Rao (2004): *Relevancy in Elementary Curriculum*. New Delhi: Discovery Publishing House. ISBN 81-7141-751-5.

Ediger, Marlow and Digumarti Bhaskara Rao, (2004). *Teaching Social Studies in Elementary Schools*. New Delhi: Discovery Publishing House.

Ediger Marlow, B.S.V. Dutt and Digumarti Bhaskara Rao (2004). *Teaching English Successfully*. New Delhi: Discovery Publishing House. ISBN 81-7141-707-8.

Harshitha, Digumarti and Digumarti Bhaskara Rao, Editors (2004). *Educational Innovations*. New Delhi: Discovery Publishing House.

Indira Devi, Author and J. Prasanth Kumar and Digumarti Bhaskara Rao, Editors (2004). *Values in Language Text Books*. New Delhi: Discovery Publishing House.

Jayasree, Kandi, Author and Digumarti Bhaskara Rao, Editor (1999). *Correlates of Socialisation*. New Delhi: Discovery Publishing House. ISBN 81-7141-517-2.

John Babu, Chikati, Author and T.J.R. Prasad, G.M. Madhukar and Digumarti Bhaskara Rao, Editors (1996). *Problem Solving in Mathematics*. New Delhi: APH Publishing Corporation. ISBN 81-7648-273-0.

Lalitha, T., Author and K.S. Prabhakaram, D.S.N. Sastry and Digumarti Bhaskara Rao, Editors (2004). *Educational Philosophic Beliefs*. New Delhi: Discovery Publishing House. ISBN 81-7141-765-5.

Madhu Bala, Jampala, Author and Digumarti Bhaskara Rao, Editor (2004). *Adjustment Problems of Hearing Impaired*. New Delhi: Discovery Publishing House.

Marja, Talvi and Digumarti Bhaskara Rao, Editors (1996). *Educational Leadership and Social Changes*. New Delhi: Discovery Publishing House. ISBN 81-7141-320-X.

Nirmala Jyothi, M., Author and Digumarti Bhaskara Rao, Editor (2003). *Non-detention Systems in School Education*. New Delhi: Discovery Publishing House. ISBN 81-7141-654-3.

Prabhakaram, K.S., Author and Digumarti Bhaskara Rao, Editor (1998). *Concept Attainment Model in Mathematics Teaching*. New Delhi: Discovery Publishing House. ISBN 81-7141-424-9.

Prasanth Kumar, J., Author and Digumarti Bhaskara Rao, Editor (1998). *Effectiveness of Distance Education System*. New Delhi: Discovery Publishing House. ISBN 81-7141-437-0.

Prasanth Kumar, J., Author and G. Sundara Rao and Digumarti Bhaskara Rao, Editors (2000). *Open University Student Support Services*. New Delhi: Discovery Publishing House. ISBN 81-7141-550-4.

Ramatulasamma, K., Author and Digumarti Bhaskara Rao, Editor (2002). *Job Satisfaction of Teacher Educators*, New Delhi: Discovery Publishing House. ISBN 81-7141-655-1.

Rama Krishnaiah, D., Author and Digumarti Bhaskara Rao, Editor (1998). *Job Satisfaction of College Teachers*, New Delhi: Discovery Publishing House. ISBN 81-7141-438-9.

Rama Kumar Ratnam, M., Author and Digumarti Bhaskara Rao, Editor (1998). *Dukka: Suffering in Early Buddhism*. New Delhi: Discovery Publishing House. ISBN 81-7141-653-5.

Rathaiah, Lavu and Digumarti Bhaskara Rao, Editors (1996). *International Innovations in Education*. New Delhi: Discovery Publishing House. ISBN 81-7141-359-5.

Ramesh, Ganta and Digumarti Bhaskara Rao, Editors (1998). *Environmental Education: Problems and Prospects*. New Delhi: Discovery Publishing House. ISBN 81-7141-423-0.

Rathaiah, Lavu and Digumarti Bhaskara Rao (1997). *Achievement Correlates*. New Delhi: Discovery Publishing House. ISBN 81-7141-385-4.

Reddy, Sudhakar Y., Author, and Digumarti Bhaskara Rao, Editor (2003). *Creativity in Adolescents*. New Delhi: Discovery Publishing House. ISBN 81-7141-659-4.

Reddy, M.S., Author and Digumarti Bhaskara Rao, Editor (2004). *Creativity in College Students*. New Delhi: Discovery Publishing House. ISBN 81-7141-697-7.

Radramamba, B., Author and Digumarti Bhaskara Rao, Editor (2003). *Problems of Teaching*. New Delhi: APH Publishing Corporation. ISBN 81-7648-462-8.

Venkata Rao, P. and Digumarti Bhaskara Rao (1989). *A Text Book of Zoology—Junior Intermediate*. Guntur: Vignan Publishers.

Venkata Rao, P. and Digumarti Bhaskara Rao (1989). *A Text Book of Zoology—Senior Intermediate*. Guntur: Vignan Publishers.

Venugopala Rao, K., Author and Digumarti Bhaskara Rao, Editor (2000). *Teacher Morale in Secondary Schools*. New Delhi: Discovery Publishing House. ISBN 81-7141-551-2.

Vidya, C., Author and Digumarti Bhaskara Rao. Editor (1996). *A Text Book of Nutrition*. New Delhi: Discovery Publishing House. ISBN 81-7141-309-9.

Vidya Bharathi, D., Author and Digumarti Bhaskara Rao, Editor (2000). *Educational Philosophies of Swami Vivekananda and John Dewey*. New Delhi: APH Publishing Corporation. ISBN 81-7648-309-9.

Books in Telugu Language

Bhaskara Rao, Digumarti (1986). *Dhrushya Sravana Bodhanapakaranalu* (Audio Visual Teaching Aids). Guntur: Nagarjuna Publishers.

Bhaskara Rao, Digumarti (1993). *Jeevasashtra Bodhana* (Teaching of Biology). Guntur: Nagarjuna Publishers.

Bhaskara Rao, Digumarti (1995). *Vignanasasthra Bodhana* (Teaching of Science) Guntur: Nagarjuna Publishers.

Bhaskara Rao, Digumarti (1997). *Vidya Manovignana Seshtram* (Educational Psychology). Guntur: Creative Press.

Bhaskara Rao, Digumarti (1998). *DSC Study Material*. Guntur: Nagarjuna Publishers.

Bhaskara Rao, Digumarti (1998). *Upadhyayudu Vidya*. (Teacher and Education). Guntur: Nagarjuna Publishers.

Bhaskara Rao, Digumarti (1998). *Vidya Drukpadalu* (Prespectives of Education). Guntur: Nagarjuna Publishers.

Bhaskara Rao, Digumarti (1999). *EdCET Teaching Aptitude*. Guntur: Nagarjuna Publishers.

Bhaskara Rao, Digumarti (2001). *Bharata Samajamulo Upadyayudu Vidya* (Teacher and Education in Emerging Indian Society). Guntur: Nagarjuna Publishers.

Bhaskara Rao, Digumarti (2001). *Bhoutika Sastra Bodhana Paddathulu* (Methods of Teaching Physical Science). Guntur: Nagarjuna Publishers.

Bhaskara Rao, Digumarti (2001). *Jeeva Sastra Bodhana Padhathulu* (Methods of Teaching Biology). Guntur: Nagarjuna Publishers.

Bhaskara Rao, Digumarti (2001). *Vidya Manovignana Sastram* (Educational Psychology). Guntur: Nagarjuna Publishers.

Bhaskara Rao, Digumarti (2003). *Patsala Yajamanyam/Paripalana* (School Management and Administration). Guntur: Nagarjuna Publishers.

Bhaskara Rao, Digumarti (2004). *Vidya Sanketika Sastram mariyu Computer Vidya* (Educational Technology and Computer Education). Guntur: Nagarjuna Publishers.